Jennifer Hanser

About the Author

A foodie who sometimes abuses hair-care products, STEPHANIE KLEIN is an acclaimed writer and photographer with a cultlike following. She is one of the Internet's most popular icons—stephanieklein.com has been featured on the cover of the *New York Times* Sunday Styles section, where she was named among the top one percent of all bloggers—and Klein's photography furnishes New York's Hotel Gansevoort. Her rise has been chronicled everywhere from *20/20* to Food Network, and her wildly popular first memoir, *Straight Up and Dirty*, is currently in development as a half-hour comedy series. While she enjoys living in Austin, Texas, with her husband and twin son and daughter, she will always be a New Yorker.

ALSO *by*
STEPHANIE KLEIN

Straight Up and Dirty

Moose

A MEMOIR

Stephanie Klein

HARPER

NEW YORK . LONDON . TORONTO . SYDNEY

FOR MY MOTHER, YOLANDA,
AND MY SISTER, LEA,
WHO FILLED OUR HOUSE WITH LAUGHTER
AND FILL MY LIFE WITH LOVE

HARPER

A hardcover edition of this book was published in 2008 by William Morrow, an imprint of HarperCollins Publishers.

FIRST HARPER PAPERBACK PUBLISHED 2009.

Designed by Janet M. Evans

The Library of Congress has catalogued the hardcover edition as follows:

Klein, Stephanie, 1975–
Moose : a memoir of fat camp / Stephanie Klein.
p. cm
ISBN 978-0-06-084329-8
1. Klein, Stephanie, 1975––Health. 2. Overweight teenagers—United States—Biography. 3. Obesity in children—Treatment—United States. 4. Camps for overweight children—United States. I. Title.
RJ399.C6K538 2008
618.92'3980092—dc22 2008002728
[B]

ISBN 978-0-06-167286-6 (pbk.)

09 10 11 12 13 OV/RRD 10 9 8 7 6 5 4 3 2 1

CONTENTS

AUTHOR'S NOTE

I'VE HELD ON TO MY ADOLESCENCE. LITERALLY.

Three puffy rhinestone-studded diaries with locks, boxes of photos, camp letters, and sheets of fight-song lyrics. Rotten poetry. *I*'s dotted with hearts. Somehow, holding on to it as I have allows me to move forward.

I always hear that you have to let the past go, have to live in the moment, focus on your now. I'm able to move forward *because* I keep my past so close. It encourages me to try new things and move in unfamiliar directions, because the past—what I knew, what I had, who I was—is always there to fall back on. And I need that, to remember who I was before I became a wife and a mother. Because as much as I might have hated her at the time, I love that girl.

I chose not to tell the story of *Moose* in quips and witty puns because that's not what adolescence is. It's awkward and tender, vulnerable and angry. It doesn't always make sense. *Moose* isn't a book about accepting yourself as you are, embracing life as a fat girl. It's not pro-fat, peppered with tips for learning to love your cellulite. It's not about overcoming eating disorders. It's about a time in my life, which I affectionately refer to as the Thunder Years, when I navigated the adult terrain of reconciling my childhood wounds and overcoming merciless monikers like Moose.

Having spent five summers attending fat camps as both a camper and a counselor, I've been on both sides of it: the first-time camper afraid of putting her face in the lake, worried she'll be homesick the entire summer, and the counselor spending her last summer before entering college teaching obese eight-year-olds how to pee in the woods and walk so their thighs don't rub together.

In the telling of *Moose,* I've compressed my experiences into a single summer at a single camp with a fictional name. In doing so, there had to be a few composite characters and a compressed timeline. While some of the names and certain identifying details have been changed, make no mistake—sadly enough, everything in this book actually happened. All the journal entries, unless otherwise noted, were extracted from my diaries and were written by me between the ages of twelve and fifteen.

Moose is a coming-of-age story that's about so much more than a summer at fat camp. It's about what we all go through, learning who we want to be and what kind of friends we want, eventually coming to terms with who we actually are, and realizing that who we are has nothing—okay, maybe a little—to do with our thighs.

PART  NE

"Because when you're a fat kid like I was" can take you just so far. You can only grip onto that excuse for so long before it becomes trite. Yes, poor you, poor over-privileged, over-fed, upper-middle everything girl. It's time to stop clinging to that shit as your identity. It's not who you are anymore. God, there's way worse out there. Just get over yourself already.

I took a step away from the mirror and politely responded, "Eat me."

—2007, age thirty-one

one

BABY FAT

"YOU NEED TO GAIN FIFTY POUNDS," MIMI SAID AS SHE plotted my weight on her medical chart. Certainly, I'd heard the words "need" and "gain" cobbled together in a sentence about my weight before. Though they were usually words in my own head and were always assembled a bit differently: "You *gain* any more weight and you'll *need* to hire someone to help you find your vagina." Mimi's new arrangement of the verbs was far more distressing.

I was standing on a scale in the medical offices of the Texas Perinatal Group. It was one of many appointments with Mimi, my preventative preterm labor specialist. My obstetrician had mandated these weekly visits upon learning I was pregnant with twins. Multiples tend to be in a hurry, he'd said as he scrawled Mimi's contact information on his prescription pad.

If I gained fifty pounds I'd weigh more than a Honda. And certainly more than my husband, which was worse.

"You're just not gaining enough," Mimi continued as she leafed through papers on her clipboard.

"Yeah, but I've got time," I said, shooing away her concern with my hand. "And I hear it all comes on in the last month anyway."

"Stephanie," she whispered, in an alarmingly real way that made my name sound like an object, "you're nearly six months pregnant. With twins. And you've only gained thirteen pounds."

I didn't know what to say. I didn't want to hurt my sweet babies, but I was frightened of getting any fatter. As it was, prepregnancy, I'd been twenty pounds heavier than my "happy weight"—that brilliant place where clothes shopping was enjoyable, reunion events were eagerly anticipated, and thin white pants seemed to be my most flattering choice. Medically speaking, before there were two pink lines, I'd been just seven pounds shy of being classified as overweight. And now I was being asked to play patty-cake with the idea of smearing on some excess plump.

Please. I might have been bordering overweight, but my dimpled ass was far from dumb. Pregnancy-brain hadn't rendered me completely useless. I'd done my research, relying on my proficient medical expert (ahem, Google), so I knew if a woman began her pregnancy overweight, as I nearly had, she should restrict her calories and gain little to no weight during pregnancy.

Despite this, I was being urged to pack on the pounds, and I was downright leery.

"Oh, yeah, sure. Eat all you want," Mimi would say now, and once I was accustomed to eating donut pudding for breakfast, I was sure she'd say, "Mmm, yeah, about that. You didn't think I was serious?"

"I'm trying," I said, stepping from the scale and returning to the chair where I'd set my clothes. With her back still turned, Mimi slid open the white drawers beside the chrome sink, peeking through each one. I faced a wall of baby announcements and hiked up my shorts. Ordinarily she left the room while I changed, but I wanted to save time and get the hell out.

When I turned around, she was still foraging. I yanked a thin shred of skin from my lip and felt calmer now that I tasted blood.

"Here it is," she said of a pamphlet outlining dietary guidelines for women carrying multiples.

"You gave it to me last week," I said, taking it anyway. "And I really am trying." Mimi glared at me as if to say the thirteen pounds I'd gained wasn't all placenta, amniotic fluid, and baby weight; it was thirteen pounds of bullshit.

"Is that what you think skim milk is? That's not trying. You need the extra calories from higher-fat dairy."

I hoped to be one of those chic pregnant women who could pull off cap sleeves and pencil skirts, ruched camisoles, or a tube dress. But my arms looked like tubers, and everything I wore made me look like a Mallomar. I figured the babies would take what they needed from my body, so the only one who'd suffer would be me. And I didn't care if my health was compromised if it meant my lard arms might make it out leaner. I refused to fall into that *I can gorge now* mind-set just because I was pregnant. "You're eating for three now" was a myth I wasn't about to choke down with my DHA and prenatal vitamins.

"It's not like I'm starving myself. I'm full all the time." I never skipped breakfast, drank far too many protein shakes, and layered my salads with white meat, low-fat pasteurized cheeses, and chopped egg whites. I ate healthier than I ever had on any diet.

"You have to force yourself to eat more."

"But I'm not hungry," I said, stretching open the nutritional accordion she'd handed me.

"It doesn't matter if you're hungry or not." I couldn't believe someone in the medical community was instructing me to ignore my body's signals and force myself to eat, even if I was full. "Are you exercising?" she asked as she watched me scoot into my sneakers.

"No, you'll be happy to know that I'm still a lazy piece of shit."

"Well, good. That's what I want to hear. The more rest the better."

I'd read articles warning women against gaining too much during pregnancy, how overindulging would make it harder to shed the excess weight after birth. Overweight mothers were at an increased risk for developing gestational diabetes and high blood pressure. Articles with titles like "Preparing for the Marathon of Labor" emphasized the importance of keeping fit. And here was Mimi emphasizing rest. Actual lying down, feet-elevated rest, not just taking it easy.

"Mimi, you have no idea how hard this is for me." *I'm fat as it is,* I was about to say aloud, but I knew she'd start in about my distorted body image. She couldn't understand. Instead, almost apologetically, I lamented, "I used to be fat."

"Well, to look at you no one would ever know it."

No, I thought, *I will never forget it.*

PART

Two

Dear Dirty Di,

How psyched up 4 camp am I? A lot!!
Today was <u>terrible</u> because:

1. *I lost my science textbook. I think it was stolen!!*
2. *Some kid called me "moose."*
3. *Leigh and I kind of got in a fight.*
4. *J.P. never called me back after I called 4 times!!*
5. *I don't think I love Barry anymore.*
6. *It rained.*
7. *I had to run in gym.*
8. *I looked like shit.*
9. *I think I like J.P. a little more than a friend.*
10. *I wouldn't go out w/ him.*

two

WEIGH OF LIFE

Today was an O.K. day. I wasn't late for one class, and I found my locker!!! I like Wheatley. I just wish that some boys would like me, too. I mean, besides geeks. I like this kid Doug, and I have a fair chance at getting him. It's just that, well, no one likes fat girls.

I was eight years old and rotund. Of course, at eight, I thought "rotund" was a type of root vegetable. Mom and I were unloading groceries onto the conveyor belt at Waldbaum's checkout counter when I began to understand the weight of things. Not simply what three nectarines weighed, but how heavy being fat could feel. When I lobbed a plastic sleeve of bagels onto the moving counter, Mom sprang the news on me, casually, as if she were talking about a new hairstyle she might like to try.

"Oh, tonight you're going to meet with a nutritionist named Fran," she said as she balanced tomatoes between cans of orange juice concentrate. I had heard Mom refer to this Fran person before, when she spoke to Aunt Iris on the telephone. "Fran gave you that recipe? Well, let me know how it turns out." Fran Levine was the "fat doctor" of Roslyn Heights, Long Island. She wasn't really a doctor, but that's what the ladies called her.

"What are you talking about? I'm not going." I didn't shout. I whined through clenched teeth and felt myself reddening. What if someone at school discovered I had to go to a fat doctor?

"Yes you are."

"No I'm not!"

"It's already settled. She's expecting you. It's not a big deal; she's going to help."

"Not a big deal," I've since learned, is an omen.

"Yeah, you know that goiter in your neck that's just doubled in size? Well, in a certain light, I can kinda make out a tail and a row of teeth in there. But I'm sure it's no big deal."

It's always a big deal when someone makes a point of saying it's not. And when Mom said it, she wouldn't even look at me.

I pushed the metal cart into her legs. It rammed into her shins.

"Damn it, Stephanie!" She bit her lower lip and leaned into the cart. The lady behind us edged forward to see what was taking so long. Mom thrust the cart through, snapped her checkbook closed, and dumped brown bags into my arms.

I shoved the bags back to her, lunged my head toward hers, and in a contemptuous, even tone told her, "I hate you, you stupid . . ." But I didn't know how to finish the sentence because I wasn't allowed to curse, especially not to my parents. "You stupid . . . mother. How do you even call yourself a mother? I'm way smarter than you are. I could make you cry, you're so dumb." I dropped the bags and raced out of the grocery store alone. I was eight, and I was good at it.

My disciplinarian father—whom Mom had us call "Poppa" instead of "Dad" because it sounded more European and not so "Ameri-KAN," she'd say in disgust—forbade swearing and raising my voice to elders, but "horrible" was gray area. I used the leeway to pick at her scab of insecurity. I was miserable with who I was, and I wanted her to feel it.

Mom had opted for secretarial school instead of college. I imagined her, the one Yolanda, sitting amid rows of Mary Sues in tight monogrammed sweaters and full skirts, their hair sprayed, teased, and smoothed into beehives. They'd punch typewriters in unison, their nails a chorus of clicks and taps. Someone would occasionally pop a gum bubble, prompting the instructor to flicker the lights, signaling silence, as she surveyed the room for the culprit with a cocked eyebrow. That was as challenging as it got for Mom, I thought. Secretarial school.

I dashed to the car and crouched by the headlights. She was going to slap me, I thought, as I waited out of breath, rocking in a squat on the hot tar. But once she was back at the car, she unloaded the bags into the trunk, wheeled the cart away, turned the key to her door, and got in. Mom started the engine, rolled down the windows, and simply said, "Get in." She had been crying. We drove the rest of the way home in silence.

FRAN'S DYED AUBURN HAIR WAS ONE FLAT COLOR EVERY-where, even the strands framing her face. She was as thin as Mom—about a size four on top, six on the bottom—but Fran looked older around the eyes.

I stepped on the cold metal doctor's scale—thankful she wasn't really a doctor, so I needn't disrobe—and exhaled as much air out of my body as I could. I thought I would weigh less if I didn't breathe.

"Let's put you on backward and measure you first." That seemed harmless; I was proud of my height, four foot nine. "So you go to North Side Elementary, right?"

"Yeah."

"My good friend Carolyn's daughter goes there, too. She's about your age, I think." What? No! Now the word would get out that I didn't just look like a chunk, I had to show up on Monday nights to be counseled for it. "Teresa Stone. Do you know her?" The blood was coming. I felt it in my face, a pulsing burn. I forced a compliant smile, nodded, and wiped my upper lip with my wrist.

"Now, let's see what we weigh, shall we?"

I turned around and watched her slip the scale's weight farther along the metal ruler of good and bad. Farther. A bit more. I stopped looking. I didn't want to know. I felt as if I was about to have diarrhea.

With her chin nearly touching her chest, her eyes peered up at the scale over the mauve reading glasses resting at the tip of her nose. She scribbled something onto a thick yellow index card. Her nails were tomato red, manicured and long. She folded the card in half and instructed me to write my name on the front. I was used to this. Adults were always asking us to write our names on everything: inside your underwear, on every sheet of notebook paper, on knapsacks and textbooks. This card was going into my pocket, but before I slipped it in, Fran warned, "Don't look inside."

On the ride to Fran's house, Mom had told me to put rolls of quarters in my pockets so I'd definitely succeed the following week without them, even if I failed. "I'm only kidding," she was quick to add afterward. Then she dropped me off and zipped away once Fran opened her front door for me. It seemed strange to me, this idea of cheating before you're even on a diet. I mean, isn't that what diets are for?

When Fran scribbled down my weight, I wondered who else she knew. I thought about Aunt Iris. How had she heard about Fran? Was she a client or were they tennis friends? *Fuddruckers!* What if they were friends and Fran told her how much I weighed?

I liked that I could call her Fran and not Mrs. Levine like every other adult. While she mostly catered to adults, Fran also offered a teen session on Monday evenings. There were about nine of us there, but I was the youngest person Fran ever had as a "client." Eight years old and suddenly a client—it made me feel older. And nervous.

About to enter the fourth grade, I didn't really need the answers to most questions the older girls asked:

"Fran, let's just say I wanted to drink beer. I mean I wouldn't 'cause I'm not old enough or anything, but if I was gonna, do I substitute a fruit and a bread?"

"Fran, when my friends and I drive to Friendly's at night after a game, what do I do when they're all eating sundaes and fries?"

"Fran, is semen fattening? I heard it's all protein, and that it's good for my hair, skin, and nails."

I focused on the image of golden salty fries dipped into cool slushy milk shakes. Warm and cold, together. I heard the other things asked—I could have repeated their questions if I had been accused of day-dreaming—but they were floating words strung together in my head, hovering for only a moment for immediate recall; nothing else registered. I didn't listen for the answers. I couldn't get past the visual of girls with pom-poms and guys in letter jackets, the way I'd seen them in the movie *Grease*. People somewhere were having pep rallies with marsh-mallow sauce and extra whipped cream. It's what popular people did. They ate maraschino cherries and smiled and never got fat or ugly. High school must have been all bonfires and backseats. Girls with ponytails, straight teeth, and slender thighs went to Friendly's for ice cream floats and flirting. I'd never be a cheerleader. No one would be able to lift me for the pyramid.

There was a slightly frayed couch and a circle of metal folding chairs in Fran's basement. The couch was deep and comfortable; I knew I'd start arriving early to meetings for a seat on it. I wanted to avoid the "So, how'd ya do?" I heard the others ask as they left the closet in which Fran hid the scale. One girl cried in the closet. She inched open the door, bulbous and sniffling. No one asked how she had done. Fran summoned, "Next, who's next?" without stepping from the closet.

It was a closet inside her carpeted basement, which was accessed from a long staircase that led from Fran's kitchen. Not unlike the plus-size section in department stores, it made me feel as if I were buried inside a Russian nesting doll of shame. The basement walls were paneled and adorned with paintings in heavy gilded frames. On another closet door hung an enormous cardboard cutout of a white tennis racket. "BETH" was stenciled on it in glitter, and signatures weaved between the strings—a bat mitzvah sign-in board. I later learned that

Beth was Fran's thin daughter, who'd sometimes attend our meetings. According to Fran, when Beth was younger she could eat anything and not gain weight: a sleeve of Oreos, sugary cereals, cartons of frozen pizza bagels. Then she had to have dental surgery, and her metabolism changed. "Now she'll always have to watch because it's in her genes," Fran said as she pinched the sides of her own thighs.

In another corner of the basement, just beyond the weigh-in closet, was a home gym. There was strength-training equipment, a StairMaster, and a polished rack of black free weights pushed flush against a mirrored wall. I assumed Fran's husband and son used this area, as it never occurred to me that women would have any use for extra weight, even if it was free. I'd never meet Fran's husband, but I'd hear all the stories. One night I learned that he refused to eat salad. Fran recounted their conversation.

"But it has no taste, so how can you hate it?"

"I just do," he said.

"Do you like ketchup?" He nodded. "Do you like mayonnaise?" He nodded again. "What about relish? You like relish, don't you?" Another nod. "Well, that's what salad tastes like. It tastes like whatever dressing you put on it."

"My husband wouldn't even eat salad dressing because it had the word 'salad' in it. So I had to mix ketchup, mayonnaise, and relish in a bowl, right in front of him. And I had him dip a wedge of iceberg lettuce in it, and you know what he said?" She paused. "'Not bad.' 'Well, that's salad dressing,' I told him. And that's how I got Mr. Meat and Potatoes to start eating salad. Now he eats it without any dressing at all. Just fresh lemon."

Yeah, in front of you, I thought. I wondered where her husband was the night she told us that story. I pictured him in their bedroom—a man with a brown face, round pink ears, thick plastic eyeglasses, a semicircle of white boxy teeth, and a mustache he just snapped into his potato head. He was reclining in bed with one leg crossed over the other as he flipped through cable channels and languidly dragged his finger through a trough of Thousand Island dressing. The son I'd never seen stood fanning his father with an oversized banana leaf. And the lesson I walked away with that night wasn't that I should eat my veggies. I learned that anything could be learned. That you could trick yourself into liking things you didn't, or at least trick other people into thinking you did.

Once all the girls were weighed, Fran turned off the closet light and joined the circle. She smelled like spearmint and nicotine, even from far away. Before speaking, she glided her hand over her hair and made eye contact with each of us. Then she placed a thick hardcover book strewn with yellow Post-it notes on her lap. It was quiet. Fran's voice was steady and purposeful as she read the story of a young man who lost his job.

"'Your head is in the sky, boy,'" Fran read with a butchered Southern accent. "'These here drawin's, they ain't no good. Do some real work; you're no good at this.'" Fran's eyes darted around the room, alive and manic as she mimicked accents. "'Desolate, he sat in his modest room and nibbled on the last of his food.'" I wondered what he was eating: brown crusts, a block of orange cheddar, a pan of pull-apart rolls? Ooh, pull-apart rolls with Country Crock spread. No. Bad. No rolls. No spread.

As Fran read the story from her lap, my eyes wandered, and I found shapes in the grooves and curves of her soft pine walls. I discovered a shape resembling a bird with one leg in the lines of the wood. A bear head with an apple mouth was in there too, even when I tilted my head. I loved finding shapes in glass and wood and in the grit between floor tiles; they were like everyday Rorschach tests. The young man from Fran's story had mice in his walls. "'One mouse crept in and dined on the crumbs.'" It had to be a hunk of cheese. Swiss. "'The young man began to sketch the mouse. His drawings were simple but quite good. He named the mouse Mortimer,'" Fran read. "'No one thought his drawings of Mortimer the Mouse were any good,'" Fran said, meeting my eyes. "'But he continued to draw, despite what people told him. And now,'" she said slowly, "'his mouse has a new name.'" She took a ruminative pause before adding, "'He's called Mickey.'" I looked around at the older girls before reacting myself; they were smiling. "That young man was Walt Disney, but once upon a time, a long time ago, he was just a boy in a room, doing what he needed to do for himself, despite what anyone told him. And that," she said, "is what I want from each of you." I smiled. "The power of will; you all have it within." She closed the book with a bang.

Annabelle, an obese teen with frosted hair and freckles everywhere, excused herself and tottered to the bathroom. I watched her trail off, pinching her clothes so they wouldn't cling. It made me itchy watching her walk. Was I that fat from behind?

Samantha raised her hand.

"Yeah, um, so, those shakes ya told me ta drink last week are detestable. I know ya said to give 'em anotha try, but I'm telling ya, they're nasty." Samantha was an Asian girl with a nasal Long Island voice. She carried a designer handbag, and she adorned her wrists with chunky gold gemstone jewelry, the kind I imagined girls got for their bat mitzvahs. I watched her fasten each one after she weighed in. Like the other girls, she was dressed simply in gossamer clothing, parachute pants and a mesh tank top. I didn't know Asian girls could get fat.

"Well, have you tried making them with ice or half a banana?"

"How'm I gonna mush up the banana?"

"Just drop it in the blender."

"I don't have a blenda."

"Well, then, how do you make the shake?" Fran's glasses were now dangling from her neck.

"I mix it in a bowl and whisk it with a fawk. Isn't that how ya supposta make it?"

"What do you mean you don't have a blender?"

WHEN SAMANTHA FINALLY REACHED HER GOAL, FRAN bought her a blender. Fran frequently reminded us to start thinking about what we might like when we reached our goal weights.

After answering any program-specific food questions, Fran told us the account of the Jelly Donut Man, a client from one of her adult sessions. At his first meeting with Fran he told her, "Now hair me. I down't wanna be hair. Period. My doc says I gotta be, or I'll die." Fran impersonated him, sounding half Southern, half trucker. Jelly Donut Man had recently had a heart attack. "I'll do whatever you say, 'cause I gotta, even eat that rabbit food, but I ain't no way, no how givin' up on my donuts. Ya hair?" For the first week Fran let him have his three jelly donuts every day. Once he saw that eating all that salad wasn't helping, he agreed to reduce his donut intake to two a day. At first, it worked. He began to lose weight. I imagined his overalls loosening. Then he reached a plateau, so he gave up another donut. "Eventually," she said, "he went a long, long time without eating any jelly donuts." After a year passed and he finally reached his goal weight, Fran surprised him with his goal weight gift: a jelly donut.

"Go ahead. Eat it," she urged. I imagined her as Eve with an outstretched hand. "Go on." Then I pictured an old skinny man with a wrinkled mouth licking powdered sugar off his thin lips.

"He said, 'Ya know, it ain't nearly as good as I remember,'" Fran ended. I still wonder if he finished eating it anyway or if he only took the one bite.

The meeting was over. Fran reweighed Annabelle to see if her bathroom visit had made a difference to the scale. "Be good, ladies," Fran warned from the closet.

I OPENED THE YELLOW CARD WHEN I GOT HOME THAT night. I became aware of my breathing, as if I were about to be caught doing something I shouldn't. I shut my bedroom door and sat on the edge of my twin bed. Written inside the card were the date—September 2, 1984—and my weight. I saw the number and slapped the card closed, almost too fast to have seen. Before that night, I was too terrified to step on a scale. Seeing my weight written in pen made me whine into a cry. I was an ugly porker. Not the cheeky pink kind bathed in buttermilk with a squeal so cute it sounded like a giggle. I was the crossbred boar kind I'd learned about at school, with angry jowls and an immense puckered ham. I looked at my pleated stomach. With the palms of my hands I reached toward my back and pulled the rolls of fat forward toward my lower abdomen. When I pushed it all together, it dimpled. My stomach looked like a yellow spotted potato. I decided I would give up Cheez Doodles.

VARIATIONS OF THIS INITIAL VISIT WOULD CONTINUE sporadically over the next four years. At first my appointments with Fran were described to me as nothing more than a nutritional education. "Just so you're aware," Mom had said. Ultimately, though, I realized it was more. My weekly attendance at these sessions was part of a "reduction program," designed to mold me into something else. In these four years, I'd attend Fran's meetings off and on, but mostly off, and after a yearlong hiatus, I decided to get with the program. In early September of 1988, at age twelve—when a shitty day meant agonizing that "I don't think I love Barry anymore"—I was determined to become the something else, *someone else,* everyone wanted me to be.

Each day Mom packed me a brown paper bag with a dry turkey sandwich on wheat with white lettuce and yellow mustard, accompanied by the dreaded red apple. The flesh was too soft, the skin too thick, and I was too hungry. I ate the damn handles: the dusty-looking parts near the stem, sometimes sucking on the core, as I watched other girls suck Fruit Roll-Ups off their index fingers. My bag contained no Fritos, no whoopie pies, no fun at all. Sometimes I was graced with a minuscule box of raisins, the kind you needed small fingers to open. I had hot-lunch envy.

I wanted a soft doughy pizza square with fries—anything under a heat lamp. Balanced on a plastic tray were corn dogs, chicken potpie, and mac 'n cheese. You ate hot lunch if you were the kid with the mustache or the boy who picked his nose, rolled a boogerball, then flung it across the room, adding machine-gun sound effects.

Popular girls did not do hot lunch. Their mothers supplied them with white-paper-bagged lunches, inscribing their daughter's name in marker. Girls with ribbons and banana curls in their hair enjoyed gourmet deli sandwiches with mozzarella, double-stacked Rice Krispies Treats wrapped in wax paper. They had soda, too, even a straw, and there was always a cutesy note from Mom. I gazed longingly at Diana Cirino's silver Capri Sun pouch, so sweet with artificial goodness that her lips turned fruit-punch red. Then I looked down at my "100% juice" box with a gloating cartoon prune on it. I finished it in one sip, then crunched my way through a bag of room-temperature celery.

Meatballs and overcooked spaghetti, ooh, and garlic bread—bring it to me. I wanted the hot nasty lunch more than the designer sandwiches, despite how in fashion they seemed. But I passed on it all and stuck to my meager meal. I wanted to know how thin tasted.

I lost six and half pounds my first week back on Fran's diet, but during that visit, upon learning of my weight loss success, I was also reminded never to use the word "diet" in Fran's presence.

"It's not a diet," she ranted. "People quit diets. A diet starts, and a diet ends. This is a program." She narrowed in on me with her eyes. "Sure, it feels easy at the beginning. You're just starting to change your habits, so it all feels like an activity, something to follow, find the fun in learning all the new eating rules. But eventually you'll tire of all of this, the watching, the record keeping, the caring. And it will feel like work." It already felt like work. "And you'll want to start a new diet if the weight stops coming off so quickly. You'll eat grapefruits all day, or hot dogs for three days, or cookies for breakfast and lunch with a sensible dinner. You'll try every fad, eating your carbohydrates and proteins at different times because you heard someone swear by it. And I'm here to tell you, diets don't work. Programs do. A program works if it's something you can stick to, forever. If you want to be thin, you'll have to see this as a Weigh of Life." She drew the words on her legal pad, then displayed it with both hands for all of us in the room.

Okay, okay. *Program.* But it's still a damn diet when you're forcing down boiled chicken and water-packed tuna on melba toast; I don't care what you call it.

She told me not to expect to lose so much every week; it was mostly water weight. I never understood what that meant. Water weight. I drank a lake of water that week, so you'd think I would almost gain weight from all the extra fluid. Then I was told I'd lost so much, but it was only water?

Fran had me choose a prize from a wicker basket. The big winners of the week chose first. The best prizes were jumbo pencils with charms on a satin string tied around the eraser. Smaller gifts were magnets, stickers, or erasers that smelled sweet. Once you lost ten pounds, you earned a glossy folder with pastel stationery, so you could pass notes in style. I was still wondering what I'd want for my special gift once I reached my goal weight of 110 pounds (according to both a glossy chart hanging on the inside of her closet door beside the food pyramid and to her rule that for each inch over five feet, add five pounds to a base weight of 100 pounds). I'd grown to five foot two since I'd first gone to Fran when I was eight. And along with the height came even more excess weight. I wore a size 16 in pants and was a long way from any big prize.

"Today is the first day of the rest of your life," Fran began. I sat perched on the edge of the couch. "You are all fat. Every one of you. You might not look fat, but you are. It's not baby fat anymore; it's fat fat. You are not pleasantly plump, big boned, or a little chunky. Just forget shapely, voluptuous, and"—she hesitated and looked up, probing her brain for just one more—"statuesque. You don't need any more sugar in your lives, if you know what I mean. Each of you is F. A. T. Admit to yourself that you have a problem and that this problem, whether you like it or not, will never go away. You can exercise and eat right, but I promise you, you will struggle with this for the rest of your life." Was this right? "And in a way, you're lucky, because you're learning to deal with it while you're young. Some people spend their lives thin, then wake one day to realize they're fat, and they don't have a clue what to do about it. You all have a chance to make eating properly a habit now. Make no mistake, though. You can become thin, but you'll never outgrow this struggle, so stop wishing some miracle pill would fix this for you. Learn to face this instead of running from it."

I WOULD NOT BE ORDINARY.

THAT NIGHT I BOUNDED UP TO MOM AND POPPA'S BEDROOM excited to share my weight-loss news. "Fran said I almost lost a size today. Well, another half a pound and I will be down one clothing size in just one week!"

"Yeah, well, I wouldn't get too excited," Poppa said while doing his crossword puzzle. "You've still got a long way to go."

I stomped off and slammed my bedroom door. In the solitude of my room, I let my ritual of cleaning and peeling begin. I scrubbed my face with Noxzema and stared at the red crease marks my jeans imprinted into my skin around my stomach, across the rolls of fat on my back. I ran my fingers over the rosy indented lines that wiggled across my hips and down the sides of my boobs. There were other lines, temporary ones, left along my shins after I peeled off my socks. I spread powder on the bumpy red patches that crept along my inner thighs. Mother called it chub rub. The boys at school called me Moose.

I dreamed I was thin that night. The dream was so vivid that once I awoke, I was startled to see I was still fat. I kept staring at the mirror, pulling the insides of my thighs in tight grips. I was making the face Grandma made when she sorted through old photographs. She'd gently pass her thumb over her face in a photo. "So young," she'd say. "Would you believe it?" I looked at myself the way old people looked at themselves, in disbelief. The person we saw before us looked nothing like what we pictured in our heads.

I pushed the fat from beneath my chin into my throat with my thumbs. "Oh, well." I sounded like a robot.

The next day I began a new diary of all the food and water and diet soda I put into my body. I didn't want to walk onto the school bus in the morning and hear the boys chanting, "Boom-baba-boom-baba-boom!"

No, really. There was actual chanting. I know it sounds a little *Stand by Me,* but when you've lived it like that, there's no point in borrowing from pop culture. We have a hard enough time forgetting our adolescence; there's no point in drumming up an alternative.

Farmer's cheese, turkey blandwiches, and one half of a hollowed-out bagel smeared with Polaner All Fruit were my new saviors. I crunched down on melon, right to the bitter rind. Chicken of the Sea, two pieces of melba toast. Half a grapefruit, half a banana. Everything was halved. Alba Fit & Frosty mornings, roughage. It was rough all right. I craved an extra piece of bread.

And I'd continue to crave "extra" for the rest of my life. Never one to order the sauce on the side, and certainly not the type to substitute steamed anything for fries, I've come to learn that "programs" just turn me into a bitch. First you crave a larger portion, an extra serving of protein. Then you want rings of Maui tempura onions pressed onto your rare cheddar burger. You begin to realize, quite simply, that life isn't only unfair; it's uncommonly cruel.

According to Fran, I still had forty-eight pounds to lose, "You know, so you'll have some wiggle room when you're trying to maintain." She urged me to keep it in the back of my mind and to focus on the near term instead. My short-term goal became hitting the 100-pound groove in the metal doctor's scale. Currently, the heavy anchor weight was lodged in the 150-pound slot. I weighed 156 pounds and change. Change, indeed.

three

Sabotaje

Tomorrow's Yom Kippur. We're going to temple because Poppa feels guilty. I'm going to fast. It won't hurt. I need to lose weight. I'm so fat. God, how I wish I was skinny. Guess I'll really have to put my mind to it!

MARIA IS AMUSING.

Pablo is very quiet.

Jose is right handed.

Mr. Navar is boring.

In Spanish class a few weeks later, our teacher, Mr. Navar, lectured on the differences between *ser* and *estar,* both verbs for "to be." *Ser,* he said, was used when describing permanent things. With your nationality, gender, or the color of your eyes, use *ser.* Tell 'em you're tall; say it like you mean it. *Estar* was a slapdash of a word describing a passing mood. We alternated around the classroom, student to student, everyone describing him or herself using a vocabulary word from the chalkboard. *Gordo, gorda, flaco, flaca.* Fat and thin were the only words on the board. *Soy flaco. Soy flaca. Yo soy flaca.* My turn: *"Soy flaca."* I didn't waver.

The next person began, *"Yo soy—"*

Señor Navar interrupted, "Come on, class. We are who we are. There's no point in pretending. No shame. It's not good or bad; it just is." He pointed to his distended stomach and said, "*Soy gordo.* Okay, Stephanie, do yours again."

I sunk into my chair, my chin fell to my chest, and I pushed out a whisper, *"Soy gorda."* The Spaniards are wrong; weight should be *estar.*

I couldn't eat at lunchtime. I stole away to the library and picked my scalp.

I WAS RAVENOUS COME DINNER. I SALIVATED OVER THE LAMB chop Poppa gnawed. Orange grease dripped down his fingers as he sank his teeth into the marbleized flesh. It would taste better with a smear of mint jelly, melting into the valleys, along the edges of the crackling fat. I rolled a lump of baked potato with my tongue until it crumbled against the roof of my mouth, fuzzy and dry, like mealy bits of bruised fruit.

"Eat the skin," Mom urged. "It's where all the vitamins are. Very good for your hair, skin, and nails," she said as she clicked hers against her glossy place mat. I thought of the "man protein" the girls had discussed during my very first meeting with Fran. The potato skin felt like a piece of paper that had been torn from a grocery bag. "Eat more," she said, "it's so good for you." I was accustomed to being told what *not* to eat, but now that I was on a "food program," I was being encouraged to eat. The skin of things. Canned foods. Powders. Things I never would have eaten before were being offered to me, a display of "it's okay." More than ever, I was being urged to eat, at the exact moment in my life when I was focusing on the nots. Eat more of this, not that. Fill up on water, sodium-free soups, fiber. I thought I was supposed to have less, yet more was offered.

I pushed the last bulb of potato across my plate, thinking I might leave it there to prove I had control. There were more potatoes in the world, I told myself. I could have them at any time. Did I really want more right now? I knew my body was sated, but my brain wanted to eat like a beast. "Go on, eat it! Fast, while no one's looking!" I edged my plate clean with the side of my fork, then went in for the plunge. I reached across the table, leaning over my younger sister Lea's plate, and sank the cool metal into the buttery basin of scalloped potatoes. Mom cooked separate meals. I wanted to be good, for Fran to like me, mostly, but I didn't want anyone else to want it for me. It was mine, like my blood and name.

Poppa waved no to me with his finger when he saw my fork hit the side of the fluted dish. Yellow oil pooled near the center; only a wedge of scalloped pie remained. I would have savored it now that I was dieting, enjoying each bite as if it were my first. Dieting made me relish things I'd previously ignored. He then puffed out his cheeks at me, pushing his chair away from the table. "You don't want that," he said, waiting to see what I'd do. "You really don't." I ate the forkful. "You're not even hungry," he said.

You're fat, too, I thought. *Why do you get to eat it?*

That's when I realized men got away with more. Men could eat piles of food and lick the marrow from bones. Gnaw ribs of meat and heave coated discs of starch into their mouths. It fed their blood, made their handshake more powerful. It didn't matter if you were fat and a man. If you were fat and a girl you were no longer feminine. Fat was masculine. *Gordo.*

I'll show you, I thought, but all that it showed was up on the scale the following week.

I MISSED THE TEEN SESSION AT FRAN'S DUE TO "INSUBORdination."

The word was written in cursive on a pink slip of paper. Mrs. Joan Trover, my eighth-grade math teacher, had lovely penmanship. We called her Roxy behind her back, because it was rumored that she had lived on a boat and had tattooed "Roxy" on part of her breast. Austen Rand, a boy who chuckled audibly at math jokes, confirmed it to me one day.

"It's there. I saw it when I went up to her d-d-desk to ask her for help before class. I saw all the way down to her hair pie." Then he snickered the kind of laugh that uses a string of *hes*. *Hehehehehe.*

After the second bell rang, signaling we all ought to be in our classes, I asked Mrs. Trover if I could go to the bathroom.

"Absolutely not," she snapped as she straightened the crease of her green attendance book. She thought we all smoked in the bathrooms, but I was known for saying things like, "Please extinguish your cigarette. I can smell your cancer." So I was put off. "Now, Stephanie, sit down and take out your homework."

"It's already out, and I really have to go."

She raised her eyebrow and squinted.

"What? I *have* to go."

"You don't have to do anything except sit down right this minute."

"I'll sit, but then you're gonna have a puddle on your floor." I wasn't being urgent about it. I could have convinced her to excuse me if I was more insistent, if I started to hold myself.

"Stephanie, I've had enough now. Stop your nonsense this instant, or you'll be visiting Mr. Dolan's office."

"Well, I suppose that would be all right. I assume *he* has a bathroom in there, and I doubt *he'll* make me explain about the puddle effect."

"I mean it!"

"Okay, then how about you give me a cup and I'll take care of it right here and now." That was pushing it.

She called the principal's office and handed me a pink slip with the word "insubordination" written on it and her signature, "Joan Trover."

"Why didn't you sign it 'Roxy'?" I could see it, just then, that broad line, creamy and thick. I had crossed the line. Definitely.

I sat and listened as Mr. Dolan told me I had so much potential, but I wasn't channeling it properly.

"Mr. Dolan, it's not about potential; it's about pee."

I was a good kid. A horrid infant, I'm told, but a good kid. I think all parents get put through it at some point. If your toddler is a lump of sugar, you'll look forward to tongue-piercing rebellions and a getaway ladder propped up against a bedroom window. I was an easy adolescent where school and drugs were concerned. To this day, I've never experimented with any drugs, including what Poppa refers to as "grass." I've never even taken a drag of a cigarette, but my friend Hillary Senft made me hold one once, in the parking lot of Roosevelt Field Shopping Center, late at night, "just in case someone approaches us, you can burn them in self-defense." I hated having to defend myself to our principal, so I sat with my hands in my lap staring at him across his expansive desk. He had kind eyes and was a gentle man.

Mr. Dolan exhaled a defeated sigh and asked me to remain after school for detention. Despite the punishment, I felt that Mr. Dolan was on my side. That secretly he, too, knew I wasn't being unreasonable. In a way, I believed he was proud of me, that if school politics weren't at play, he'd have patted me on the back and applauded my inherent assertiveness. I thought rude was justifiable if you were right.

Of course I was wrong, but at the precocious age of twelve, I simply rolled my eyes and agreed to stay after school, believing, without equivocations, that I would be extraordinary.

"Precocious," by the by, is the go-to term used by ordinary adults who were never categorized as gifted. "Snotty" is far more accurate.

Since I had spent that Monday afternoon in Mr. Dolan's office, I wasn't able to make it to Fran's teen session. So I attended the adult session on Wednesday night. To accommodate the larger group, the adult session, like Weight Watchers, was held in the basement of a church instead of at Fran's house. A folded Japanese screen surrounded the scale. I heard a man say "M.S." before he stepped onto the scale that night. I never heard anyone say anything before weighing in because at the teen sessions the scale was in a closet. I also had no idea men would ever see someone to lose weight.

"Henry, do you know what M.S. stands for?" Henry knew that when people walked up to the scale and said "M.S.," Fran subtracted three pounds automatically. Henry didn't answer Fran. The ladies in the class were poking one another in the sides with their elbows while covering their lips with their fingers, implying we should all be quiet to hear what was happening behind the screen.

"M.S. stands for menstrual syndrome, Henry." With that, the silence broke into laughter. Henry came out from behind the curtain carrying his shoes.

"Hey, it was worth a shot," he said, a shoe in each hand by his hips.

He sat in front of me. His wife rubbed his back and whispered, "That's what you get for being a smart-ass." That night his wife complained to Fran that she didn't understand why she wasn't losing weight. "Henry and I eat the same exact thing. He loses weight, and I end up gaining weight. How is that possible?"

"If you eat what he eats, you're going to weigh what he weighs. More, actually."

"You do not. You don't eat what I eat," he protested. "You ate a whole jar of fruit spread the other night."

I wish I could have seen the wife's face after Henry said that. The room became silent, and even Fran said nothing. She just peered out over her reading glasses. It was clear, that night, the wife would not be eating what Henry ate. Henry would be gnawing a bone, all on his own, nibbling on rawhide in the doghouse into which he had just cast himself.

The adult session was much less relevant to me than the teen class. I didn't need to cook separate meals for my husband and children. And I didn't care how many calories were burned if you vacuumed the house. I raised my hand and asked Fran, "What do I do about the fact that my mother always buys my father goodies? And it drives me crazy, and even though she'll try to hide one, I always find it and eat some. The other day I found an apple pie in his bedroom dresser!" I didn't mention the fact that I'd gone in there to grab his *Truly Tasteless Jokes* book. I'd read passages for detailed scenarios then masturbate to words like "bush," "spread," and "cream."

"And when I asked her not to buy stuff like that, she said she can't deprive my sister or father of their goodies just because I'm fat." I had gained three pounds that week. All the adults looked at me, sitting on the metal folding chair in my nylon sweat suit. It was quiet, and when I finished talking, they all looked to Fran, waiting for her response.

"You ask your mother, if her daughter were an alcoholic, would she serve your father a beer with dinner?" Fran was a pro. "Obesity is a disease the same way alcoholism is. Obesity can even be harder because—well, as you all know, you can't go cold turkey with food." It was the first time I'd heard the expression. Cold turkey. I pictured Grandpa seated at the head of our dining room table with an awkward serving fork, surveying a holiday platter for the dark meat.

Fran cleared her throat and began with a story. "'Jane was an overweight teen with a beautiful face. "Such a pretty face" sounded like a compliment, but to Jane, when people said it, all she heard was that while her face was pretty, the rest of her wasn't. It was just a backhanded reminder that she was a disappointment—not living up to her potential.'" Apparently it was going around. "'Jane had enough.'" Fran stopped reading, looked up, and alternated stares with each of us for emphasis, then continued. "'Jane decided she wanted to lose weight once and for all. Her face and sweet personality afforded her a handsome boyfriend named Roger, and she wanted to look her best for him. As time went by, people took notice of how great Jane was looking. In the hallways at school, compliments were no longer reserved for what a great game Roger had played the previous night. Jane was beginning to lose weight, and people took notice.'" Then Fran paused, looking up, before continuing. "'One day, she opened her locker to discover a box of butter cookies that hadn't been there before. Jane had tried hard for weeks to avoid her favorites. She couldn't understand why someone would do this to her. Upset, she went to the principal and explained the situation. She couldn't think of anyone who would do such a thing to her. The principal gave his word he'd monitor the situation.'" It was no surprise that it was Roger who was sneaking the goods into her locker. All I could think about, in that moment, were Girl Scout Cookies, how Mom froze them by the box, hoping to prevent all of us from devouring them in one sitting. She'd shove them far back in the freezer, behind the bulky meats and plastic-wrapped holiday appetizers. My arm began to sting when I rummaged for too long.

I imagined the cookies in Jane's locker were Trefoils, buttery Girl Scout logos, the kind you put in your mouth and just suck on until they collapse into a buttery paste.

"Sabotage," Fran said sternly, snapping me back into the moment. "There will always be people trying to sabotage your progress. And in most cases it will be the very people you would hope would be your biggest supporters."

When I got home that evening, I sat at the dining room table with a large piece of construction paper and a Magic Marker. The table was polished and smelled of lemons. Fruit was piled high on a long silver banana-leaf serving plate. Tangerines, waxy apples, and yellow freckled pears. The squat donut peaches smelled fake, like the sweet perfumed hair of a plastic doll. I ate a banana and knew the reason it was there was to bring out the yellow highlights of the surrounding paintings on the walls. I drew a calendar of the week with slots for breakfast, lunch, and dinner. I wrote "banana" in the Wednesday evening slot. On the back of the paper I wrote:

I am not going to be Moose any longer.
I will not come home and eat three bowls of cereal.
I will do something active every day.
I will drink my water.
I will not be sabotaged.

I stuck the food calendar to the refrigerator using a Popsicle-stick magnet I'd received as a prize from Fran the previous week. The stick had a strip that looked like a fortune cookie printout attached saying STICK WITH IT. There was also the miniature cupcake wrapper with the magnetic Reese's peanut butter cup magnet placed inside it. Attached to the cupcake paper was a strip that read SUCCESS IS ITS OWN SWEET REWARD. There were magnetic rolling pins, avocado halves, cracked eggs, and a lobster with a missing claw. There was a papaya, some pigs, and lots of cows, too many. And in the center, a stupid battery-operated bulldog guarded the fridge and barked every time the refrigerator door opened. This was Mom's idea.

"What? It was on sale."

four

Sloppy Seconds

I am so psyched up for camp! I'm making out lists of what I want to bring. I'm going to a new camp! I am psyched! Camp doesn't start for another three months. Meanwhile, I must have called the number 540-0001 forty-eight times, and it's $2.00 the first minute and $0.45 each additional minute. I met this guy Pete on there. He thinks I'm 16 years old. In case you haven't guessed, I'm not. He's 19, almost 20. I talk to him on the phone. We've never met. He talks about "eating out" and blowjobs, and I don't mean blowing up balloons for $0.20 a balloon.

I BOUNCED FROM DETERMINED TO DEFLATED TOO OFTEN. Here's how it went: I combed through beauty magazines with a pair of scissors, the long silvery kind with a Q tail, used for clipping locks of hair. I'd cut out images of things I might like to wear once I became thin. Asymmetrical Benetton sweaters with miniskirts and white slouchy leather boots. I'd reward myself with fashion, or beg my parents to, instead of gratifying myself with food. Mostly, I chose images of navels. Not oranges. Abdomens. I wanted a vertical belly button.

Mine looked like a horizontal coin deposit slit. I was a walking piggy bank. I'd affix the images to the bevel of my full-length mirror then stand naked in front of it, distending my stomach, examining, and comparing. "Oh well," I'd say aloud, then climb into my fat pants, which were becoming looser. They were still fat pants.

When I was at school, though, watching girls with ribbons in their hair eat moist brownies, I wanted that too. Walnuts. The hard edge of a corner piece, dipped into cold milk. I stopped caring about my thinspiration mirror and cared only about the now. I'd heard it all the time, "Live in the moment." But if I did that, I'd weigh more than a dump truck. Losing weight wasn't about the moment at all; it was about having faith in the future. It was about knowing there would be another meal in a few hours. I could wait; I needn't stuff the day's nutritional values into my Hostess-hole all at once.

Fran had told us about a client she once had. "A concentration camp survivor," she whispered, shaking her head. "She couldn't leave food on her plate." I wasn't surviving anything but puberty, and I ate like I'd survived locusts. "So I had her eat on smaller plates, so she wouldn't feel guilty about not eating all her food." Then she emphasized, "Portion control." Fine, I'm eating one brownie, not a tray. Deal.

That's when I dealt with the plateau. "But I'm doing everything the same," I lied when the scale moved in the wrong direction.

"Well, maybe you need to vary your diet more," Fran instructed after assessing my fallacious food diary. Yeah, I'd eat blondies instead of brownies. Great idea, Frannie. I wanted what tasted good more than I wanted thin. I wanted them both, really. So I'd have the brownie and even out the crooked piece of pound cake from the fridge, thinking I'd starve myself the next day. It's called pound cake for a reason, and you can't eat it and have it, too.

It was a lesson my paternal grandmother had tried, more than once, to instill in me over the holidays. "Now, that's way too big, Stephanie," she'd say of my slice of chocolate layer cake. "You can't eat all that."

"Oh, yes I can too." I knew she didn't mean I was incapable of finishing my portion, but I'd pretend not to understand the implication.

"Now, now, you share that piece with Grandma," she'd say as her fork cleaved its way through my dessert. "Tell her, Nenda," Grandma once said, looking to Mom for solidarity.

"Nenda" was the name Aunt Iris took to calling Mom when they were younger, at an age where "Yolanda" was too much name for such a small mouth. When Poppa first broached the subject of marrying outside the Jewish faith with his parents, he used the name "Nenda." He didn't want to divulge that the name of the woman he intended to marry was "Yolanda," fearful it would betray her Hispanic heritage. "European," he'd said when probed for more details. "Yeah, Greek." He spoke in half-truths about Mom's half-Greek, half–Puerto Rican lineage. When Grandma discovered that Mom was Puerto Rican, she refused to speak to Poppa for six months and had to get a prescription for Valium. She worried that her grandchildren would come out black.

"Nenda" shrugged when asked about the size of my serving, sweeping off into the kitchen to clear the mostly untouched plates of food she'd spent weeks preparing. In the days preceding a holiday, our freezer and fridge teemed with foods we weren't to touch. "No, those are for the guests, girls! Here, you can help with these," Mom urged, directing Lea and me to help construct the spanakopita.

We'd work at a hurried pace, stationing ourselves at the kitchen table, unwrapping cool strips of phyllo from a damp cloth, spooning the runways of dough with melted butter, then pressing on a new layer. It felt like the thin skin on the backs of hands. Phyllo, zigzag butter, drizzle, phyllo, butter, phyllo—it all had a rhythm. Mom sang "Silver Bells" while she oversaw the construction, warning us not to add too much of the spinach-feta mixture. All that work only to add a single spoonful of filling, folded up in its triangular pocket like a gem hidden in a handkerchief.

And it all went half-eaten. Intermittently, Mom stuffed cherry tomatoes with crabmeat, but religiously, for the Jews, she set out a crystal bowl lumped with chopped liver and flanked it with Carr's Table Water Crackers.

"These are delicious, Nenda. You've really outdone yourself. What are these?" Grandma asked, her outstretched hand covered with a crisp, half-eaten triangle atop a poinsettia-print napkin.

Because I loved attention as much as food, I interrupted with the answer, "Span-ah-co-pee-ta." Upon hearing a foreign name, Grandma's face clenched into a stiff smile. I watched, wondering if she'd swallow.

"Spinach triangles," Mom hurried to reassure Grandma as she glared at me. Bad. Bad girl for letting your Jewish grandmother know she was eating something "ethnic." It wasn't as if Mom were serving intestines. Mom had to wear fabric armpit guards beneath her holiday silks because Grandma's nervous constitution made Mom nervous, too. "You know, just a little spinach and cheese," Mom encouraged, sounding as panicked as Grandma looked.

Grandma finished chewing, but she never asked for more.

Instead she asked, "Where did you get this chopped liver? It's tastier than last year's." She opted for the organ. Who remembers what last year's liver tasted like?

With the company gone, the kitchen immaculate, and everyone sacked in their beds, I was finally able to eat. The moon outside the kitchen window looked as though it had been poked in place with a Q-tip. I ate from a bakery box in the dark.

The lights flipped on, and I froze, the fork still in my mouth.

"What are you doing, Stephanie?" Mom asked.

And without pause, I distinctly remember mumbling, "Grandma didn't let me have my cake because she ate it, too."

Mom opened the cabinet beneath the kitchen sink, pulled out a long sheet of aluminium foil, and used her hands to wrap up the cake, wedging it into the freezer. She licked icing from her fingers and left the box on the counter. Before shutting the lights, she said, "Now come on. Time for bed."

I was still sucking on my fork as I heard her make her way up the stairs.

AFTER THE HOLIDAYS, FRAN LECTURED ABOUT WILLPOWER.

"I just couldn't take it anymore," she confessed during a teen session. "I tried. I did. But I had to get that cake out of the house. Out. Out. Out."

I'd eaten mine for breakfast. Frozen.

"You all need to try it this week," Fran said to the group. "See how liberating it is to say no to something. To just upturn your plate and let the cake flop out into your garbage. Let the frosting stick to all those garlic skins, onion peels, and carrot shavings." I would have eaten it if that's all she had in her garbage. She should have said other things. I wished I had her willpower.

She lost me completely once she mentioned the coffee filters she'd dumped in on top. I felt an eyebrow poke up, wondering how it might taste: the fine grain of strong coffee, the sugary luxury of chocolate. I'd need a whole lot worse in my garbage can to prevent me from digging through it.

I sometimes found slugs on our walkway. I'd cover them with salt and watch them shrivel and ooze. That's what had to be in my trash if I was going to toss something as delectable as cupcakes and be expected not to root them up afterward.

Despite her willpower, Fran didn't seem pleased with herself. She explained that it would have been better if she hadn't been driven to spoil the things she loved. She said it took more willpower to keep things in the house and resist them than it did to rid your shelves of all that you coveted. Fran said "willpower" as if it was the ultimate goal. Resisting temptation is what made you a success. True success seemed to come from the ability to prepare food, to have a stare down, and, ultimately, to resist.

I imagined Fran wrapped half-finished wedges of pie, first in a layer of plastic wrap, then in an armor of aluminum foil, just like Mom. Fran would tuck it away in the back of a freezer. That she kept in her garage. Which was always locked. The key is somewhere inconvenient. Like the neighbor's garage. "If you're really good," she confided, "you wouldn't need to hide or bury things." You could bypass a tray of frosted cupcakes as if they were lima beans. La-di-dah.

To be successful at that game, I'd need to hide the goods beneath the fleck on the speck on the tail on the frog on the bump on the branch on the log in the hole in the bottom of the sea. I wasn't good at hiding food. I was better at finding it.

THROUGHOUT THE REST OF WINTER AND INTO SPRING, I rewarded myself with food when I lost weight, which only led to a gain the following week. Even if I starved myself the whole day of weigh-in, it couldn't hide my celebration feasts: nachos at the movies tented in spicy cheese sauce, curly golden French fries showered with the sweet sting of ketchup, puffy Cheez Doodles tucked into my cheeks as I sucked them into a cream. I didn't show up for Fran's meetings for weeks. "Too much homework," I pleaded to Mom and Poppa. This was absolutely true, the bit about homework. I couldn't get a grip on Bacon's Rebellion. Reading about backcountry farmers made me crave soft-boiled eggs with crackling fatty bacon strips. Cheesy grits with moons of butter. Brushing up on American history was impossible. I masturbated as I read texts on global studies, trying to speed through the passages.

I gained weight and feared returning to Fran.

"Can't I go to Weight Watchers instead?" I pleaded with Mom. And she complied, but when I did try Weight Watchers, I learned it wasn't personalized. The leader didn't stare at me; she was too concerned about her lecture, thumbing through index cards. She didn't recount motivational stories or read from books. Instead she requested that the group participate, asking simple, obvious questions to involve everyone and let them do all the talking. Really, it seemed like making someone else do your work for you. "Share with me some of your negative self-talk.

Raise your hands and let's make a list of all the mean things we say to ourselves." I could do that at home and didn't need to hear how I was crueler to myself than I'd ever be to others.

To me Weight Watchers was an idea whose supporters seemed to be clumps of housewives in church basements who didn't mind eating meat Jell-O. I was pretty sure I'd seen a recipe for herring in aspic beside a pedometer. They sold powdered shakes and then drew food pyramid diagrams on jumbo memo pads. Women in tapered jeans, wearing sweaters with cowboy tassels, asked if they had any additional treats for sale in the back. And the lecturer wouldn't dream of saying, "Why don't you try to forgo all snacking this week since you gained today and see if you can manage eating three healthful meals instead?" Fran would have. Fran made me accountable.

Fran reminded me of everything I avoided when I looked at myself in the mirror. She was my cellulite, the fat flippers on my back, my subconscious telling me I had to face it all and deal. I knew it was time to go back to her. And as sure as I knew it, I was just as terrified—terrified of becoming the teary-eyed plum pudding in her basement closet. I imagined returning to Fran, after missing weeks upon weeks, and being stared down through those half-moon glasses of hers. I became a mind reader: *Fat. You are a husky girl, and you've got no business ever missing a meeting, tubby. You weigh more than I do.* When I did return, Fran said, "I'm glad you've decided to come back." She touched my hand. "You'll do it this time."

She was wrong. I didn't lose anything except my resolve. "Well, you've hit a plateau," Fran said, still glancing at my yellow card. "But don't get discouraged. I think you've grown." Five foot three and it was nearly summer again. 1989. I was now thirteen; I'd grown, indeed.

✿ GREAT SUMMER CAMP ✿

If you are 8 to 16 and need to lose weight try Yanisin.

Have fun and lose weight. Great food, no hunger.

Call Kevin @ Yanisin 800-FIT-CAMP

IT WAS CIRCLED IN RED AND POSTED ON THE REFRIGERAtor door beneath a frying pan magnet: my introduction to summer 1989. Actually, it was for both Lea and me.

I'd gone to sleepaway camps before, camps where I ate burnt marshmallows off a stick, attended organized evening activities of chocolate pudding wrestling, and had canteen time with my own harvest of candy. But these camps I asked for. Back in 1985 I'd wanted more than anything to experience a sleepover party that lasted a full eight weeks. I had to plead with Mom and Poppa, though. They thought I was too young to spend an entire summer away.

Really, I think it was less to do with my nine-year-old status and more to do with the fact that I was a chronic bed wetter. They'd tried everything to cure it. Mom and Poppa moved beyond the rubber sheet to restricting my intake of fluids: no liquids after 8 P.M. And, before bedtime, they'd wait outside the bathroom door, insisting I empty my bladder. It didn't help. I'd still awake wet and warm.

Eventually they'd found a metal contraption that sounded an alarm when wet. The slim electrical mat was slid beneath my sheets, a thin stash of wires peeking out, connecting to the black boxy alarm.

Middream, I'd spring up, startled to realize I hadn't been using the toilet as I'd imagined. I'd click off the alarm and run to the bathroom. Then I'd cover the small round wet spot with a towel and fall back asleep. The bedwetting tapered off. I'd have the occasional relapse, but overall I was in a better position to negotiate for sleepaway camp.

I strategically placed reminder notes throughout our house, begging to go to Camp Summit like my slightly older cousin Jessica. I taped a note to the milk carton saying, "You won't need to buy as many groceries!" I wove one through the teeth of Poppa's comb saying, "I promise to be well groomed." They were everywhere. I placed one into the cuff of Mom's gold bracelet in her jewelry box, wrapped one around Poppa's steering wheel, and even taped one beneath the toilet seat. They sent in the money for my first summer away from home.

Shortly after securing a spot at Camp Summit, my parents let me have my first sleepover at Teresa Stone's house—the very same girl Fran had mentioned at my first session. Teresa wore spandex pants with heels once she was in high school. Our senior class yearbook predicted she'd be "Owner of Terry's House of Spandex in 2013." I'm convinced Teresa added them to her wardrobe as a prohibitory measure against having to change her clothes in front of others for gym class. This was an idea I could get behind, but not at the price of electric blue latex. Maybe she read a magazine article on how to dress when you're full figured. "Don't wear oversized clothes; you'll look like a tent." Although she was only marginally overweight, maybe Terry wore spandex with the hope that she'd look like a tent pole.

In grammar school she was the kind of girl who'd lean over her paper during tests, assuming everyone wanted to copy from her. "Ooh, ooh" regularly escaped her mouth as she held one arm over her head, straining to give our teachers her perfect pigtailed answers. Today, she's most likely the woman at the gym who times people on the elliptical machine. She'll interrupt their workout with a perky, "Oh, I see you've got two minutes left." Then she'll tap her sports watch and flash a disingenuous smile, clenching her small workout towel as she stands waiting instead of just using the stationary bike.

In fourth grade we were paired together for a science project. After school we had to grow our own crystals from salt—something involving a string and the sun. The project took a week, so Teresa suggested we get together over the weekend to check its progress.

"Well, why don't you check its progress and tell me about it?" We *were* talking about salt.

"But then we're not doing it together, and this is a group project."

"But there isn't anything to *do*. You want me to come over and just look at the salt?"

"Yes."

"But then what will we do after?"

"We can play with dolls or do a puzzle."

I wasn't the most popular girl, but I had standards. Playing dolls with Terry meant she'd want to dress them and pretend they were at school solving mathematical word problems that referenced oranges and cups of milk. I'd want to undress them and make them have orgies. Teresa and I were very different girls, but I agreed to a sleepover. Maybe this Teresa girl had a hidden side.

Or not.

"Ew, that's gross," she said in reaction to my suggestion of having Barbie sleep with Ken's dad.

"Fine, she can sleep with his mom, then."

Teresa pranced to her dressing table and counted as she brushed her long plume of brown hair with her Mason Pearson brush. I put the Barbies down and slept in the guest room. It was the first house I'd ever been to where a room was devoted to and solely used by guests. I left early in the morning, whispering to Mom over the phone to please hurry and pick me up.

Days later I was at North Side Elementary School Park, just around the corner from my house, with my best friend Hillary Senft. We were playing Don't Touch the Rocks, a game where we'd hop from slide to swing to ladder without ever touching the pebbled floor of the playground. The sky began to darken, but we decided, instead of running home, that we'd lie on the big tire swings and twirl until everything became unfocused and we somehow felt as though we were more part of the sky than we were of the earth.

When I looked up and steadied myself on the swing, I saw Mrs. Stone, Teresa's mother. Mrs. Stone yanked Teresa by the hand toward me.

"Are you going to tell her, or am I?" Mrs. Stone asked in a shrill voice to her daughter. Teresa stood silent, looking at her shoes.

"Hi, Teresa," I said.

"Hi," she said to the pebbled ground.

"Well, Teresa doesn't want to have to say anything, Stephanie," Mrs. Stone continued, "but if you're not nice to her and make people like her, she's going to tell everyone at school that you still wet the bed."

I whipped around, looking for Hillary, wondering if she'd heard. She was steadying herself by the fence across the way, picking gravel from her shoe.

"Do you know we were on our hands and knees scrubbing your piss from our mattress? That the smell is still there?"

I don't know if I blinked or shrugged, but I didn't speak. "Well, do you?" *Circle, circle, dot, dot* repeated in my head. Kids would be giving out cootie shots in my presence. They'd call me Crotch Rot and ask to see my diaper rash.

"Well, what do you have to say? Are you going to make people like her or not?" I didn't say anything. "You had better, or rest assured, the entire school will hate you instead of Teresa."

I still cannot believe Mrs. Stone was a friend of Fran's. That she slid into her car that day, dragging Teresa with her, making sure seat belts were fastened as she drove to my house, planning to say the reckless things she did. Or that she reinforced, not only to her daughter but also to others, that Teresa was disliked, hated even. And although I didn't have the words just then, I was certain my parents would.

I zipped home from the playground in a crying frenzy. Hillary followed, unsure of what was going on. "I hurt my knee," I told her. As I ran up our front path, I glanced through the garage windows, looking to see if Poppa's car was there, but he wasn't home yet. I raced upstairs into my parents' bedroom and relayed the events to Mom, hoping she'd know just what to say. Not just to me, but to Mrs. Stone. Surely I'd hear her say "How dare you?!" in a stern phone conversation, along with a "some nerve," a reminder, even, that I was just a child. And then another "Really, how *dare* you?! If you have a problem with my child, you deal with me; you don't threaten a nine-year-old."

But this was Mom, for whom the phrase "How dare you?!" was as foreign as Burma. Apparently Mrs. Stone had first gone to our house looking for me, and when she shared with Mom her plans to spread word that I still wet the bed, Mom said there was no reason for it to come to that, that Teresa and I would work things out ourselves. But Mrs. Stone didn't see. Instead, she left our house and then accosted me on the playground minutes later. And when I told my parents, they never thought to make that follow-up "How dare you?!" phone call. No one was on my side, and I felt ashamed.

Poppa worried I was wetting the bed for attention. Had I wanted attention, I might've considered doing cartwheels and overblown cheers, worn a squishy clown nose, or stuck with the tried-and-true tantrum. Becoming known as "Miss Tinkle" wasn't the kind of attention I hoped to garner. Poppa tried to intellectualize it, combing through books in self-help aisles. "Genetics," some books said. "Love," others reasoned. Mom insisted it was hereditary, and "nothing to get so neurotic about. These things happen." I might have received more hugs, but I still awoke in a wet ring of urine.

"Kegel exercises," my pediatrician had insisted during a wellness exam.

"What do bagels have to do with anything?"

"No, *Kegel,*" he said, this time more slowly. He instructed that when I urinated during the day, I only allow small amounts to escape before quickly holding it in again. When I did this, I still imagined a bagel, visualizing myself peeing through the center of it with each new blast. Even my bladder was lazy. I figured it was better than a lazy eye. At least a lazy bladder you could hide.

And as it turned out, Teresa hid it for me; she never told anyone. Still, I couldn't quite look at her ever again. Sure it was summer, and Mom and Poppa decided to let me attend Camp Summit after all, but I knew the end of the school year wouldn't wipe the slate clean with Teresa Stone. You don't just forget something like that. She knew something about me no one else did, and that intimacy, the way she knew that part of me and could at any moment push it and hold it against me, wasn't something I could easily forget either.

I continued to wet the bed during those early summers at the normal sleepaway camps, waking in the blunt of night, ripping sheets off my cot in the dark, hoping I wouldn't be discovered. I sometimes slept on towels and remade my bed after breakfast. If anyone noticed, no one said anything.

And now, four summers later, in the spring of eighth grade, a small part of me still worried I might relapse. My body was lazier than ever, and this time I was no longer the one threading notes around the house in unusual places. This time it was Mom and Poppa who left them right there on the refrigerator door: their demand for sleepaway camp.

It wasn't Jew camp with Friday nights ensconced in white, lighting candles and reciting prayers over bug juice and braided yellow challah, as Camp Summit had been. This time there would be no bug juice. This time there was a toll-free number incorporating the words "fit camp."

I ate three bowls of Crispix, sitting at the kitchen table with the box and the milk, staring at the posting. "Lose weight," the advertisement said. There was a photograph of a boy standing sideways, his head turned to the camera, smiling. He was wearing what appeared to be Jolly Fisherman pants, holding them out in front of him. It was his "after" picture. I didn't know how to feel about it. I wanted to lose weight, but knowing someone else hoped I'd lose it too was like saying the words aloud: "I am fat." I didn't like admitting it. It's why I sometimes wore one of Mom's girdles to school. I could know I was fat, but when anyone else acknowledged it, I felt ashamed. Going to Fran was one thing, but a whole summer away with a horde of fat kids felt like a punishment. "Great food. No hunger." It seemed weird seeing an advertisement for sleepaway camp that didn't tout horseback riding, friendship, and tradition. Instead it focused on need: *Need to lose weight?*

As long as there was a fat camp out there that would "fix it," I wouldn't need Fran anymore. I wouldn't have to worry about losing weight on my own, about willpower, about her staring me down through her mauve spectacles. Fran was wrong; there was an easier solution. There was a fat camp in the woods of West Stockbridge, Massachusetts, that would force my body to move, would serve me the meals I'd need to eat. I wouldn't have to make decisions, just show up.

I glugged down the remaining yellow milk in my cereal bowl. Now that there was fat camp, nothing else mattered. Now there was a sausage-sized container of raw cookie dough for the taking. Everything bagels with jelly and an extra-thick layer of whipped butter. Now was time for sloppy seconds, no napkins, licking from my fingers. In the coming weeks, I began to do as they said and lived in the now. Only I did it with a can of Easy Cheese in hand.

When the brochure for the camp arrived, I ripped it from its envelope for studying. I'd pass it to Lea once I'd committed each page to memory. The booklet seemed outdated; girls in butterfly shorts with ribbing along the edges, frosted winged hair, square bathing suits. It looked like a plumper and homelier version of *Three's Company,* with nary a Suzanne Somers in sight. There were knee socks pulled to the actual knee. I kept returning to one photograph: kneeling in front of a young girl in a pink floral swimsuit, a nurse with cropped hair studied the numbers on the tape measure she wrapped around the girl's thighs. It was the one image in the brochure that really showed it, the addressing of weight. The other photographs featured archery, boys playing basketball without shirts, just flaps of fat covering their waistbands, kids coated in shaving cream. Arts and crafts activity, with tongues furled in concentration; treasure boxes made with Popsicle sticks; girls sitting in a circle threading lanyards. Go-karts. I didn't see sweat. War-painted faces, feathered hats, campers in a band of locked arms, jumping into a lake off a floating dock. There were some skinny people, but mostly the kids were fat, fatter than I was. Measurements. Yikes.

The packing list made me frantic. I kept returning to the photos in the brochure, squinting at the cubbies in the cabins. What did they have in there? I needed everything on that list, laid out in stacks on my bedroom floor to see. Because unlike at my prior camps, no one from home would be there. No one knew me; I had a fresh start, and my wardrobe, I knew, would be my social life. That and my bedding. Thankfully, I no longer needed a plastic sheet. Now I needed something plush and perfect. I'd learned from my last camps, with the mistake that was my reversible Strawberry Shortcake sleeping bag, that your bedding defined you. Something simple and practical worked. Navy blue. Waterproof. But let's face it; you're not making friends with simple. At a camp where no one knows you from home, you can be anyone you want. I wanted to be Laura Ashley.

All that was left was a bathrobe, slippers, and washcloths—even though at home I never used one, I would have three washcloths as the list suggested. A netted bag for panties, safety pins for socks. Then Mom bought Lea and me new black trunks from a camping supply store where they had a "complimentary" service of labeling everything purchased with your child's name. Socks, shirts, pants, sleeping bags. Everything was overpriced, so Lea and I got to hear a lot of, "Damn well better be complimentary. And they better sew your name on using eighteen-carat-gold threads." Yet my parents had no problem justifying sending me to a fat doctor or fat camp, at any price. "It's your health," Poppa said. "For your health or education, any price is worth it." At that age, even though my thighs seemed to be the other white meat, I didn't correlate fat with health. Fat meant unpopular, not unhealthy.

Aside from my best friend Leigh, my crew of have-to-have friends were the sloppy seconds, the unpopular leftovers of our grade. Imagine viola cases and kids who sat in the front row of the bus and befriended the driver as part of their bodyguard regimen. Throw in an image of high-waisted stonewashed jeans, always-white sneakers, and an overloaded knapsack worn over both shoulders. We made room for one another, the have-to-haves and me, or else there would be parent-teacher conferences, and instead of hearing "insubordinate," our parents would be faced with "antisocial." One such have-to-have friend was the aforementioned Austen Rand, who didn't have acne but looked as if he should; his forehead and nose had pores you could see from an arm's length away. His face was slick with oil and shone from across a room like a polished coin. Despite the fact that I was madly in love with Barry Wagenberg, I kissed Austen in our classroom utility closet one day just before lunch. His tongue had rivers running through it, deep cracked lines like the surface of a meat patty, and it was wider than I'd expected. He darted in, poking his tongue through my lips. I wiped slobber from my mouth with the back of my hand. I didn't care if I seemed rude. I had just been Hamburglarized.

Just before I pushed open the closet door to leave, Austen made a request. "How about sloppy s-s-seconds?" I knew he didn't mean he wanted a second kiss, only this time even sloppier. He meant he wanted to sidestep second base and go straight to licking my boobs. I simply told him, "That does more for the guy than the girl."

"Really? I thought the nipples were an erogenous z-z-zone." Clearly he'd pawed his way through several books on how to pleasure a woman.

"Well," I said with one hand on his chest, "not for me." I pushed him away, then opened the closet door; it was over.

Later that week, I was with more of the have-to-haves behind the stage in the auditorium. The lighting was gym yellow, and the ceiling was high, so backstage, there was a dim comfort, as if it were rainy outside and you were left to read a choose-your-own-adventure book. A velvet burgundy curtain was drawn closed, and the wood of the stage was smooth and worn slippery with use. Our musical instruments were stored there, some locked in a metal cage, others aligned along the wall in their black-handled cases. It smelled of trombone oil and rosin. We'd hang out there after lunch doing homework problems together while the athletic kids played dodgeball.

Barry Wagenberg, Meryl Ferrara, Austen Rand, and a few others were back there with me. We were seated cross-legged with open textbooks and blue binders as we answered homework questions. I was acutely aware that Barry's knee was touching mine, so much so that I hardly noticed when the conversation turned toward sex. Austen overheard Meryl say she liked it when boys licked her boobs. Then she removed her bottle of Wite-Out from the clear zippered pencil case toward the front of her Trapper Keeper binder. I remember thinking there was no way Meryl had ever even kissed a boy; her thunderous mother taught Catholic school. Meryl believed in saints and prayed to them before midterm exams.

"Wait, wha-wha-what?" Austen asked while blinking wildly. "I thought g-g-girls didn't like it when b-b-boys s-s-s-sucked their titties!" He sat perfectly still, but his words came out stammered and frenetic, betraying him. I pretended not to understand his look. He thought I had it in for him, thought I was misleading him in the ways of women.

"You know, it's not all about the g-g-guy, Austen. Of course g-g-girls like it," Meryl threw back with a cruel authority native to twelve-year-olds.

"I don't understand," he said, more to me than anyone else.

"Maybe you would if you stuck with English instead of Klingon, you moron," Meryl added before snorting.

I was embarrassed that I didn't enjoy "sloppy seconds." How was it that every bit of me was emotionally sensitive—I could cry from just watching movie previews—yet stimulating my nipples, a physical erogenous zone known even by middle-school boys who couldn't kiss, did nothing for me? I was anxious, worried someone in our group, especially Barry, would know that I'd kissed Austen. I wanted to change the subject. I didn't have to. One of the boys farted.

I grew to like most of the have-to-haves over the years. We were stuck with one another, in the same classes, sharing locker space and seats on the bus. The have-to-haves' favorite pastimes included staying after school to predict the weather with the earth science teacher, practicing their woodwind instruments, and bonding with the phylum Arthropoda, pinning insects to Styrofoam boards and labeling each genus and species. I was lobbed into their crowd, I assumed, because I was fat *and* smart, which isn't the same as fat and funny or fat and rebellious. Funny might have landed me a seat beside popular, at least for entertainment's sake. But smart and fat might as well have been fava beans. Smart did nothing for my social life.

The only real social life I had was spent on the telephone. I used my free time to call 900 numbers, one in particular: a party hotline, the equivalent of chat rooms back then, but over the phone. I was a glutton for attention from strangers. When I found a deep, seductive voice, I called out to the moderator asking to connect us to a private line. That's when we'd exchange numbers, so we wouldn't accrue any more of their exorbitant fees, and begin to . . . begin to nothing. Nothing ever came of it.

Except once.

His name was Pete. According to my diary, his birthday was April 17, and he lived in Far Rockaway, Queens. These are probably the only PG details he shared with me once we spoke outside of the party line. He sounded older, the kind of older a boy can't fake. There was a texture in his voice, a deepness, and sense of control. He claimed to be nineteen, nearly twenty, and his voice never conveyed a hint of anxiety. We'd talk dirty to each other for nights on end. "We'll see each other soon," he said, and I agreed. "And when you come over, I'm going to penetrate you slowly."

"No," I interrupted. "I'm still a virgin."

"That's okay. I have a special pillow we can use. It props you up, so it won't hurt."

"I'm not having sex with you!" I yelled. Even during the erotic exchange of fantasies, from the safety of my childhood bed, I didn't like to imagine having sex. I did, however, enjoy imagining everything else.

"Well, can I put you on my special swing? And then we can just try different positions until you're more comfortable."

How totally fucked up. I'd like to say I stopped returning Pete's phone calls. That I was completely disturbed by the content of our hushed talks. That I returned to the party hotline, and upon recognizing his voice, I outted him as a phone sex predator to all the strangers on the line. But that's not what happened.

I continued to call Pete, wanting more, wanting, mostly, a boyfriend. I wanted someone who desired me and thought I was pretty, and over the phone, I could have that. Pete's phone was disconnected, and I never heard from him again. When I racked up a $504 phone bill trying to find my next "boyfriend," my parents removed the phone from my room. So I spent the rest of my free time in my parents' room trying to get the Playboy Channel to come in clearly.

I hadn't seen much of the channel. Sometimes I'd catch it at the very beginning before it was scrambled, and I'd watch a buxom woman in a bikini dive off a waterfall only to emerge without her top. I loved the way my vagina pulsed when I saw her large round breasts. But then snow would blast on, and I'd be forced to imagine what came next. I could never think of anything.

"Watching Playboy is gross," my friend Leigh told me when I suggested we watch it at her house. "It's for boys, not girls."

Aside from Leigh—who was also overweight, but unlike the rest of the have-to-haves, wasn't a nerd-fest—I'd have gladly traded away my adolescent associates for a chance at popular. Maybe a summer at fat camp was my chance.

Leigh and I stowed away our fat differently. She had remarkably large breasts that made fabric pull. No, not just large, *shapely*. Whereas mine seemed to be invented by my body, out of necessity, to accommodate extra fat. *Yeah, no problem. It's all under control. We just went ahead and added two additional storage bags.* They were ovals that sagged outward, and my nipples looked like blushing house spiders. I didn't look like a woman at all; I looked like a redhead.

I'd never really seen a naked redheaded woman. Although she's a natural redhead, too, Mom's complexion is far darker than mine. She has olive skin, she tans in the sun, and now that she's older, her hair has darkened to a rich auburn instead of a strawberry blond. The bare women I'd seen on television had thick dark piles of pubic hair and compact brown nipples. Any chance I had at seeing a naked woman up close was with Mom, but she habitually dressed in her closet, secretively. When she caught my sister and me trying to spy on her, she'd crow, "What are you two looking at? Stop being such pests," as she snapped to cross her arms over her exposed breasts. I presume when she discovered us watching her, Mom never thought we were curious, but rather thought of herself, ashamed, wondering what we saw when we looked at her. She imagined the worst and always knit her brow when she stood before a mirror, even when only inspecting her lipstick.

Unlike my modest-peaked mother, however, Leigh had comic book cleavage. While I was fascinated with her breasts, it was too much for me to feel them, and I told her so. "Hugging you is like feeling you up," I told her. "It's like we're locking horns or something."

So when we embraced, she learned to hug me from behind. "Okay, Stephanie, is this acceptable?" She made me laugh about it. "Stephanie, guys like big boobs," she said, and I remember thinking, *Yeah, if you're slim, not when you look like we do.* But I loved Leigh's breasts. I thought about them at night, when I was alone. I wanted to suck them because her nipples were brown and so different from mine. And when she changed her clothes, I pretended to do something else, became busy all of a sudden, even if it meant hurrying over to pick up a misplaced magazine. I looked, though. I fantasized about her beautiful globes, the way they hung. I wanted her to dangle them above my mouth and let them rest on my face, heavy.

On my last night home, before leaving for camp, Leigh and her knockers came over to help me pack. We reviewed the packing list together, just to make sure I had included everything. We were sitting on the floor of my bedroom when Leigh read through the list aloud.

"Canteen. Poncho. Folding plastic cup? Are they kidding, a plastic cup? For what, brushing your teeth? They're telling you how to change your life, how to fit in a smaller size pair of pants, and now they're telling you how to brush? Chapstick? Small musical instruments? Wait, what the hell, a poncho? Like a yellow one or something from a hippie store?" Leigh didn't want me to go. "Let's forget packing and go to the grocery store, get some raw cookie dough, and go eat it at the movies with spoons." I rolled my eyes, and then we rolled everything else into the camp trunk. "Less wrinkling when things are rolled," she said.

"Thanks," I said, but it sounded like an apology.

"I wish I were going with you. I can't believe they're sending your sister, too. Lea doesn't even need to lose weight. Promise you'll tell me what you eat, so I can do it along with you from here." Leigh was going to summer school.

"I promise," I said, but a part of me didn't. A part of me wanted to be thin without her.

I packed my bag for the bus: stationery, headphones, a DO NOT OPEN UNTIL YOU'RE ON THE BUS letter from Leigh, sugar-free gum, and a thick stack of fashion magazines. Beside the bag, I laid out my outfit: a tie-dyed T-shirt, a black Champion sweatshirt, Timberland shit-kickers, worn-in Levi's. I was ready.

I couldn't sleep. Lying in the dark, I kept opening my eyes. It was my last night in my own room. The shadow of two green duffel bags looked like bodies bent in slumber. I ran through the list: shorts, boots, fishing pole, hair scrunchies, formal gown, stamps. My outfit, flat on the floor, looked like a deflated body, the elbow of the sweatshirt bent with attitude: "What exactly are *you* looking at?"

five

Bay of Pigs

I have decided that I'm going on a strict diet. I want to feel good about myself. I'm doing it for me. Barry will like me if I'm thin. I'm so huge!! "Guys will be breaking down the doors," Mom and Poppa say. Yeah, just go on a diet. I'll get a guy, I figure, if I lose ten pounds before camp. I'll lose about forty pounds by August. 120 is good. I think the reason I'm so excited about going to camp is because I saw pictures, and well, I think I'll be the skinniest girl there. There is a first for everything!

THE BUS LEFT FROM A PARKING LOT IN YONKERS, NEW York. "In front of the Baskin-Robbins," the directions said. Well, of course they did. Cram seventy-five kids from the tristate area into a parking lot faced with thirty-one flavors, then punt 'em off to "you're finished eating" camp. Or was it finishing camp? It felt as if I were leaving home for boarding school, seeing children in navy sweaters and ripped jeans, Oxford shirt points poking out in triangles. Braided leather belts. Burgundy loafers stuffed with pennies. I had my fan and a pillow for the bus resting in my lap as I watched from the backseat of my parents' Cadillac. It was overcast; colors seemed to pulse, especially mine. I wore a tie-dye shirt with an iron-on peace sign and an anklet with silver bells that chimed when I walked. I threw the anklet on at the last minute because one of my friends from school had a cool older sister who wore one. I repacked the Timberlands and settled on a pair of hand-painted leather sandals, the kind that loop only around the big toes. They had daisies painted on the toe loops. After seeing what everyone else was wearing, I unclasped the anklet and slipped it into my bag. I could be anyone this summer. I wasn't going to start off on the wrong note, especially not one that chimed in with the Grateful Dead's "Scarlet Begonias."

"My God, you cut your hair!" one girl squeaked while pawing at another girl's urbane bob. Mothers make their children get camp haircuts before leaving home. "Everything grows like weeds in the summer," Mom had said after scheduling my butcher chop. "And when your hair is too long, Stephanie, you look like a country-western singer." It was eight weeks away from home, not a lifetime, but while under the watchful eyes of our mothers, we allow them to do the Last of the Mohicans on us. It's the last bit of mothering they'll do for a while.

Most of the kids raced in squeals toward one another, bumping together in knotted barreling hugs, squalling through the parking lot. They pointed at their Keds sneakers, boasting how their colorfully beaded friendship pins were still affixed to their white laces. Wiggling beside one another, they looped their arms together while signaling to their handlers to come closer. Parents shook hands, patting one another's children good-bye. These were what I later learned were called fat camp champs. They returned each summer, sometimes weighing the same, sometimes lighter, usually heavier. Gluttons of food and for punishment, I thought, eyeing some of the boys as they exchanged rooting gestures and complicated hand-slap routines. Their jeans were too big, even for them. It began to rain.

It was rumored to be at least a three-hour bus drive to camp—which, to a tween, meant in the same amount of are-we-there-yets, I could get to Disney World by airplane. Or better yet watch six back-to-back episodes of *A Different World* while Kobayashiing my way through a Costco-size box of Cookie Crisp cereal. Or I could just listen to a mix tape on my Walkman, beside a window, with a stack of magazines in clutch. Lea would be sitting with a friend of hers, Bridgette Anne DaBella, a googly-eyed girl with a mop of curls, tall for her age. I found an unoccupied bench of seats toward the middle of the bus and tucked myself behind a young boy whose green sweater resembled a damp towel draped over a bowl of dough left to rise. He was holding back sobs, his face drained, his eyes bloodshot.

Parents and younger siblings stood together in the gray parking lot, a band of arms around torsos and shoulders, huddling beneath makeshift umbrellas of slick windbreakers. My parents were thinner than the others. Mom has always been thin. Tall, eats like a truck driver, weighs nothing, and wears elegant clothing people notice for its rich drape. Poppa's belly was as round as a Vietnamese pot-bellied pig's, but it didn't sag or hang over his belt like the other fathers'. He looked five months pregnant, and when I was an infant, he says laying me on it was the only guaranteed method of alleviating my cries. People said I looked like him, which made me wince and worry. *How can I look like a man? He has a mustache,* I thought as I unconsciously ran a finger along my upper lip. When I went to the mall with friends, if it meant waiting an extra hour for Mom to be the one to drive, I'd wait. "Why don't you just let Poppa drive?" Mom asked one day as she finally tied her tennis shoes near our front door.

"Because he's bald," I managed to say after swaying for a bit. I was embarrassed of his balding head, fearing he looked older than a father of a thirteen-year-old should. And I looked like *him,* people said. I wiggled in a fit beneath Mom's hands whenever she tried to pull my hair into a French braid. With all my hair pulled off my face and behind me, I felt bald, too.

Later that night, when I was climbing into bed, Mom asked me to apologize to Poppa. "Stephanie," she whispered, "he heard you. You really hurt his feelings." That's when swallowing became hard, when I wanted to cry a little but knew I wasn't the hurt one, so I wasn't allowed. What I felt, exactly, was crestfallen, before I knew the word existed. It felt as if the ribs in my chest were ceiling beams, collapsing into their own structure. I didn't move. Instead I clutched the covers and went to sleep in silence.

As I looked at him from the bus, I wished I had apologized for that, wished he knew how normal he looked amid the heavier parents with their booming laughs and meaty handshakes. That's all I knew of normal at that age. Everything came down to how you looked, even your parents, who loved you despite your awkward years, and in part because of them. Normal, back then, meant not fat. Not slow. Not last at everything. Not wheezing at the smallest exertion. And that's how I felt on the bus to fat camp: like the normal one.

Hands pressed against the steamy glass bus windows; I left behind a labyrinth of fingerprints. I would miss Mom and Poppa, but at least I was the one leaving, with a summer stretched before me. It always seems easier to leave than to be left behind. Because when others leave, you're left with negative spaces, left to focus on what was once there. Your routine is the same, while they're off exploring and experiencing something new. You can't help but feel abandoned, despite all the rational thoughts in your head. The hardest part is the unknown. I know things like this now.

Mom told me years later that once the camp bus was out of sight, she cried in Poppa's arms. I hadn't realized, not beyond the obligatory "we're going to miss you; be good" sentiments, that she'd actually miss me, or that I'd miss her too.

THE BUS RIDE BEGAN IN HECTIC GREETINGS AND EAGER questions. Which school district, grade, favorite band—the usual. I was caught off guard when a collegiate brunette with creamy skin and an enviable flip of hair approached me with, "Virgin?" Her hand on her hip, she stood beside me waiting for my response. She had a side part and broad shoulders and looked as though she was the lone girl in a house of boys. She smelled of apple hair shampoo, and if she were a dress, she'd have been a silk dupioni halter in hibiscus pink with lime green trim. I caught my reflection in her tortoiseshell sunglasses. My forehead wrinkled in a defensive reply.

"What, you so are a fat-virgin; it's practically written on your belly," she added while pointing to mine. No, that was a peace sign on my shirt, associated with Woodstock, Lennon, and free love, not virginity. "It's no big deal, ya know," she said, now smiling. *Oh, no, the dreaded omen.* I wondered if the Greek letters on her shirt said something different. "What I mean is"— she took the empty aisle seat beside mine— "you're a first-timer to the whole fatty farm thing, right?" *Oh.* It was strange hearing her refer to Yanisin as fat farm instead of fit camp, as the brochure touted. "Yeah, I'd know if you were here last year because you're on the thin side," she said, and I felt myself start to smile.

"Well, I've been to camp before but never, never fat camp."

"I knew it. Fat-virgin," she said, louder this time, while turning around in her seat, addressing others sitting behind me. "Pay up." She tipped her hand into a stiff position, waiting for a pile of crisp bills. On her wrist, I noticed a translucent ring worn as a bracelet. It was the plastic bit used to hold together a six-pack of beer. Instead of being issued money, her hand was slapped by someone from behind. "They thought for sure you've been doing the rounds, fat camp hopping. Not me. I'm a fat-camp-champ here, so I'm very in tune with these things." It was her sixth summer—Wendy Fink, now a counselor in training— and, as I later came to learn via rumors, in the arts and crafts shack three weeks later she'd stop being a virgin of any kind, with Tanner Becker, a fleshy lacrosse player with a shorn head and noticeable space between his two front teeth. "As a CIT, I'll basically spend the summer wiping homesick noses and un-short-sheeting beds. So you're what, twelve?" I was thirteen going on twenty, but I still had much to learn. My education began when this inquisitive young woman introduced me to my first fat-hyphenated word. Once you're at fat camp, you learn to add "fat-" to nearly everything, like adding "in bed" to the end of a fortune cookie proverb. Fat-camp, fat-virgin, fat-camp-champ. I was beginning to understand. She was my new guide, and as it turns out, a CIT in my division of thirteen- and fourteen-year-old girls.

Things quieted as the lots of land began to ramble by. Each of us settled into his or her waiting position. Some of the kids had brought light blankets, their pink faces peeking out from beneath the folds, tucked in like sweet little pigs behind crisp yellow pastry dough. I leaned my head against my pillow, watching browns roll into green, feeling the deterioration of the roads as we left the silky paved highways. Bobbins of hay twirled into large wheels, stumpy houses cobbled from stone. Half-finished fences, tractors, and the smell of grass. The first sighing began when we approached the "Entering W. Stockbridge" sign, then someone yelped, "The red barn." I turned to search, seeing others rise, sitting on their knees. We were getting closer. Girls gripped one another and squirmed. All at once, the inhabitants of our bus became wild. When we passed the truck stop, boys hooted. I would later learn that the morbidly obese who were too heavy for the camp scales were weighed at the truck stop. They began to sing camp songs they all knew by heart, their own pledge of allegiance. It was the Bay of Pigs invasion without helmets.

We drove through town, past Queen Anne Victorians with fancy spindles and hanging flowerpots. Then a quick silence drew through the air, an audible inhale, as if we were waiting for our signal to attack our enemy. Some of the campers had seen a hickory sign whose letters, made of twigs, spelled YANISIN, which steadied all the other kids but made me feel anxious. It was the one-mile marker sign to camp, the one I'd spend each day of my summer touching on the mandatory "sign and back" two-mile walk. There it was, in the branches of trees, my summer, spelled out before me.

We welcome you to Camp Yanisin.
We're mighty glad you're here.

We'll sing you in; we'll sing you out.
To you we'll raise a mighty shout.
Hail, hail the gang's all here—
And we welcome you to Camp Yanisin.

WHEN I GOT OFF THE BUS, I SAID MY NAME TO A WOMAN with a clipboard and a hanging plastic whistle. She barked back, "Upper Camp, cabin twelve A" and pointed to a hill that was not only massive but incredibly steep. I laughed when I saw it, half-toying with the idea of asking her to steer me toward a ski lift. The photos in the brochure couldn't capture this. Lea got off easy and was assigned to a cabin in Lower Camp, "in the valley," where the younger girls were housed.

Forming one end of a semicircle, my bunk was on the edge of Girls' Hill, beside about a half dozen other cabins. There was a metal playground in the center with monkey bars and a double-wide seesaw. I was left alone to walk a tree-lined gravel path running from the white benches in front of the office to the focal point of camp: the dining hall. The path separated the boys' side of the camp from the girls'. It took me a good twenty minutes to wheeze my way up the hill to my cabin. The bunk smelled of wet wood and minerals; it was painted white with red trim, and it was divided into two rooms with a shared bathroom. There were two entrance doors—side A and side B. I wiped my palms on my thighs before opening the screen door of 12A. It contained three brown metal beds and three bunk beds; only tops were available. Tops were problematic for both bedwetters and butterballs alike. At least I'd outgrown one habit.

I chose the top bunk by the door, above Kate Hart, a girl from somewhere Southern enough to give her a drawl, who made me feel as if I had no right to complain about being fat. Kate had beady eyes that were too small for her face, expressive half-moon brows, and a jovial unkempt way about her. She managed to blow her indecisive strawberry-blond waves into woolly wings she kept tucked behind her ears. Her freckles were plentiful, and the ones near her eyes looked like smudged fingerprints. That summer I slept above Kate, and when I farted loud enough for her to hear, she'd push her feet into the springs of my bed, giving me a joy ride. "Quit it, Klein!"

Marguerite Bennetts, from Maryland, sat on a top bunk across the room picking at her braces and plucking her corrective dental rubber bands. She was sniffling into a Kermit the Frog doll, her legs dangling beneath her, kicking the air. Later in the summer, Marguerite hurled her penny loafer at my head from atop that bed, right across the room, because I'd taken it upon myself to hang Kermit by a noose in the shower. A farmer also shot at her when she snuck off camp, picking her way through fields, over fences, and through barns for a cold slice of pie from the general store. I imagine her now as a social worker who insists on using a rubber ball, instead of a chair, to strengthen her core. She's probably plagued with a nervous tic, unfashionable glasses, and hair that always needs to grow out.

My clothing trunk and duffels arrived on a gardener's truck driven by a man named Chester with summer teeth (sum'er here and sum'er there). People always whispered "the Molester" after saying his name. Certain fat-camp-champ boys volunteered to unload the trunks at Girls' Camp, yelling, "Men on campus. Don't cover up." I watched from the camp porch that connected 12A and 12B as they delivered the trunks door to door, then I heard my name.

"Stephanie Klein?" I smiled, taking a half step back. "Welcome, pop-tart." It was Adam, Wendy's fifteen-year-old brother. On the bus ride, she'd shown me his photo in the summer 1988 camp yearbook, smiling at the camera with a girl in profile. They were a soigné couple, draped in evening clothes, both his hands on her waist at a dance. She was wearing a hot-pink bubble dress with white taffeta bows on the sleeves. He had long floppy hair and looked like a Brooks Brothers advertisement, in formidable dun colors. Now he was standing before me in a kelly green button-down shirt that was flapping open, revealing a thin white undershirt. I wondered if he'd ask me to dance at a social. Adam had a buzz cut, dark caterpillar eyebrows, and a very wide toothy smile—one you'd expect to see on a second grader. He was broad, tall, and tan. I wasn't sure if it was muscle or fat, but it all looked good to me. "Adam Jackson Fink," I whispered to myself at night.

Most of the girls had arrived earlier and had already unpacked. It was my turn. I examined the new pair of "goal jeans" I'd flipped into my trunk, tags intact. It was the largest size the "normal store" carried, and although I could only pull them up to my knees, I begged Mom until she agreed to buy them. All the girls at school wore them and I hoped I could, too. I folded the jeans and gave them a home deep inside my cubby.

Halfway through my trunk, I discovered a thin brown paper bag sandwiched between two sweaters. I looked over my shoulder before looking inside. Leigh had outdone herself.

Once the unpacking was complete, I slipped into a bathroom stall to change into warmer clothes. I hated this about camp, having to undress in front of people. I opted for a pair of distressed jeans, boots, and my XXL black Champion sweatshirt. As I undressed in a bathroom stall, I watched a brown moth flap in the corner of the door.

"Push it out, Klein," Kate said from outside the stall, assuming I was actually going to the bathroom. We'd agreed to walk around campus as other kids from different parts of the country continued to arrive. Once I emerged from the stall in my warmer clothing, Kate said, "Oh, you'll tucker from that in like a week. I never thought I'd bare this white ass to a crowd, but we never say never 'round here." Then she smacked her ass, adding, "Giddy-up."

We negotiated the steep hill, our arms slightly raised for balance.

"How the hell am I going to get up this hill every day?" I was thankful I'd changed back into my Timberlands.

"No shit, Sherlock. That's how we all lose weight. They starve us and have us climb for our supper. Those flaming assholes." Kate had "Yanisin'd" the summer before.

"Seriously, I'd rather stay in the cabin and miss a meal than have to come back and walk up this monster."

"Huh, you think this is bad. Wait until you fix to meet Bitch."

"Bitch?"

"You'll see," she said, shaking her head. "Oh, you'll see." Kate was in her own head, stuck in a memory. The way she spoke, something about her, gave me the impression that she was poor. I knew her family had enough money to send her to camp for a summer, but I still suspected she came from a large family stuffed into a small rustic house with threadbare wall-to-wall carpeting. I wasn't considered rich at home, just normal. But around Kate, I felt like I'd always get the mansion (not the apartment, shack, or house) while playing M.A.S.H. I imagined her family kept their potatoes and onions in sacks near the back door and took pride in their display cases of shotguns and shot glasses. Kate, I would later learn, was the youngest of three, with a brother named Jim who'd lived with their grandma since Kate's mom kicked him out, and a sister named Elizabeth who drove a used Cavalier Z24 with a LeBra front-end cover. Kate had a photo of a two-door Pontiac Grand Am tacked to the window behind her bed. "Someday," she'd say, as if she was staring at the body of a supermodel.

Once we were down the hill, we swung past the valley of cabins with the younger girls my sister's age, past the tennis courts, and headed up a hint of a path near a campfire pit. From there we negotiated the hill toward the dining hall steps, which emptied out to the gravel trail bisecting the campus. Kate and I stopped walking to catch our breath.

"Now get ready, darlin'; you're about to be fat-flocked quicker than two jiggles of a jackrabbit's balls."

"What?!" Kate knew things. Disturbing things. Things about the teats on a polecat, dead coon dogs, greased hogs, and the Lord.

"Oh, you'll see."

Fat-flocked? Should I cover my head? Were there birds that could smell fat? I learned soon enough it wasn't about birds, or feathers, or anything from a barnyard. It was about boys. A covey of sizable boys swarmed me with questions, smiles, uncomfortable fidgeting hands, feet kicking at the gravel.

"Why are you here? You're not fat," a few of them said.

"I'm sorry, are you blind?" was my constant reply. My hand sat on my hip.

"How much do you weigh?" they asked.

"A lot." Even in a size sixteen, I was thinner than most everyone I saw. Each toss of my hair inspired. I was suddenly beautiful.

THAT NIGHT OUR COUNSELOR, HARPER, SLEPT IN THE CABIN with us. Once we were all folded into our beds, in the dark, she asked us to turn on our flashlights and point them toward the center of the cabin floor. I pointed mine up toward the ceiling first, examining the names carved into the wooden beams.

Angie wuz here, but now she's gone
She's left her name to carry it on
Those who knew her, knew her well
Those who didn't can go to hell!

"Look at the lines of light on the floor," Harper instructed. Then I repositioned myself on my bed, aiming my flashlight toward the center of the room. I was excited, just then, being tucked into a sleeping bag, in the dark. "They're fuzzy and continuous, and they're there as long as your light is." She lowered her voice. "That's the circle of hope." It was the perfect setting for a ghost story about Chester the Molester. Instead she continued, "We're going to go around the room, and each of you should say aloud what you hope this summer will bring for you. Everything said in the circle of hope stays in this cabin." Harper was from Oregon but pronounced it "Organ." She attended Harvard undergrad and looked more like a Jane. She smelled like Liz Claiborne eau de toilette, and to this day, when I see that triangular yellow bottle, I think of her. "Who wants to begin?"

Tara Tennenbaum began without saying "I do." "I hope that I lose gobs of fat this summer, and that I make nice friends, and . . ." I imagined Tara pulling gum from her mouth in a long string as she spoke. She was quick to correct anyone who didn't pronounce her name "Tar-uh." "And I hope I don't get too homesick for my mumsies." Tara was from Newton, Massachusetts. Now she's probably a tanorexic, a woman who always asks for the booth with the newest bulbs at the tanning salon, then covers her face with a towel and reconfirms her Botox appointment. She most likely wears men's oversized watches and only nourishes her Maltese, Dior, with bottled water and fresh meats from Lobel's on Madison Avenue. In her world, every weekend is "a-maz-ing" and every acquaintance is totally her BFF. She's rude to anyone in the service industry, but people most likely tolerate her because her pavé-set platinum heart is always in the right place.

Candy Williams of Jacksonville, Florida, slept above Tara. She was the first black girl I'd ever known besides my housekeeper's granddaughter. I thought it was bad planning on her parents' part naming her Candy. It was like dooming her to a lifetime of fat pants. She began, "Before I came here, my mama made me go bra shopping. I'm a 38H. That's not even funny. I gotta lose weight. It feels like I'm lugging around honey-baked hams." Candy was athletic, fearless, moody, and buxom. That summer the boys called her Candied Yams behind her back. I called her Hams to her face, at which point she'd sometimes grab her breasts and make them dance a happy jig. When teams were chosen, she was always picked first.

Marguerite Bennetts and Joy Colwin said "I hope" at the same time. "You go." "No, you." Someone go already. Joy's overprocessed blond hair hung in crimped forked branches. She dressed in bleak colors, showcased photos of Harley-Davidson motorcycles behind her bed, and would become a chain-smoker by the following summer. "I hope people start to confuse me with my thin sister." Then she spit out, "And that Grayson Spoon isn't as bitchy this summer." Who was Grayson? I'd need to learn why someone named Joy hated her.

"Girls, be nice. This is about you. Your hopes for yourself," Harper warned. "Now you, Marguerite."

"I hope my parents change their minds and pick me up," Marguerite said, still clutching Kermit. "I didn't even realize this was a fat camp before I got here. My parents dropped me off and left before all the fatsos came off the buses. I went to that rec hall to get pop, and it's all diet!" she said, still in shock. "I can't believe they tricked me. Man, this place sucks." *Who's she calling fatso?* My arms were only half the size of hers, and I wanted to be there. How could she not?

"Beulah, you're next," Harper coaxed after some silence.

Beulah Tsaoussis had matted bangs that covered her pimpled forehead and eyes. She wore a black Minnie Mouse T-shirt the entire summer. Every day. Beulah smelled like her name. There is always one girl who doesn't shower, who gets private talks with counselors in the shade. She walks with a lifeless gait, hoping each step will go unnoticed, her head down, crowned by an overgrown bowl of hair that throws her face into shadow. Invisible is her best defense. Beulah didn't respond. She just rocked her head in an anxious tic.

As jaded as I was, in the day-to-day trenches of fat camp, I wondered if any of these girls would become my real friends. Not have-to-haves just because we were at camp together, but true lifelong friends.

Jessica Fallis wore leg warmers, even in summer, and painted each of her fingernails a different color. She might've looked babyish, but she had a sexy voice that sounded both hoarse and musical at once. If she had been my friend at home, I would have made her record my outgoing answering machine message and pretend she was me. I knew she'd be my competition for the lead in the camp musical. I was also jealous of her dark straight hair. Of all the girls in the cabin, she was the prettiest. As she spoke about wanting to lose weight, I thought about what I'd say. I wanted to be clever and well liked. I hoped I'd fall in love, that my clothes would fall off, that I'd discover my collarbones. "I hope I can get my jeans on without using a hanger," I said. I knew this would prompt questions.

"A hanger?" Jessica repeated.

"You know the tiny hole in the zipper pull of your jeans?" I heard a "yeah." "Well, there's a hole, and sometimes my pants don't fit. I try to get the zipper up, but it hurts my fingers. So I lie on my back, and my stomach flattens out. And I stick the tip of the hanger through the hole. Then I grab onto the rest of the hanger and pull. It works." I had things to teach these girls.

When Kate spoke, I wiggled out of my sleeping bag and flipped onto my stomach, then looked down at her. "I hope my mother doesn't die this summer." She said it in a whisper. No one said anything. I quickly lifted my head. I couldn't believe she had said that. We all went to sleep in silence.

six

YOUR WORTH IN WEIGHT

I think I have changed into a grown woman at 13. I'm fat, and I want to be skinny. I look at things differently. I feel that this time in my life is only a fraction, and it doesn't matter. From now on, I'm going to be myself. I feel myself changing inside.

"OH, PISS OFF," KATE MOANED FROM THE BOTTOM BUNK when she heard it. It was the sound of reveille snapping through the morning over a scratchy loudspeaker, followed by an unnaturally high man's voice.

"Everybody up, up, up. It's a beautiful day. Rise and shine, campers. This is your wake-up call. Look to your neighbor and say, 'Good morning, neighbor!' Line up at the flagpole in fifteen minutes for Lower Camp and twenty-five minutes for Upper Camp." Then Billy Joel's "We Didn't Start the Fire" filtered through the speakers.

Our counselor, Harper, was already dressed, her hair swept into a high lacquered ponytail, the laces of her running shoes double knotted. Her legs were muscular and defined, slender and smooth. She could be a counselor anywhere; I wondered what she was doing at Yanisin.

"Come on, girls. Time to get going. Brush everything and get ready for breakfast." She paced the cabin, clapping, using a singsong voice that's repellent anytime, but particularly so when you're being forced awake.

"To hell with that," Kate added before stuffing her head beneath her pillow.

It was colder than I'd thought it would be. I didn't want to slip out from my cocoon of sleeping bag, so I lay there for a few minutes until most of the girls were up, changing out of their pajamas.

"Move it or lose it," I warned as I dismounted the upper bunk bed, stepping on Kate's elbow. She remained unfazed, waiting in bed until they called us to the flagpole for lineup. When she stirred, she was a morning blur of lavender and pink with images of cherry-topped sundaes, Popsicles, and chocolate chip cookies printed on her long flannel pajamas. And she was about to wear these very pajamas to breakfast, adding only a pair of hiking boots to her ensemble.

The other girls in the cabin were flossing—which I didn't realize people did more than once a week—brushing their hair, sitting on bottom bunks, waiting. They were dressed like I was, in nylon shorts and extra-large cotton shirts, sneakers with pom-pom socks. I stared at Kate as she pulled on the tongue of her boot while the others left the cabin.

"What, like I've got someone to impress?" This made me think of boys, of Adam. I didn't know what it was about him, but I found myself eager for our next encounter. Would I see him at the dining hall? I added a smear of number 44 lip gloss—an almost-white, thick pink frost as indigenous to the girls on the North Shore of Long Island as the icy blue eyeliner we applied to the very inner rim of our eyes—then looked to Kate.

"All right, let's bump and grind with the baby Jesus." This was her colorful way of suggesting we get moving.

The grass was wet on my ankles, the sky still gray. It was cold, and I wished I could go back for a hooded sweatshirt. We walked the dirt road down Girls' Hill to the valley. A volleyball court with a sand surface was to our left, along with a concrete hockey rink and two large fields with soccer goals and football goalposts. Harper stood just beyond a large oak, conducting a pointing tour to the girls of our cabin.

"Equipment shack, arts and crafts, the weight room. And obviously, that's tennis," she said, pointing toward the gated courts to our right.

"What about that one?" Tara asked of another, smaller, red-trimmed shack beside the Snack Tree. The Dutch door was chained closed with two padlocks.

"That's the canteen," Harper said, ushering us up the next hill toward the flagpole.

"She means the *can't* teen," Kate said. "All they've got in there are stamps, batteries, and diet slushies."

Once we panted our way up to the flagpole, Harper asked us to form a straight line. Lower Camp had already done this and was winding through the side entrance of the dining hall, a white building with red ornamental stickwork and a steep, gabled roof. As the youngest girl cabin of Upper Camp, we stood at the outer margin of the crowd, beside the girls of 12B. Wendy and another counselor were at the helm of their line, straightening their campers into order.

"Put your hands on the shoulders of the person in front of you," Harper said, facing us. "Now drop your hands to your side and take one step forward."

"What's the big deal?" I asked Kate's shoulder. We didn't have flagpole lineup at my other camps.

"The straightest line goes in first, Klein."

They rewarded us for being quiet and straight. With food. Who was I to pull a Fran and lecture on the wrongs of this? It was summer. I was on vacation. "Mum's the word," Harper said before pulling her index finger to her mouth in a "shhh." To this day, I despise when people say this. "Mum" is not the word. Pick a new one.

Then the camp owner, whose jubilant castrato voice I recognized from the morning wake-up announcement, welcomed us all to Yanisin, broadcasting how our counselors would be walking us through our day's activities over breakfast. The owner looked beefy, which seemed like bad business to me. A former camper, indeed. He clearly overdid it with the bench press—he looked as if he'd been squeezed, really hard, in the middle, forcing the bulk of him up toward his neck, like a cartoon. After we finished our breakfast, he explained, we were to return to our cabins to clean. Then there'd be inspection followed by a morning camp stretch.

Although entry into the dining hall was staggered, the line of people still stretched into a curly swirl, and we were toward the front of it.

"Which one's Grayson Spoon?" I asked.

"See a girl so ugly she'd run a dog off a meat wagon?" Kate said without turning. "Grayson's always the one next to her."

"No, really."

"Yeah, really. She surrounds herself with the uglies to make herself look better."

"Be serious."

"Fine, just look for a polo horse in her upper left corner. She only wears that Ralph Laurant crap." Grayson, if I had the right girl, had the body of a bowling pin, all ass and thighs. She had tanned skin and silky chestnut hair that swept her shoulders like a soft kiss. She looked fantastic in pink, and when she caught my gaze, I whipped around.

Once inside the dining hall, I followed suit and grabbed a plastic tray and moved along the assembly line. The walls were littered with laminated food pyramids and simple line drawings of kids doing jumping jacks beneath arched slogans written in puffy letters. "Fitness is fun! Spread the word." Then another drawing of a boy with clouds of hair juggling **A**pples, **B**ananas, and **C**arrots: our new fitness alphabet. It was almost enough to make you lose your appetite, but this was fat camp; we ate everything anyway.

I was served a Styrofoam bowl of purple yogurt, a single-serving box of Rice Krispies, and a banana. I had the option of taking a miniature box of 2-percent milk. I declined, smiling at the thin man in the hairnet. Then I felt an elbow in my side. "Take it, Klein." So I did.

Our bunk sat together at one end of a long rectangular table, beside other girls. I looked for Adam across the dining hall, for cute boys in general, but it was mostly a mass of hats and tangles of brown hair beneath camp banners and old color-war flags, painted toilet-bowl seats hanging from rafters.

"What, they don't have their cereal with milk where you come from?" Kate asked. Because of my time with Fran, I was used to skim milk and didn't want the extra fat, especially not from milk. Fat from cheesecake, fine. But now that I was at fat camp, there was something particularly disturbing to me, knowing my milk was thicker and had more fat in it. Shouldn't they be giving us nonfat milk? Isn't this a diet camp? The extra fat reminded me it came from an animal. I remembered Fran once telling us that humans were the only animals who still consumed dairy after infancy. No wonder so many people have problems digesting it. It made me question if I should be having dairy at all, but when I asked Mom about a soy alternative, she ignored me. She might have said something about when I live on my own. Most parents employed this logic when it came to a drum set or purple hair dye. "When you have your own house, you can layer yourself in soy cheese, but under my roof, you'll eat cow enzymes and like it." Mom never said this. Instead, she expressed that she wasn't preparing separate meals, other than one for "us girls" and one for Poppa. She hoped my dairy-free request would lose steam if ignored, which is exactly what happened. Maybe this summer I'd become dairy free. But this would leave me with only a banana and a box of cereal. I stirred my Krispies into my bowl of blueberry yogurt and set my carton of milk onto Kate's tray.

"Jesus in a manger! Not out in the open," she snapped as she returned it. "First open it." I watched her pull at the waxy carton and then pour its contents over her cereal. Then she traded her empty container for mine. "And that," she said, "is how it's done, hon." All that for an extra serving of lactose? She belonged here. I was beginning to wonder if I did.

As soon as our dining table was full, our division leader, Gina, lectured us about the Anti-Trade Agreement. "Is that understood?" We all nodded our heads at Gina, a butch woman with cropped hair and a thin braided rat-tail. Looking at her in her jean shorts, I found another meaning of the word "cutoffs"; hers cut off the circulation to her heart. "'Cause I don't want to hear that you didn't know. I'm talking not even green beans for carrots." As she spoke, I couldn't get past the fact that she'd stuffed a paper napkin into the collar of her shirt, as if she'd been offered the two-pound lobster for breakfast. This was our leader, someone capable of punishing us, and she wore a bib.

None of the counselors could discipline or reward us with food. Far worse, I imagined, if they caught us trading food, they'd force us to do knuckle push-ups in the rain, the muddied boot of a counselor thrust into our backs. But to my relief, they couldn't discipline us with exercise either, seeing that their goal as a camp was to introduce us to the fun world of exercise. So instead, if a rule was violated, you got ETB, early to bed. No free play after dinner. Free play, the time after dinner but before the all-camp evening activity, meant tetherball competitions and pickup games of basketball. It also meant mingling, sharing a paddleboat with a boy on the lake. It meant you had a chance to escape the "anti-PDA rules" and display your affections out of public scrutiny, behind the boathouse on Lovers' Lane. I would never trade food again, not even for money.

The returning campers sang and pounded their fists and fingers on the table. There was spontaneous metered clapping. Then words I didn't know. I began to clap and thump too. I'd learn the words; I could almost hear new ones in my head. "Knit one. Purl two. Oh, Adam . . . Stephanie Klein loves you."

After eating, I went to clear my tray and return to the bunk. Harper corrected me, saying none of us was to leave until we'd all finished eating. I eyeballed the empty trays of our table. All of us *had* finished. "No," she said with her hand fanned out toward the rest of our long table, toward girls I hadn't even met yet, "we haven't *all* finished."

"You mean we have to wait until every single person is done?" I asked Kate once I was back in my seat. "But those girls just sat down."

"Yeah, why d'ya think I wanted your milk? For my health? Please, it gives me something to do." Even at fat camp there's eating because you're bored.

"They want us to eat with purpose," Joy said in a studious voice while adjusting her imaginary eyeglasses. She simpered, then said, "Slowly, paying attention to the way it tastes in the front of our mouth versus on the roof of our mouth or the back of our tongue, aware of each flavor and sensation."

"Oh, I got a sensation all right," Kate added. "It's called pins and needles. And they can come and kiss it, right here on the sweet keister our good Lord gave me." To make the time pass, I would load up on extra vegetables from the all-you-can-eat salad bar for lunch if I could. And I'd hold on to my milk from now on, tasting each sip.

Once we were excused from the communal table where sharing was prohibited, we headed back to our bunk and were introduced to the daily work wheel.

"Here we go," Kate said as she zonked onto her bed, ignoring Harper's request for us to huddle near the makeshift paper-plate wheel. First Harper pointed toward the center of the inner plate, at a small pie chart, sliced into equal portions, each sliver bearing one of our names. The outer circle was segmented similarly except instead of names, there were tasks assigned to each section with a number scribbled alongside the chore indicating the "shower hour" lineup for later that evening.

"Every day I'll turn this inner wheel with your names on it," Harper said while demonstrating, "so you'll each have a new chore and its corresponding shower slot."

LATRINE meant wearing yellow rubber gloves, provided to protect your hands from staph and germs, but, as I'd come to learn, the mere act of snapping them on felt nothing short of vile.

"Wait, excuse me," Tara interrupted, "I was told there was a cleaning service that took care of bathrooms. That we just had to make our beds and fold our own clothes."

"I'm afraid not," Harper said.

Tara looked to me, widening her eyes. It was one of those looks that said, "We're in this together, you and me, so you better say something now." I hadn't even spoken much to Tara yet, but I knew she was looking to me because, of all the girls, I seemed the most similar to her. I was Jewish and knew that Gitano, Jordache, and Sassoon weren't dance moves.

"Whoever's got Latrine will start by cleaning the shower and will finish up with the bathrooms," Harper continued.

Inevitably, shower duty meant encountering a matted hair flower sprouting from the drain. Yanking the black hair from deep within the shower's throat was by far the least offensive part. After spraying tile cleaner on the flimsy shower curtain, there'd be the task of plucking dead moths that had been smashed against the bathroom walls. There'd be Comet and a small mildewed sponge, which somehow made you think you were infecting rather than disinfecting. Sanitary napkins, I soon discovered, weren't sanitary at all. And to speak of the "trail mix tracks" that stained the inside of the toilets—well, it was a wonder that LATRINE only secured first shower. You needed at least two after that job.

First shower meant first to finish getting ready for dinner, which equated to more free time for socializing in front of the dining hall before lineup. While FIRST SWEEP showered second, DUSTPAN showered third. I thought it should be the other way around; playing bitch to FIRST SWEEP should entitle you to some shower power. GROUNDS picked shit off the ground. Not feces, just sugar-free gum wrappers and the like. PORCH showered last, as your only duty aside from a cursory sweep was collecting damp towels or bathing suits from the porch railings. I wondered if there was an anti-trade agreement when it came to chores as well. I'd have sooner been LATRINE and showered first than been PORCH or GROUNDS, forced to yield my free play time and bathe after dinner.

I didn't have daily chores at home beyond clearing my own plate. Sometimes Mom demanded I set the table, in that mock-threatening tone that never went anywhere. She'd throw in a decorative "or else" and wave a menacing wooden spoon. "Set the table," she reasoned, "and then you can eat." I'd reach over her, sticking my hand into the tin of food she'd covered and kept warm, tented beneath aluminum foil. "I said no, Stephanie." But that's all she did: *said*. "Just wait until your father gets home" never worked. And when neither Lea nor I stirred to help her, she stepped nearer, waving her spoon. "Do you know what this is for?" Mom once threatened in a grave tone appropriated only for dreaded things.

Lea's eyes lit up, her face swollen with excitement.

"Well, do you?" Mom said, drawing nearer.

Lea looked like an August plum, and after several wide-eyed blinks asked, "Ooh, you mean you're going to make rice pudding?"

And with that, Mom set down the wooden spoon, usually reserved for stirring her homemade confections, and broke into a stream of uneven laughter, so hard she couldn't breathe. And I was jealous of my pip-squeak sister just then. Because it was the best feeling in the world, delighting our parents enough to make them laugh, even if done unintentionally. Even if it was only our mother. *Only* because she never really felt like a mother. Not to me.

Sure, when I was sick, she was the person I called out to in the middle of the night. She brought me matzo ball soup, ginger ale, and a Charms lollipop for my throat. I'd search for hidden pictures in *Highlights* magazine and play with the Yes & No Invisible Ink book, then I'd whine, "Stay here with me and hold my hand."

"Stephanie, that's how germs spread, through the hands." She'd sit on the bed, but she wouldn't hold my hand, so I'd clasp her wrist instead. Mom would flip through a magazine, and I'd be afraid to change the channel on TV, worried the change might make her look up and notice the time. She'd want to get off the bed to do the things that mothers did. She'd stay, though, and I'd appreciate it when I was sick, more open to affection, but when I was back in the pink, I didn't need her.

Mom watched movies with Lea and me, the three of us huddled beneath one comforter. Sometimes she'd interrupt, asking the questions of a child, things no one could answer because they hadn't yet been revealed in the film.

"Does he survive?"

"I don't know, Mom. I'm watching it right along with you, remember?"

"What did he say?"

"I don't know; if you weren't busy talking . . . ," I'd whisper impatiently. Incidentally, I've since picked up this maddening trait and currently irritate just about everyone with my abuse of it. But when I complained about Mom doing it, she and Lea would exchange scolding glances, then one of them would stick her tongue out at me.

"I saw that!" I'd say, whipping my head around.

"You're a bitch on wheels," Mom once snipped.

I wasn't driving a car or riding a bike. I didn't quite understand where she got the wheels bit. For some strange reason, I imagined a dessert cart when she said it—the glass kind found in upmarket restaurants. I wondered how I'd fit on it. Then I darted out of the room, tattling to Poppa that she used the word "bitch."

Our weekends were spent with her as our chauffeur, driving us to dance and singing lessons, drama class, piano, and painting, and schlepping Lea off to Maccabee soccer. She made holidays fun, sewed costumes, and always offered to drive when other moms wouldn't. Mom was a cool older sibling, the kind who took us to rock concerts and stood on her chair, but when she tried to pile on the demands and play the part of mother, her pleas went unanswered. I'd defiantly laugh at her requests. And as I got older, I bloomed into even more of a brat.

When I eventually became thin, I would steal her favorite clothes and wear them to school without permission. "Not nice," she'd say, shaking her head. "I'm sorry," I'd lie, and proceed to do it again. I'd accidentally stain one of her cardigans, slipping it, unwashed, back into its drawer. "Not nice," she'd say again. My mother: the queen of "said." And through most of my life she would remain that way.

I wasn't accustomed to cleaning up after others. But at camp, I liked the formality, the relatively just shower system, the regimented schedule. I liked striving to have the most shipshape cubby, being awarded with an extra fifteen minutes come curfew. I loved the clean order of things, knowing exactly how to excel. When Marguerite asked why she had to make her bed at camp when she didn't have to at home, Harper told her that Camp Yanisin, and ultimately her job, was to teach us to take responsibility for our own lives. And as ironic as it was, for the first time in my life, at fat camp, I liked pulling my own weight.

Adjacent to the work wheel hung a chart of our daily schedules. After the all-camp stretch—where we resembled marooned sea cows, left on a concrete hockey rink to grunt and twist on our backs—we'd have three activity periods, each lasting for an hour and fifteen minutes. Afternoon lineup and announcements were followed by lunch and rest hour. Then after another divisional activity, we were able to break off from our division into afternoon clubs and clinics, where the focus shifted from losing to acquiring. That is, the emphasis of clinics was no longer on losing weight, but on acquiring or improving a skill. Archery, tennis, and basketball clinics, for example, didn't include drills or sprints with counselors badgering us for blood, sweat, and tears, but were instead designed to encourage follow-through and proper form. Then we'd welcome shower hour, dinner, free play, evening activity, curfew, lights out. The schedule dictated wardrobe: bathing suits or sports bras? Due to the high number of yeast infections the summer before, we were allotted five minutes between activities for changing our clothes. In that time, bathing suits were stripped off, then draped on the porch. Dry clothes, baby powder, a hair band, a stick of sugar-free gum. Smear on more sunblock. We exchanged jelly shoes and goggles for sneakers and baseball gloves. "Today, though," Harper clarified, "we're not following the schedule. But you should start to think about which activities you'd like to do during your elective periods after lunch. Today we've got orientation, so put on your swimsuits." The cabin fell silent, as if a coffin lid had just closed.

Once assembled outside our bunk, we headed in a chunk to the recreation hall, a dilapidated building on stilts with decorative half-timbering. It smelled of rain and Elmer's glue. We were there to have our "before" pictures taken. Long curved lines of girls in bathing suits, flip-flops, and roomy airbrushed T-shirts formed inside the building. A smaller room within the rec hall housed a diet soda vending machine and a Ping-Pong table. The far wall of that raftered room had a white paper backdrop and photoflood lights. A mustached man named Leslie sat on a stool with a Polaroid camera and some cardboard boxes, calling out, "Next." I was uneasy and very quick about peeling off my clothes. Like new skin beneath an old Band-Aid, I was tender and pale in my black swimsuit. The fabric near the straps was already pilling. Mom had urged me to buy a new suit before camp, but I couldn't bring myself to try on anything else. Someone would want to see how it fit; a saleswoman would pull on the straps and examine my crotch. "One's enough."

I sucked in my stomach and pushed my chin out to avoid the double chin while Leslie instructed me not to smile. As my smile eased, he snapped my photograph. I supposed they wanted us to look miserable before. We had nothing to be smiling about, but after, oh after, we'd have new Yanisin bodies and smiles. That's when they'd prompt us for one by reminding us of food: "Cheese!"

I stood cold on the white paper, unsure of what to do with my arms. At my feet, a white cardboard sign read YANISIN 1989. Leslie twirled a free finger, indicating I should turn so he could get my profile. I bit my lower lip, looking toward Harper, hoping she'd say it wasn't necessary. She smiled back with a face that bordered on genuine apology. She might have winked. I imagined a yellow tag pinned to my ear with identifying information reduced to a number. The sign at my feet fell facedown. He'd see my rolls congeal if I bent down toward it. So I pivoted as told, wishing I had something to hold besides my breath. Beneath my breasts, sweat rings bloomed; I could feel the wet crescent marks on my suit. Leslie fixed the sign and stepped away. I wondered if I smelled.

Once the camera was down, I scampered to the corner of the room to dress. "Not just yet," Harper said. In an attempt to hide my cellulite, I'd moved around the room without turning and had missed the ominous presence of the scale. It wasn't like Fran's tall balance-beam scale. The neck of it reached a freckle on my thigh, and the metal platform was wide and worn. It looked old-fashioned, as if it belonged in a country kitchen beneath a hanging ornamental cow. It was an antique meat scale, something for livestock. I wondered if they wanted me to step on it with my bare feet or if they'd slip a piece of waxed paper down first. One hundred and sixty-four pounds. I weighed more now than I ever had with Fran. I might have been an inch taller, but I still had more than forty-five pounds to lose, and in medical terms, I was officially obese. All those dry turkey sandwiches for nothing. I weighed almost as much as my father.

Poppa made it a point of letting me know things like this. He'd say it with his thumbs tucked into the waist of his jeans. "Stephanie, soon we can start sharing dungarees." But he usually said it in private. One evening our family went to the Ground Round, a franchised theme restaurant that served its food in red plastic baskets and displayed vintage cartoons or Laurel and Hardy episodes on a movie screen as families dined at wooden booths complete with personal jukeboxes and all-you-can-eat popcorn. When we arrived, a host greeted us with a handful of balloons.

"Welcome, folks. Today is pay what you weigh day for children twelve and under." People who say "folks" should not be permitted to leave the house. "Well, pretty lady, why don't you just step right up?" he said, motioning to me as if I were the circus act. I wanted to pull the yellow smiley-face pin from his suspenders and stab all his balloons. I was nine at the time, but I was sure I appeared older because of my height. I looked up toward my parents, hoping one of them would save me.

"Does she have to get on the scale?" It was Poppa, gallantly rescuing me from the shame of wobbling onto the scale. "'Cause I think if I have to pay what she weighs, I'm going to be losing out on this deal."

Some kids pull the silent treatment. Some throw temper tantrums and cry and hit, screaming until strangers look. Others refuse to eat. All this, hoping to punish their parents. My refusal to eat that night had nothing to do with my parents. I'd lost my appetite, and when a waiter tried to restore it by offering me a balloon, I whimpered. I was too old for a balloon, too young to be treated as an adult. I was stuck in puberty purgatory with a father who was prejudiced against fat people. "So is most of the world, babe. You'd be much happier . . ." And then I zoned out until the check arrived.

"YOU'RE ALL SET. YOU CAN GO NOW." THE WEIGH-IN AND "before" photos were complete. "Just sit at the bottom of the steps, and then we'll make our way to the pool for swim tests."

Requests to stop at our cabin for nose plugs and goggles were denied. Schedule, schedule, schedule. The boys our age had just finished their swim tests and were threading their way to the rec hall for their pictures. Male counselors flirted behind their wet towels and large mesh sports jerseys. "Why, hello, ladies. My boys know CPR if any of you are interested."

I pinched my shoulder blades together upon remembering Mom's advice: "Good posture can shed a good ten pounds." I was too timid to look at the boys, to see if Adam was there. Instead I gripped my towel and watched our counselors. Harper and Wendy slapped hands with the boy counselors. There was a comfort there, between them, as if their sex didn't matter. They could roll their eyes and make fun of how slow and hopeless we all seemed to be, share smiles, and somehow understand one another in a casual encounter, dressed in shorts, walking in lines, as a group. Leaders. I wanted to be older.

We slogged across Girls' Hill, just past our cabin, to another road leading to the pool and lake. Once we reached the pool fence, I strained to look back. Adam's head was bobbing, his arm around another boy's shoulders. I imagined they were singing guitar solos. I wondered if he'd noticed me. Maybe next time, I'd look up.

THE "BUT I HAVE MY PERIOD" EXCUSE WASN'T GOING TO work. "So do I," our division leader, Gina, sang out from the center of the pool, treading water. "It's called a tampon." And this bit I remember well: one of the girls said tampons were the work of the devil. Her mother believed using one was a sin. Then under her breath one of the other counselors said, "Welcome to Hell."

"Everyone is getting in the pool. I don't care if it takes all day," Gina said with a smile. I already hated her.

Most of the girls refused to disrobe, fearful that the boys weren't completely out of sight. Once they were assured the coast was clear, campers sporting skirted bathing suits toddled toward the edges of the pool, their shirts still on. They moved like grandmothers, shuffling in small, metered steps, as if one careless move would lead to a fractured hip. All that was missing were floral bathing caps with chin straps. Lea still tells me when she first came to camp she was jealous of these skirted trendy numbers and felt like an outsider. "I thought it was what the cool kids wore. I didn't realize it's what the fat kids wore." I sat on the pool's edge, my feet fluttering in the water, as I listened to the rules.

The camp pool was half the size I was used to at our country club back home, where I'd learned to swim when I was three. Swimming was the only sport at which I excelled, but I didn't learn this until one afternoon at the club, when more than anything, I wanted sugar.

The summer of 1976, Mom and Poppa were initiated into North Hills Country Club of Manhasset, Long Island. One of Mom's sisters, Iris, and her husband, Lenny Messina, arranged for Poppa to meet some of the members, as an issue had been raised about Poppa's profession. They weren't sure if there was room in North Hills for another "moving and storage" guy. It's not as if just anyone is accepted to North Hills; it's like Manhattan co-op real estate. The family's history, income, and social standing are put before a committee. I imagined photographs and papers filed in a beige folder with a tab reading "The Jews" passing hands in a wood-paneled boardroom. I wonder if my fat would have been a consideration. If the committee could prognosticate that the Kleins' first child would be shoveled off to a fatty farm one summer, would they reconsider the membership? "Bad genes," someone would whisper. As a third-generation club member, Lenny had some pull at the club, and with his father on the admissions committee, it was no time at all before Mom played tennis with the ladies and Poppa spent the days inside the men's grill playing gin rummy for money.

Throughout those North Hills summers, trophies were awarded in every category. There were wars over who would win the Family Cup. We never won because it was just Lea, Mom, and I who participated. Poppa was always at the card table; his award was a bankroll. The Corollas won almost every year, with their four daughters and three sons. At first my trophies were for deftly balancing a Ping-Pong ball on a spoon while racing to the finish line. Mom was an A tennis player and received many golden trophies on Awards Night. Lea won at knock-hockey and Connect Four. I never really cared about winning, until the day I did.

There was a Girls 12 and Under swim race. Mom was on the tennis courts, which were close by but hidden behind tall spruce trees, aligned along the fence like soldiers. Sugary ices in long plastic tubes were awarded to everyone participating in the race. The winner got first pick of which flavor ice she wanted. Mom and Poppa never let me eat anything sweet. One of them spoke with all the snack bar staff, alerting them that I wasn't permitted to charge anything fried or with sugar to our account. But this ice, they would have to give me. The ice was the only reason I even mounted a starting block.

BANG. It's all I heard. After that, I became deaf to all sound. Breaking the surface, I felt a slam and arctic water. Shock. Rhythm somehow took over, and there I was pumping and moving fast, feet pointed. Something was different. I felt strong; I felt it in me for the first time, that ability to really haul. Only after my hand slammed into the edge of the pool was my sense of hearing restored. All I heard was yelling. Mr. Buckly, a middle-aged pool activities director with a shiny head and white athletic socks hiked to his knees, was on the microphone, saying, "And ladies and gentleman, we have a winna!" But who? I couldn't tell if I'd won; I was distracted, caught in gasps for breath, looking beside me to see who it had been.

"For the first time this summer, Stephanie Klein in first place." I was surprised they were making such a big deal out of it. Even the older women who played bridge all day, whom Mom called the Cackling Hens, got up from their game to congratulate me. Later that night Mom told me she heard the loudspeaker from all the way on the last court; she said it sounded like a horse race. I didn't care what it sounded like; I was a winner.

From there I joined the swim team and competed against girls my age from other clubs on Saturday mornings. Again, I didn't do it for the glory of a win, for the exhilaration, for the sport itself. I did it for bagels smeared thick with scallion cream cheese, covering the hole. For slivers of Entenmann's New York–style crumb cake. For apricot-glazed hazelnut danishes and slices of lemon pound cake, left out on wicker trays to feed spectators as they cheered their children. And I was somehow actually good at it, both the gorging and the swimming. After my race, I'd steal away to a lawn chair hidden behind the rowdy crowd. I'd unwrap a croissant from my napkin as Mom rooted for one of my cousins. It would melt away against the roof of my mouth and along the wet walls of my cheeks. Success tasted like butter.

"SO DO WE HAVE TO SWIM A LAP, OR WHAT?" JESSICA FALLIS asked the thin blond lifeguard at the camp pool while most of the girls stood on the cement, squinting and shifting their weight.

"Not quite yet," the lifeguard responded in a thick Australian accent. This was Paige, one of the many foreign counselors sent to camp for free room and board and a chance to stay in America for a summer. She looked Scandinavian and had a tattoo of Gumby right above her pubic bone and, if I remember correctly, was thrown out of camp two weeks before it ended when she was found smoking on the steps of the Pig-Out Room, a storage closet attached to the back of the dining hall, where underweight siblings and thin counselors spent their free time devouring graham crackers, peanut butter, and cups of chocolate pudding.

Marguerite Bennetts refused to put even one foot in the Yanisin pool; maybe it was the sign WELCOME TO OUR OOL. NOTICE THERE'S NO P IN IT. PLEASE KEEP IT THAT WAY. Miss Marguerite claimed she'd never swum before and refused to disrobe. She crossed her arms and rocked in a frightened trance. Her face was a terror-stricken cherry truffle, and I delighted in seeing her squirm and moan, wailing as they drew her closer to the water. I couldn't wait to see them force her in. Would she scream or silently tremble, as her eyes grew wider? Perhaps she'd slug someone in a frenzied attempt to break free. Or better yet, bite someone, breaking skin, drawing blood with her braces. I hoped someone would just push her.

Paige instructed us to enter the pool, insisting we go only where we could stand, and one hand had to be on the ledge of the pool. I thought she'd call our names and make us swim a stroke the length of the pool.

Instead, she commanded, "Okay, now everyone get out." Was this a joke? We weren't permitted to use one of the two ladders in the deep end because, Paige reasoned, "You might get a cramp and won't be able to swim that far."

The plumpest of the portly girls panicked. You saw it in their snarled lips and widened eyes. They looked unnerved, as if oxygen bags had just fallen from the ceiling of an aircraft. Bereft of upper body strength, they were unable to hoist themselves from the water, so Paige and a few of the other counselors spent twenty minutes teaching us how to help one another out of the pool.

"It'd be a lot easier if you took off your clothes," Wendy announced as she wiggled off her shorts. "Not your suits," she was quick to add, "just your shirts. We all look more or less the same anyway." With both hands, she squeezed a large roll of fat just beneath her breasts. "See? So big deal. I have a second set."

"Yeah," Paige agreed, "there's no reason any of you should be wearing shirts to hide what we all have." But Paige didn't have what we did. She had what we all wanted. "Now, again," she said with a clap, "Belly up, elbows grounded, kick your feet, and throw a leg up. Roll on out." Our first swim test was learning the "Yanisin Roll."

I knew how to exit a pool. I'd been suffering the humiliation of rolling out for years. I exited a few times, feeling the fabric of my suit, along my belly and chest, biting the cement, and when I finally pulled up, I could see that the pilling of my suit had worsened. I felt like Velcro. I wanted to look like Paige, a sun-ripened Nordic blonde with a red racing suit and a shiny silver whistle dangling between breasts that stood high and proud without having to be positioned. Mom called Paige's style of suit a French leg, which meant if you were thin it made your legs look a mile long. But on me, I decided, it was a dead end.

In Paige's sight, I rolled out a few more times, then stayed in, pushing my crotch against the water jet. The water shot out, like an underwater faucet, in a strong steady stream. I leaned all my weight on my forearms, holding half my body afloat like a buoy, my forearms pressing on the ledge of the pool, for so long the top half of my body dried. My legs clung against the side of the pool, toes pointed, legs stiff and straight, scissor kicking through the water as I reached orgasm. No one noticed. I pushed myself from the ledge and floated, wondering how many calories I'd just burned.

I liked the way the water carried my weight. I wasn't fat in it. I hated getting out, though, especially at North Hills. It wasn't because I'd turn cold or because I had to squish my wet feet into sun-soaked nylon sneakers and dry off. It was because people could see I was obese. Even my puddles were fat. I slopped up the cement, as if the mass of me held more. I tried to drip off in the pool, lingering on the steps, to make leaner puddles. But at camp, I too had to roll out. At least here, I was beginning to realize, I would be better at sports, and certainly swimming, than most others. It was kind of like being who I'd always wanted to be at home. This place was totally radical.

Before clawing my way out, I peed in their "ool." I liked how warm the water felt, and I hated how dirty and wet the floors of the bathroom became, like wet bread. The sting of chlorine in my eyes, my waterlogged lungs, the smell of Aquamarine hair conditioner, and the stickiness of Solarcaine on my freckled skin were always summer regulars. I had decided. During elective periods at camp, I would opt for swimming.

seven

BLAME IT ON THE RAIN

Hey, how's life? Mine is awesome at Yanisin. I am considered very, very popular. Everyone is frenz w/ me—not to brag (of course!).

DURING REST HOUR THE FOLLOWING DAY THE OLDER GIRLS were having a leg-shaving party. Wading in pools of natural light, they sat V-legged on a slate path in front of their cabins. I wasn't allowed to shave. Poppa believed that shaving led to perfume, which led to makeup, which led to sex. While perfume was outlawed, scented powders, bath soap, and lotions snuck in just under his regulation line. They were driver's permits.

I wasn't much for abiding by his rules now that I was away at camp. Come to think of it, even at home, I managed to do what I wanted—well, within reason. I'd been secretly cutting the hair off my arms and legs with scissors since fourth grade, when I had my first tongue kiss with a boy named Anderson Cruise.

"Cruise up her shirt," kids sang when they saw us on the Camp Summit tetherball courts together. I was nine, and I wasn't wearing perfume. I was making jewelry boxes from Popsicle sticks, lopsided bowls in pottery, and an embossed leather bracelet I decided to stamp with the phrase "When the going gets tough, the tough go shopping." I was also wetting the bed. And on Love Rock, with the rich odor of horse manure from the nearby stables wafting over us, I was tongue-kissing a boy whose nickname was Cruiser. There's something distorted to me about this: a girl who was still wetting the bed was also French-kissing a boy. This is what happens at sleepaway camp: girls *think* they become women. And like everything else, it only gets grander at fat camp.

The line of older girls sat spread-eagled on the pavement with basins of foamy water, shaving cream, and orange Bic razors. I was bleaching a pair of jeans and my black Champion sweatshirt, setting them out to dry in the sun. A boom box blared Milli Vanilli's "Blame It on the Rain" as plump teens swished plastic razors over their meaty legs, hoping that night someone else might be touching them for the first time. Back at home, they weren't noticed for their legs unless it was for their cellulite. At fat camp, the playing field might have been wider, but it was leveled. And far from the watchful eyes of their parents, left in the care of teenage counselors with their own libidos and agendas, campers would spend the summer exploring and discovering a bit more than their bodies, themselves. They'd explore the opposite sex. Thus 350-pound romances would ensue. And it would extend way past dirty dancing at the DJ dances. "In loco parentis," I'd learn in the coming weeks, translated loosely to "petting past curfew." Soon there would be evenings spent naked in groups, in bushes, pranks leading to chunky dunking in the lake, sex in cabins, wiggling to fit two on a single cot without making the bed squeal. Tramp out in the woods behind the infirmary, and you'd see camper sex—imagine two pigs fighting over a Milk Dud. But for now, there were shaving parties and a slight possibility of an afternoon thunderstorm.

During thunderstorms, we weren't allowed to shower. It had something to do with being struck by lightning through the showerhead.

Crap plumbing happened to be a splendid conductor of electricity. Our counselors insisted that someone, somewhere, had been electrocuted in a camp shower. I pictured what it might be like if it happened to one of us. "Hey, Shake 'N Bake, quit hoggin' all the hot water!" someone would yell through the shower curtain. We'd assume the thud meant she was just about to start shaving the other leg.

In lieu of showering, the girls used those same yellow shaving basins to collect the rainwater to facilitate mudslides down Girls' Hill, and for a "natural shampoo." Harper swore the rain softened her hair, and as her campers, we followed suit: in bathing suits, to be exact, we used our shower caddies and basins to collect rain as it fell in ropes from cabin gutters, then shampooed one another, our feet in the mud, rinsing clean under buckets of rain. We'd all agree later that night that our hair was remarkably softer. We wanted the ability to discern the slight differences in beauty that older girls, girls with sorority letters on their shirts, could detect.

There's something warm about thunderstorms. The heavy fall of rain on roofs, the chime of it in tinny drainpipes, white veins in the distance. Throughout the summer we'd hide behind our windows, watching as the storm made its approach, stewing in plump clouds; the first drops would build into a downpour, making the whole of camp look white.

Storms meant blankets and bunk time. Listening to Tracy Chapman songs on my boom box as we played jacks on powdered cabin floors, sitting on one another's beds, asking about the photos another camper had posted on her walls. Towels brought in from the clothesline, porches cleared. It meant coming in wet, peeling off our clothes, and wrapping ourselves in towels, then sweats. The rain made camp smell of camp, of mud and lake, the way it smells inside an overturned canoe. When it rained everyone shut up.

Sometimes we played Sardines, where one person hid and everyone was it. If you discovered the girl who'd been hiding, you were supposed to join her, packed together as tight as sardines. But there weren't many hiding spots, so the game never lasted long. When Marguerite was annoying us, we let her and her Kermit hide, then sat on our beds writing letters. No one wanted to find her. "I'm gonna find you!" Hams would sing from her bed, as if she was trying. Then we'd all exchange silent laughing faces, thinking we were the cleverest girls in the Berkshires.

When we weren't pretending to play Sardines or actually playing Jacks, we'd sometimes be coerced into Slimnastics at the rec hall or ushered off to the weight room. With rows of rain boots by the door, we'd lie on the padded floors, doing leg lifts as the rain spit in through the window screens. But for the most part, not much was expected of us. The rain meant lazy. The only thing they really forced us to do was write home, even if it was just a signed postcard.

This particular afternoon, Harper arrived with some mail and a care package for Tara. Mail time might actually have been even more of a daily highlight than meals. I suppose it depended on what was on the menu that day, but overall, mail was the bee's knees. While packages were handed to us sealed, counselors were required to witness our opening them. They checked canisters of tennis balls to ensure that they were new, and if not, they handled each ball to ensure that Starbursts hadn't been stuffed into them. Sugary wheels of bubble gum tape were seized. I wondered what they did with the hijacked items. Did the counselor hoard them for herself, pushing a moist peanut butter puck in her mouth as she watched us execute suicide drills on the tennis court? Would she flush the brown and orange wrapper in the recreation hall bathroom, or would she push it through the cracks of the cabin floor? Perhaps she'd relinquish the convenience-store goodies to her superiors? If everyone at camp was supposedly behind the merits of healthy eating, where would they hide the confiscated Hostess and Mars products?

As the summer progressed, parents would receive informational newsletters designed to educate them about our nutritional goals and exercise routines, encouraging the entire family to be part of the program to help facilitate a smooth transition home at the end of the summer. In addition to emphasizing that parents couldn't expect their children to maintain a healthy lifestyle if parents didn't themselves lead by example, the newsletter instructed them to send "appropriate" items to show they cared. "Appropriate" didn't mean menus from the latest restaurant opening in their hometown, yet somehow, without fail, on cold nights, beneath a flashlight, we'd have one of the girls in our cabin recite items from a menu.

"Strawberry shortcake with homemade cream cheese ice cream?!"

"No, it must say frosting. You dweeb, you're reading it wrong."

"No, ICE CREAM. Do you hear me?"

"Read it slower!"

"No, go back to the appetizers. Read that eggplant one again."

"Ew, gag me with a spoon. Eggplant?"

"Let her have the dang eggplant. I want the hanger steak with the golden crisp fries and garlic . . . whatever it was."

"Aioli."

"Oh, snap! You're really just going to take the meat like that?"

"Duh!"

"Then you get last pick of desserts." It became a kind of poker match, where instead of cards, we'd end up divvying up our dreams. Then we'd stray from the menu, besting one another with our cravables. We'd recount our favorite foods in detail—as if speaking of a dear friend with whom we'd had a falling out. We spent our days hurrying across fields, scrambling up a hill known as Heart Attack, and on gymnasium floors doing front lying leg lifts and ass-boosting clenches. And by nightfall we'd calculate the immeasurable ways we could undo it all. We'd have the sweetest dreams.

"It's, like, only because I totally like you that I'll let you have the country-style rigatoni. That's right, the one with the loose sausage meat."

Along with the menus, parents sent teddy bears, glitter bracelets,

Lisa Frank stickers, new Swatch watch face guards, puff paint, Bedazzlers, and Mad Libs. Grandparents, though, couldn't quite help themselves, answering the pleas of their *bubbeleh* grandchildren, sending tins of homemade walnut brownies. And when they were confiscated you'd hear the screams from the next cabin. "But they're still warm! Can't I just have one?"

Tara didn't whine. At the sight of *Soap Opera Digest,* she jumped. Our entire cabin throbbed.

At home, when Lea and I would fight, there was a very strict rule: *No slamming doors!* Poppa feared one of us would lose a finger. At fat camp there was another strict rule: *No jumping in the cabin!* Maybe they feared someone would fracture a floorboard or cause a bunk bed to topple. Harper instructed Tara to sit down or she wouldn't be permitted to view the remaining contents of her package until after dinner. I thought about writing down this rule in a letter home.

Dear Mom and Poppa,

What's up? It's hot here. Camp is fun, except they won't let us jump in the cabin. And during swim tests, instead of swimming, they taught us how to push one another out of the pool. Please send more stamps. Anything else will be impounded and force-fed to a malnourished kid named Wubbah.

Love,
Stephanie

P.S. Send electric blanket because freezing doesn't burn as many calories as sweating.

I didn't write this. I was, however, handed an envelope; I could tell it was from Leigh from her bubbly writing.

ALTHOUGH SHE MAY NOT THINK SO,
I REALLY DO:

Miss STEPHANIE KLEIN
Camp Yanisin
West Stockbridge, MA 01266

Below the address on the envelope, she'd taped something she'd cut from a magazine. A profile of a smiling cartoon mother pig, with writing on her body: "It's not what you're eating—it's what's eating you." Three baby piglets suckled from her teats, and they were named FEAR, ANGER, and DEPRESSION. Gosh, what happened to names like Wilbur? When it came to being overweight, someone was always trying to analyze the "why?" of it.

Who the fuck cares why?

I was so sick of it, all the fatnalysis. Who cares *why* I overate? It couldn't all be about pointing a finger inward or outward toward marketing or Mommy or inclement weather. I didn't care what caused me to be overweight. I just wanted to know how to fix it. "History can help predict the future," a flabby counselor argued in an Easter Sunday voice. Ugh, go suck an egg. I didn't want to hear it anymore. Move more. Eat less. Burn more calories than you take in. Gee, thanks. That's so helpful. I already knew to eat clean and listen to my body, to only eat when I was in a calm mental state. *Everyone* knew. But when you're fat in the head, it's never about knowing the answers. It's about living them.

And I didn't know how. At Fran's adult session, I'd heard that "overeating to fill a void" had to translate into a different action other than eating. Instead of consoling herself with a Valrhona chocolate fondant, Fran told us she'd go accessory shopping for a pair of chocolate-brown crocodile pumps. So, what—when the kids called me Moose and Poppa puffed out his cheeks at me, I should go buy some Nikes?

My chub rub and fatty side pockets were created by something I stuffed into my mouth—no one forced me—and until I changed my eating habits, I'd continue to look as if I'd eaten too many popcorn balls off the Christmas tree. And it wouldn't matter why. Not to me, and certainly not to anyone else, including Leigh or the emotional piglets taped to her envelope.

Her letter, after expressing her disappointment in the failed marriage of Madonna and Sean Penn, was a recap of what I'd missed on *General Hospital.* She asked questions about the boys, demanding to know if I'd kissed anyone yet. Then she inquired about the other girls in my division and whether I'd lost any weight. She mostly complained about the weather and her hair. She was considering dyeing it red.

My bed shook. I dipped my head down to see what Kate was up to. She was lying on her stomach, her face in her pillow. I could tell she was crying. I didn't know if I should say anything. I turned around and folded Leigh's letter, slipping it back into the envelope. I eyed my bookshelf to ensure that the package she'd tucked into my clothing trunk was still there. It remained on the shelf, but now my fashion magazines shrouded the brown bag. Someone had moved things. My stomach turned.

I glanced down at Kate again. She was now on her back, sitting with her legs crossed. I wondered if she'd gotten bad news about her mother in a letter or if she was just homesick. I was afraid to ask because I was afraid she'd answer. Her face was wet.

"Oh, holy night! What is it, Klein?"

"Nothing." I tensed up and stared at the wooden ceiling beams. Kate used her feet to push the springs of my bed. I laughed, and when I looked back down at her she was smiling again. "Those aren't pillows!" I screamed as if I were playing Steve Martin to her John Candy in *Planes, Trains and Automobiles.*

"Funny, she doesn't look Druish!" Kate yelled back. It was the routine we'd established, quoting lines from John Candy films.

"What are you looking at? You never seen a guy who slept with a fish before?"

"I don't know if you've noticed, but I've got a slight weight problem."

"What movie's that from?"

"Stripes." I blinked down at her, then shrugged. "No way! You haven't seen *Stripes*?" I shook my head. "I don't know if we can be friends."

"Well, what if I know something you don't?"

"Impossible!"

"Well, if I did, would you want to be friends?"

"What are you talking about?"

"Is any of your stuff, I dunno, different?" I whispered.

"Speak up. I'm not a superhero, ya know."

I motioned for her to lean in closer, then whispered again, "Is any of your stuff missing or in different places?" Kate froze. Her eyes darted before she sprang into action, like an animal released from a trap. She sprawled on the cabin floor, then eased her tennis racket out from under the bed. She unzipped its cover, slipping her hand in, then molested the racket frantically. Her shoulders dropped, dipping her head in defeat.

"Jesus tap-dancing Christ!" While we were being weighed the afternoon before, a counselor had inspected our cabin for food. "Must've been right after they weighed us, when we were on our way to the pool. No wonder they wouldn't let us stop for goggles." Tampon boxes, coat pockets, even tennis racket covers had been frisked for food. "Snickers. Damn. What'd they take of yours?"

The package Leigh had snuck inside my trunk was still there. The counselors must not have seen it. I tilted it toward Kate so she could see.

"It's what they didn't take," I said.

AFTER REST HOUR, WE ASSEMBLED ON OUR FRONT PORCH, shoelaces tied, baseball mitts in hand. I feigned athleticism and familiarity with the sport, punching my right fist into the pocket of my orange mitt. I could be anyone. Shortstop, even. I could chew a wad of sugar-free gum and spit heavy strings of saliva on the ground, kicking my feet, producing clouds of dirt and giving the illusion of readiness. In fact, I'd insist on shortstop, despite being warned that it was one of the most skilled positions. I liked it because you weren't actually held accountable. There was always someone else you could blame. The first baseman had way too much action; you couldn't feign skills if you covered a base. As shortstop, your world was grounders, and if I happened to miss a pop-up, it would be a first, as far as they were concerned. "The sun blinded me," I'd say, squinting even in the retelling of events.

Who was I kidding? You can't fake hand-eye coordination. You can't pretend to be athletic, even at fat camp. But as I came to learn, the next hour was for doing just that: pretending to be someone you weren't.

I thought we'd be heading to the baseball diamond behind the cabins, but I had it all wrong. We'd do that during the next period, when they'd emphasize technique and remind us all simply to try our best. "It doesn't matter who wins the game," our counselors would lecture, "because as long as you participate, you're a winner." I knew this was a phrase designed to comfort and encourage kids like me, girls who'd been traumatized by participating in organized sports back home. But it seemed so *Little Engine That Could,* far too scripted and patronizing. God, I thought, it's not like we're *that* bad.

But before baseball, we were led to the middle of Girls' Hill, where we were instructed to stand beside at least one person we didn't know. Our leather mitts were pitched to the ground behind us as we clasped hands, stretching into a fat kindergarten circle near the metal playground. I really hoped we weren't going to play Duck Duck Goose, because seriously, that shit was tiring.

"Truth or dream?" our division leader—or DL as we'd come to refer to Gina—announced. We were now sitting as she explained from the center of the circle this version of Not Quite Truth or Dare. She told us to reveal two truthful things about ourselves and one "dream." Our peers would be charged with guessing which detail wasn't true. We'd begin with whoever's birthday was next. I watched Gina as she watched the circle, her head nodding as if she were counting. She had a neck like an American white pelican, and it reminded me of my grandma's arms. I couldn't help but think of a dare for one of the other girls: *I dare you to poke her wattle. Ooh, I dare you to walk right up to her and gobble!* "Raise your hand if your birthday is in July," she instructed. Five of the girls raised their hands. That had to bite, the summer birthday. I imagined it ranked right up there with being a New Year's baby. No one really celebrated you. During the school year, you got to distribute cupcakes, or at least protest homework. Your family was there to make you feel special. But at camp—worse, fat camp—you were in it alone. Just a solitary candle in your meager slice of turkey meatloaf. No icing licked from fingers. No sprinkles. No celebrating with food.

As we went around the circle, a blur of uninteresting truths and dreams was stated in mumbles and unconscious snorts. I was bordered by a resident of New England, the youngest sibling of six, a portly girl who insisted she was a trained classical dancer, on track for Juilliard. I was eager to hear what Grayson Spoon would say, wondering if she'd reveal three truths, forcing us to choose our own dream from her real life. She resided in a Manhattan brownstone beside Diana Ross, "Near the Met," she said. At the end of summer, she'd pass through Switzerland on an alpine tour with her older brother, Dalton. "I'm adopted," she added as her third and final fact.

By now, I imagine, she's tracked down her birth mother and lectures her sons on careless sperm donation. I suspect she's the type to vehemently deny ever attending fat camp and has been known to order her foam on the side, "in a cup," she tells the barista. People just believe and do what she says.

Grayson was wearing a moss green polo shirt, the slit near her collar piped with a thin strip of plaid. Girls like Grayson were born in tartan, and even when revealing their lack of blood lineage, sounded as if others owed them something. When pressed about her "dream," she revealed that at summer's end she wouldn't be going anywhere but to Choate. Up until then, I thought Choate was some type of chocolate powder. Most people would have categorized Grayson as conceited. I categorized her as popular and wished that I, too, was being sent away to boarding school, where girls smelled of library and triple-milled French soaps.

When my turn came, I thought about mentioning my ethnicity, sharing that I was a quarter Russian, a quarter Austrian, a quarter Greek, and a quarter Puerto Rican, but the truth is, being Puerto Rican was something I said only in a whisper. When people asked, I'd offer a more general and European "Spanish," but even that was on a need-to-know basis. I inherited ashamed from Mom, who when young herself refused to wear dangling earrings, insisting they made her look "ethnic." It also didn't help that her father had roasted a goat in her front yard. Instead, I revealed to the circle of girls that I had recently been chased down the streets of New York when someone insisted I was Tina Yothers.

"You mean Jennifer Keaton from *Family Ties*?" Gina probed. Yes, and it was true. This wasn't my dream. Toward the end of eighth grade, my class had gone on a field trip to New York City, where we were instructed to visit different neighborhoods. Our class divided into groups of eight to ten people, which were then assigned to one high school senior. At the last minute, our guide became sick, and we were stuck with our goody-two-shoes social studies teacher as our escort.

"I promise to be cool," she said as she hiked up one of her knee socks. "You can even call me by my first name," she added, as if our spirits would somehow be lifted with the knowledge that we could call her "Bernice." She warned the class never to separate from at least one buddy, to avoid Times Square at all costs, not to take the subway (buses only), and not to buy fireworks in Chinatown. Times Square was infested with XXX video shops, peep shows, prostitutes, and pickpockets. No one cautioned us about overeating, though. I gorged my way through the city, devouring dirty water dogs from pretzel vendors at the perimeter of Central Park, licking Little Italy from my fingers, and finally packing in rolled pancakes of crisp Peking duck, threaded with strings of scallion and dabs of sweet hoisin. I didn't just visit New York; I ate it.

When it came time to meet up again with my grade at Penn Station, the girls of my group were determined to purchase porn. Okay, that's not quite right. *I* was determined, and felt like the only one, until Leigh joined in my enthusiasm. What else would a middle school kid bring back from a Manhattan trip sans parents? Fireworks and pornography seemed like no-brainers. Apparently, not to everyone. I wasn't aware then of how advanced I was sexually, but I certainly noticed the difference between what felt normal to me and, well, the desire to purchase a bobble-head doll.

Of course I know now that my interest in sex began earlier than most. As far back as second grade, even, I remember Maria, the only Hispanic girl in our class (if you didn't count me) was having a vagina party against the corner of a desk. Our teacher reprimanded her, demanding she be seated. I knew exactly what Maria was up to, knew why she wouldn't obey our teacher until she "finished." It wasn't just a cursory interest, explored in games of doctor in bushes where I'd show my genitals to another girl. At night, even in second grade, I remember rubbing myself to orgasm. Most girls weren't interested in sexual things until junior high, perhaps. They played cash register and teacher in their classmates' basements. Their diary entries were limited to detailed accounts of the school dance. Crushes and the idea of being kissed, wondering how it would feel. Practicing on their hand. But my body knew what felt good, and by eighth grade, it was far beyond just a transitory curiosity.

Other kids brought home Yankees hats and snow globes, miniature statues of the Empire State Building. I heart NY T-shirts. The last thing I wanted was a snow globe. I grabbed Leigh, and we purchased stacks of expensive smut with as much money as we had left.

"Don't get that one. I already got it. Ooh, get that one over there." Leigh and I quickly tucked the magazines into their brown bags. The man behind the magazine counter was all too happy to help us.

"What about this one?" he said, holding up a magazine with an enormous-breasted French maid on the cover.

I nodded, insisting he add it. These weren't tame magazines with centerfold spreads of airbrushed women. They were raunchy fetish magazines, presenting detailed action scenes and close-up head shots of women's faces covered in thick webs of semen.

While the rest of the girls in our group completed their touristy purchases, I wandered to the normal magazine section. A man who looked as if he sold knockoff watches and bundles of white athletic socks—three for a dollar—stared at me. I wondered why the rest of my have-to-have friends weren't eager to see the porn. I couldn't wait to get home and devour the pages, each magazine spread open to my favorite section, fanned across my bed as I masturbated. I felt different from the other girls my age in my desire to look at these things. The man in the tourist shop continued to stare, so I hid my face behind the cover of *Seventeen.* Maybe he'd seen me buy all that porn and was aroused.

"We see you, Tina," he finally said. "Tina Yothers, we know it's you." Once I realized he was talking about me, I became excited and feigned a little shyness, the way I imagined a real celebrity would respond. Mostly, I was excited that someone thought I looked that angelic and argyle—that *white,* really. I was a freckled redhead, but I didn't see myself as white. I worried that others saw me as strange, as ethnic, just as Mom had feared. Still, I was not thrilled about being likened to Tina Yothers, despite how white-bread she appeared. Because everyone knew that Mallory's little sister Jennifer was anything but little. She was a pudge. Grown strangers began to concur with the man, talking behind cupped hands, pointing. Eventually a crowd formed, and I ducked out of the magazine stand, racing toward the 2:35 train to Mineola. A shouting mass of people followed me. "Tina, can't I get an autograph?"

I narrated my Tina Yothers story, my truth, to the girls of my division without mention of the porn purchases or the hand-over-fist way I had eaten. I stuck to the mob-scene chase, and just as I finished speaking, I noticed all their heads cocked to the side. Each of them looked for recognition in one another's faces. They began to study me, smiling. "Totally," one girl said after squinting for a bit. They too were convinced that I resembled Tina Yothers. Tina Yothers was fat. They thought I looked like her.

I hadn't shared the story hoping they'd agree. I told it because I liked that I was chased by a host of strangers in New York City; it's what teenage dreams are made of. I just wished I hadn't been likened to someone that fleshy and round, so when I saw all the campers agree, I started to eat my cuticles. My story didn't illustrate that I was special. Instead, it reinforced the exact reason I came to fat camp in the first place: I was dumpy. And throngs of fat kids were letting me know it. I wasn't that different from any of them, even if I was on the thinner side of fat.

After the icebreaker, we were dismissed, half of us sent toward the baseball diamond, the rest to the soccer field, reminded that we'd reconvene later for our evening activity. "The Miss Yanisin Pageant," Gina gobbled. Would one of us be nominated to represent the division in a Bold, Big, and Beautiful contest? Not quite.

DAN MESSING'S TUFTED BROWS PINCHED TOGETHER IN an expression of agony at Grayson's suggestion of reshaping them. "If you want to win, you like, need to own it," she said as she helped to transform Dan into Miss Shapen for the pageant. Or would it be Miss Behave, Miss Understood, or Miss Fit? We had time to decide; for now, though, Dan would be Danielle.

"See how we suffer for beauty?" Beulah added as she picked at her own mole with a pair of angled tweezers.

"It's not easy being beautiful," Jordan chimed in, pronouncing "beautiful" as if "beauty" was actually "full." She shook a canister of shaving cream in her hand.

"What's that for?"

"We're gonna have to shave your legs," Jordan said, clicking her nails on the can. Jordan was *jolie-laide,* beautiful and ugly at the same time, with a narrow horselike face, wide glistening eyes, and full—what I knew boys referred to as blow-job—lips. Lip gloss always gummed up at the corners of her mouth. Jordan was Grayson's aide-de-camp, sleeping in the bed beneath Grayson's in the cabin beside mine.

"Let me tell you somethin', sista," Dan intoned. "No one's gonna be checking out my legs if you give me some nice titties." Dan wasn't an ass or legs man; he was definitely a breast man, and truth be told, he himself already had boobs. Ample man-boobs, in fact. The kind the boys at home would've joked belonged strapped behind a "manssiere." They drooped outward and bore a striking resemblance to semi-inflated whoopee cushions. "Don't give me any of those gnarly shoulder pads or socks in there, either. They need to look real," he demanded while manhandling his borderline C-cup breasts.

"Lots of cotton," Jordan said. Grayson nodded in agreement. "And we'll tape pencil erasers in place for the nipples."

"I don't know about that," I interjected. The primping girls in the cabin stopped what they were doing and looked up at me. "I mean, like, what look are we going for?" I circled Dan, eyeing him as if he were Charlotte's humble pig. "We need to decide: hornet or wasp?" I'd just thought of it myself. "You know, small polite WASP boobs can make you look really mint."

At the time, it was my idea of femininity, of what it was to be the ideal girl. Small breasts meant being refined and articulate in a string-of-pearls, country-club, my-family-arrived-on-the-*Mayflower* kinda way. Sloppy boobs that hung like ferrets, as most of ours did, didn't have a place beside proper posture and poise. "All the other cabins are totally gonna give their guys hornet boobs. You know. *Whore*net. We need to make him look different if we wanna win."

I was thinking he'd look nice in pastels, with my yellow cable-knit draped over his sunburned shoulders. Dan had trim boy hips and carried most of his weight in his abdomen, arms, and second chin. I wanted his hips. Ironically, it's what I thought of when I thought of feminine: *narrow.* Narrow was ladylike and courteous. Hips like that said "excuse me" in a sugary voice and were invited to join the Junior League. Thin, petite, small, and narrow—all the things we were not—were feminine. Breasts that made blouses buckle were sexual.

"Whorenet. Definitely," Dan said as he flashed a pod of icy blue eye shadow in my direction. The rest of the girls agreed with his proclamation and returned to fashioning him into a floozy, complete with an artificial beauty mark, harlot-red lipstick, and a black feather boa, compliments of Hams.

"And he might as well use my bra," Hams added as she unhooked it from beneath her shirt, slipping it through the armholes. She handed him a quadruple-hooked beige bra with thick elastic arm straps, still warm. There was an intimacy in her gesture, one she didn't see. Her breasts were boilerplate as far as she was concerned. And I envied it, her comfort with her body, just as it was. *Maybe it's because she's black,* I remember thinking. Hams had mentioned wanting to "free her girls up" when we'd gone around the cabin in our circle of hope, hinting that she'd like nothing more than to wear thin tank tops and never have to pause for thought of support. But as I watched her slip him what looked like a grandma bra, I realized she was more comfortable than she'd let on.

Nothing felt commonplace about my body, except maybe my ankles, wrists, and knees. Basically, I was fine with my smaller joints. Undoubtedly, though, if I had to reveal any of my undergarments to someone of the opposite sex, I'd be certain they weren't beige. A black bra, at that age, was a big deal. It had nothing to do with being ideal for a certain sheer dress. If you owned a black bra, it meant you hoped someone else would see it. It was the kind of purchase you made on the sly, at the mall with your friends in nervous laughs and quick movements, your bags tightly gripped. It wasn't a feminine purchase; it was sexual. I didn't think it was possible for feminine and sexual to simultaneously exist. Thin was feminine and dainty. Fat, as much as I didn't like it on myself, was sexual. And I wasn't the only one aware of it.

Most of the girls at camp were proud of their boobs; it was their one advantage over the slim, flat-chested girls back home. So when their chance came to decorate and define Danielle, they chose to fashion her in their own image, hoping to create someone worthy of receiving beauty accolades.

Batting his false eyelashes and making a dramatic curtsy toward me, Dan asked in an Irish brogue, "Girly, whad'ya tink of me hornet hooters?" He had trouble balancing in the heels, so he staggered and finally fell, his stout legs straddled out in front of him like smoked turkey drumsticks. We all agreed he definitely wouldn't be Irish. Instead, on this day God created Danielle, the well-endowed daughter of a well-to-do Southern aristocrat, who was due at her debutante cotillion—the likes of which Camp Yanisin had never seen. Hello, Miss Taken!

A half hour later, Hams's 38H bra was packed with plump water balloons and stretched over Dan Messing's broad-beamed body. Along with the other boys and counselors in drag, he spoke in falsetto, floundered with his footing, and insisted on world peace and access to the Pig-Out Room for "y'all of mankind." Back in his cabin, much later that night, when he'd washed Danielle off his face and returned to being Dan, I predicted that he would pass the silky bra to his friends. I imagined one of them smelling it after holding it for a minute or so. The next morning, it was reluctantly returned. Only Hams had to retrieve it from the top of the flagpole during breakfast lineup.

Danielle's hornet breasts didn't lead to victory that night. Though the discussion of said breasts did lead to an invitation, by one Miss Grayson Spoon, for me to sit beside her at the close of the evening activity, by the campfire.

"You were right," she said as she tossed a young green stick into the fire, "we should have done WASP boobs." I loved that Grayson had initiated a conversation with me.

"Thanks."

"Come sit with us."

I casually took my place among them, watching Grayson slip her abbreviated hair behind one ear. She was wearing a pinky-apricot button-down shirt tucked into ironed Levi's. A man's navy-and-green striped necktie for a belt. Cowboy boots peeped out from the fray of jean, like lizard tongues ready to lick. She was playing with a purple slap bracelet. I wished I had straight hair. Hoping for beauty like Grayson's was like being a kid who'd just thrown bread at the ducks only to run back and watch from afar, clutching her mother's leg. It was something I wanted to be a part of, but worried I'd never be able to get close. It was exhilarating and disappointing.

And then it began to rain.

BACK IN MY CABIN, AFTER FACE WASHING, JOY ASKED WHY I was associating with Grayson. "I'm just saying," she said as she sniffed her dental floss, "watch out. She's a two-faced little ass-wipe."

When I was younger, Tricia Caggiano, a neighbor of mine, once called me two-faced, and I remember being harshly offended. It wasn't her attack on my character that troubled me. I was certain "two-faced" meant I had two faces, as in two chins. It was a fat remark, I was sure. By now, I understood what Joy had meant. I just didn't know where it was coming from.

"What happened between you two must've been wicked bad, huh?" I'd learned "wicked bad" that night. I'd heard Grayson say it at the campfire before we raced back to our cabins to escape the rain. I loved this about camp, the way we gulped down one another's words and phrases, repeating them as if they were our own.

"Nothing happened," she said, now on to dousing a cotton ball with Sea Breeze astringent. Then she flinched from the smell and added, "Just watch out. That's all."

And this is how it went, being an adolescent girl at camp. There were groups of popular kids, whispers and backtalk, rumors and irrational reasons not to like people. All of it wound tightly around my self-esteem. I wanted to be liked, which I knew meant being thin, even at fat camp, where we were all supposedly accepted just as we were. All of us had our own truths and dreams, even the ones we wouldn't share aloud. We projected the images we wanted to see, behind the masks we wore. We were girls who thought we were women, girls with dreams of who we wanted to be, masquerading behind eye shadow, trying to figure out who we were. And as far as I was concerned, I was in, becoming exactly who I wanted to be: popular.

eight

SHRINK-WRAPPED

I've got an awesome boyfriend named Jared. He is an awesome kisser. Last night I said "okay kisser." Tonight I say "awesome." We were kissing (tongue) for 15 minutes straight! His hand went up my shirt, and I had on a wire bra. He wuz having trouble getting into it!!! It was awesome. I wuz creaming in my pants. I felt his dick against my leg, and he had the biggest boner! Anyway, he finally felt me up. My hickey is still here!! It isn't that big, but it is noticeable. Jared is really cute! I'm considered "hot" at this camp. I'm going to get so much booty when I get home—don't get me wrong, I'm <u>not</u> a slut! I just have a hard time saying "no."

P.S. Drew Longo and Geoff Katz were told by Jared that he really, really liked me!!!

"YOU CAN'T CHANGE YOUR HABITS UNLESS YOU KNOW what they are," Valerie said as she pointed to her white easel pad. Valerie was the camp nutritionist, a wholesome twenty-something grad student often spotted braiding the hair of six-year-olds. She doubled as a nanny for the owners' children while also playing Camp Mother, attending to the wails of homesick campers. Her marker made a dot beside the word "rituals." She wanted to know ours. This wasn't our regularly scheduled nutrition session. Usually we'd gather on Mondays. But due to Olympics Day, a mini–color war in which all of camp was divided into teams of competing countries, they'd rescheduled our required rap session to Sunday, just one day after weigh-in. First they measured our fat; then they analyzed it.

Jessica Fallis wasn't sniffling into a tissue because she just learned what her last name meant. She was blubbering because she'd only lost a pound. "Only?!" Valerie said, pushing four sticks of margarine into Jessica's hands. "You lost all that." Kate shed a sack of potatoes. Hams dropped a gallon of milk. I was down eight sticks and two tablespoons of butter that week, making a total loss of a little more than eight medium cantaloupes. This was their way of showing me that I'd lost 2¼ pounds that week, totaling 13 pounds in the two weeks I'd been there. I knew I should have been focusing on my goal to get past the use of the 150-pound anchor weight, but I couldn't stop staring at the margarine in Jessica's hands. I wanted to liberate a stick of it from its waxy paper and dip it into Joy's five-pound bag of sugar. Homemade frosting.

I knew there were patterns of familiarity in everything I did, from shampooing first thing in the shower to the why and whens of my eating. I'd already analyzed all of it with Fran and didn't care to anymore. It all came down to what I would do about it, not what I thought about it, but not everyone had had a Fran before they'd been to camp. Truth be told, I didn't mind these shaded rap sessions so much; they were a respite from calisthenics, conditioning, and caterpillar drills. Or in the case of Sunday, it saved me from an all-camp game of Capture the Flag. I sat picking piles of grass as I was force-fed a session on "rituals and triggers."

Fran hadn't only had me detail everything I consumed in a food diary; I sometimes kept a record of my *whens*. *When* I was at the movies, *when*

I came home from school, *when* I loitered by the PTA baked-goods table. The triggers, apparently, mattered. The idea was if I could identify what prompted the onset of eating, aside from actual hunger, I could find a way to avoid it by altering my behavior. But no one has actual hunger on the Gold Coast of Long Island. We ritually made dinner reservations at our favorite Chinese restaurants come Sundays. With a Shirley Temple in hand, I'd slip into the red banquette seating and eat pupu platters off lazy Susans until the onset of food coma. And that's what we were good at, being stuffed; being hungry had no place in my life.

That summer, most girls from school were on Teen Tours getting full, playing Jewish Geography with teens from other states, certain they had to know Sloane Goldstein from Livingston, New Jersey. They were off visiting amusement parks and "must-see" destinations. I was in tween group therapy.

Forced to analyze the whys of my weight, I shared with Valerie and the others my after-school ritual, the way I'd race home, dump my overloaded knapsack on the entranceway floor, then zip to the refrigerator, hungry or not. I'd stare for a while, leaning against the door as I examined the jars of duck sauce and mayonnaise, the clear half-empty packages of walnuts, wheels of waxy Laughing Cow cheese, a sticky cylinder of orange-blossom honey. And that's what the inside of the refrigerator door was for me: a medicine cabinet, teeming with orange cylinders, there to anesthetize my day. I wasn't hungry; it was habit.

I had more of them. On cold winter mornings, I ate a steamy bowl of milky farina. The smooth white grain held the dent of my spoon, thick, pooling with dribbles of honey. "It's ready," Mom would belt up to us from the kitchen, still in her robe, assembling our bagged lunches. It was my trigger, my "you're allowed to eat." I waited for the farina to cool as I loaded my textbooks into my book bag. I had a ritual of allowing a creamy seal to form on top. It's still my favorite part. I'd skim off the first layer with my spoon, then I'd step away, continuing to bundle under clothing as a new milk skin formed. I stabbed my way through it, eating in rounds, waiting for each new layer to scab. It became an activity, the teen version of playing with your food. While it was there to nourish, really it was there to entertain. Eating was how I passed time.

Once I began my sessions with Fran, my farina breakfast was replaced with a sensible half an English muffin with cottage cheese, artificial sweetener, and a shower of cinnamon, melted in the toaster. "No one needs more than a half," Fran insisted. I brought my bundled muffin half to the bus stop, where I waited with the warmth of it in my hands. The cold weather became a trigger. I ate to pass time and to keep warm, to forestall the eventual hunger that would hit with an intense frenzy come lunchtime. These were the apparent first layers of *why* on the analytical journey of excavating my inner fatty. This is why they sent us to camp, to figure out all the *whys,* then do something about them. I didn't care about the *whys.* Just limit my indolent arse to a four-ounce portion of skate, I mistakenly thought, and everything would improve. Ew. Skate wing.

Valerie asked us to raise our hands and contribute more of our rituals to her white pad. Mine weren't one-word answers. Like with everyone else, eating was a social event for me. I ate to entertain others, to comfort and calm, to procrastinate, to unwind, to celebrate and commiserate, to stuff down something to prevent feelings from bubbling to the top. But mostly I ate out of habit and expectation. I didn't eat because of FEAR, ANGER, or DEPRESSION, the reasons attached to the piglets on Leigh's envelope. I overate because I'd learned to. I was unable to sit through a movie in a theater without popcorn by the fistful, even if I'd just finished a meal. I couldn't quite sleep until I satisfied a desire for a sweet little morsel, despite how full I was from dinner. Dessert wasn't "on occasion"; it was every occasion, merely out of habit. And I needed to unlearn it.

"Alternatives," Valerie said as she added the word to the top of a fresh piece of paper. This was how we did behavior modification. We first identified the ritual, then we imagined alternative actions. Identify and modify: after school, instead of plunking down my textbooks by the door, I would need to change my route, lug them up to my room and set out my first homework task. Only then could I return downstairs to the kitchen, to open a can of low-sodium, fat-free soup, dump it into a bowl, and microwave it. "The heat will help send a signal to your brain that you're not hungry, and because it's hot," Valerie said, "you'll eat it more slowly." Yes, this seemed sensible indeed. There was a problem, though. I was still eating, despite the fact that I wasn't hungry.

"Paint your nails," Mom would suggest in the coming fall. After my summer at Yanisin, she'd witness that same ritual, my leaning in front of the opened fridge. "You're not going to go rummaging through the refrigerator when your nails are wet." Mom had the strongest, best-kept nails. "And then go use some mouthwash." It was the only time someone suggested replacing eating with another activity. And it worked. Some of the time. I was also in the habit of rewarding myself through the homework. *If I just get through this passage, I can eat.* But now I'd need to replace the eating with a different procrastination, and in practice, there was no way doing push-ups was going to work. I'd need to do quick things I actually enjoyed, like making a phone call, reading a magazine, or, I guess, painting my nails. But eating sounded like way more fun than taking a brisk walk around the block.

At Yanisin, we didn't need self-monitoring systems; our counselors did it for us. We'd play at these what-if scenarios with a nutritionist, but we didn't need to change our habits, not then, not at camp. It was theoretical. In the day to day of our practical camp lives, we didn't have an opportunity to exercise self-control. They did it all for us, in scheduled activities of Slimnastics, sign 'n' backs, and 3.8-mile loops around camp. It was a vacation from decisions and our pudgy little lives, despite being surrounded by more overweight children than any of us had ever known. It's why so many campers returned each summer, heavier than the last, unable to keep off the weight they'd shed. None of us could practice living thin lives full of wise decisions and alternative routes home to avoid all that tempted us. We lived in guarded cabins with routine food checks. There weren't cupboards at camp, or refrigerators, or hidden goodies for our fathers and thin siblings. We didn't have a chance to choose anything for ourselves. Everything was dictated.

During our time with Valerie, I listened as other campers divulged that in their homes the cabinets and refrigerator doors were padlocked. Their parents scrutinized their behavior for them. One mother sprinkled baby powder on the kitchen floor to reveal an incriminating footprint made in the middle of the night. And look how well it worked. Several girls groused that their parents resorted to bribery: a new wardrobe, gemstone jewelry, even a new Mercedes. They shook their heads in the telling, still pissed that their parents didn't fully accept them. Gasps. My reaction wasn't one of outrage. I wasn't appalled, didn't think to extend empathy in a telling eye gaze, nodding in agreement with just how hard the lonesome plight can be. Instead I thought, *How 'bout I take those wretched parents off your sterling-silver plate?*

The one thing we all had in common, though, was that none of it worked. Despite the bribes, sneers, and the slapping of our hands as we lunged in for seconds, we were still fat. And all the other attempts at controlling our eating had failed. It was nice being able to talk about it for once. To sit among other girls my age who knew what it was like to be miserable made me feel less alone. I watched Beulah grab at her rolls and ask if anyone else's fat was feeling gooier. There we were all sitting cross-legged beneath a tree, not braiding hair or giving one another the chills with *"Crack an egg on your head; let the yolk drip down, the yolk drip down, the yolk drip down . . ."* but noodling our stomachs, grabbing handfuls of our fat, reading one another's faces to find an answer to Beulah's question. Indeed it was; we were getting gooier. I imagined that the fat inside each of my butt cheeks looked like a head of cauliflower, and it was now breaking apart into florets.

"Look," demanded Hams with both hands squeezing her bare belly, "mine looks like a pumpernickel bagel."

"Quick, Jess, pass her your margarine."

Then we laughed until Valerie and our counselors had to clap us back to the task at hand, focusing again on our rituals and how we'd need to exercise self-control to unlearn the behaviors we'd relied on for so long. I thought about the role of self-control and wondered if I had any. I didn't know it then, but in the coming weeks, I'd learn more about it than I'd ever cared to.

LATER THAT NIGHT, I CLIMBED ONTO MY TOP BUNK AND cued up a subliminal hypnosis cassette I'd brought from home. It was designed to guide me through exercising more self-control in my life. The recorded man's voice prompted me to imagine myself at a buffet, witnessing others loading up their plates. *Savages.* I would not do this, he insisted in a tone that implied *I* was far more cultivated. *I* was someone who used a napkin and could distinguish her forks. *I'd* only fill my plate with nutritious foods, just enough to leave me satisfied, not full. *I'd* put my fork down between bites and stop eating when a "pleasant warm feeling" came over me. *My* attention wouldn't be directed toward something as uninspired as food. No, *I* would focus on the delightful ("sparkling," as he called it) conversation. As his voiced piped in through my headphones, I thought about the boon of the smorgasbord: the scarce rules, the expectation of several trips, and the welcomed ability to make mountains out of molehills. I could begin, if I so chose, with dessert and skip the salad business altogether. A warmed bread-and-butter pudding. Something sensible from the crêperie station: a smear of Nutella, caramel-shellacked bananas, and a pocket of cool almond cream. Fondant. Petite éclairs, napoleons, and profiteroles. Profiteroles made me think of rolls, mine to be exact. The ones on my back that bloated into flappy grips when my jeans were too tight. I had to rewind the tape. I'd worked my way up to the carving station and built myself a meat sundae by the time he mentioned "new rituals."

Before eating, he eventually came to say, a new ritual would take place: I would drink a glass of water, then take a deep breath in through my nose, hold it for the mental count of ten, then exhale through my mouth slowly, counting back down to one. These numbers would send signals to my brain. "Behind the words, there are subliminal messages being sent to reprogram your thinking. Just listen to the tape for thirty days, and your habits will change," he promised. Monotone Man assured me I'd feel completely content with my choices and never favor the old favorites, slick with fat enjoyed with my eyes closed, now that I was in a healthier state of being. This was as likely to happen as my taking a bath to stave off hunger. He was persistent, though, repeating that if I followed the steps he'd laid out, I'd control myself by being more mindful. I supposed it couldn't hurt. Maybe it was that simple, and then I wouldn't need a nutritionist or a counselor to do it for me.

The counselor on duty that night was Harper. Being on duty entailed keeping watch for trespassers, dodgy strangers who might penetrate the barbed-wire periphery of camp. She composed mix tapes on our porch—"Pinball Wizard," "Desperado," "Hotel California," and "Fire and Rain"—while wrapped in an unsightly afghan, burning a citronella candle, with a bundle of stationery and envelopes of stickers at her side. When we made too much noise, she'd threaten us like an impatient young mother: "Don't make me come in there."

Kate couldn't lift herself onto my cot, so we both sat cross-legged on hers. Everyone was getting ready for bed, performing their evening rituals: brushing teeth, applying facial masks, and readying flashlights. Once the lights were flicked off, and Harper was on the porch, I eased the secret glossy magazine Leigh had slipped into my trunk out of its bag to show Kate. "No shit," she said in a voice louder than she'd intended. Joy leaned in. Suddenly there were six of us around the bed; young fat girls, covered in green facial masks, huddled around Kate's lower bunk watching a man spurt his load onto Svetlana's immense breasts. Girls who didn't have older sisters had one in me now. I was important and suddenly popular. My life was no longer lived alone in my room with my private rituals. Now there were girls who wanted to be around me, who'd ask to sit with me at meals and to be my swim buddy at the lake. I shared my smut and felt older. I knew things about sex, and I had access to it, right there in our cabin, and that made me cool. I wanted to take this new life home with me.

"I'm not kidding," Harper warned from the porch in the dreaded low tone. Please, what was *she* going to do? It's not like she could send us to bed without supper or discipline us with hand-clap push-ups. *Empty.* Her threats were as empty as Mom's. She wouldn't dock us, sending us to bed early the next night, because doing so meant that she, too, would have to retire to the cabin to supervise us. Just the same, her warnings had each of us scattering to our corner of the cabin, our mattresses squeaking as we climbed into our beds. I tucked myself into mine with a smile and stared at the ceiling as my eyes adjusted to the dark.

I couldn't sleep. Before clicking the play button on my cassette player, I switched on my flashlight and reread Leigh's most recent letter.

She'd been exercising self-control by wrapping her tongue in Saran Wrap. She read somewhere that fat was absorbed through the tongue and that you could eat whatever you wanted, as long as your tongue didn't soak up the calories. She'd been charging up and down the steps in her house with a pedometer clipped to her waist. She'd lost two pounds that week, she added, using three exclamation points. She asked how much weight I'd lost so far, but I didn't want her to know how well I was doing. I drafted a quick letter in response, complaining that I'd lost only three pounds in the two weeks I'd been there. I didn't want to share thin with her. I feared that if she learned how well I was progressing it might motivate her to lose more weight, and then we'd be equal. Then nothing would change. Or worse, she'd have lost weight all on her own, without the stigma of being sent to a fat farm. She'd try harder, hoping to keep up with me. We'd compete for thin. Certainly I'd win if I was the only one playing. I became one of those women I detest, the kind who refuses to reveal her beauty rituals or weight loss secrets. "Oh, I really just forget to eat most of the time." Giggle. Giggle. *Yeah, you so totally snack on Ex-Lax, lady.*

I hoped once Leigh saw the new thinner me, she'd be overwhelmed, and maybe that would change the balance of things. Between us. Between me and everyone at school. I wasn't sure how. In my letters, I continued to lie. "This camp sucks. I ate fewer calories at home with Fran." I wanted to be envied for once in my life, for someone at home to want to be me. That night I fell asleep smiling to the hypnosis tape, imaging myself at a buffet-style cocktail party, with collarbones, in a form-fitting backless dress.

TWO DAYS LATER, WHEN I RETURNED FROM THE LAKE, HARPER handed me a slip of paper. At first glance I thought it was a message detailing a phone call I'd missed during our scheduled cabin phone time. Instead it was a note instructing me to visit the camp shrink—the Brain, the kids called him. More analysis of my eating rituals and habits? Did they make everyone have these one-on-one sessions? I didn't even know camps had shrinks. They had a graduate student teaching nutrition. A nurse with swollen ankles too daft to recognize when campers were feigning dizzy just so they could get some extra calories from juice. But a proper therapist on campus?

He actually called himself Doc. He had a corona of white hair with sprawling eyebrows and a knuckled chin. Evidently he founded the camp a few years before I was born, and now he spent the summers as a figurehead, with an office, a dog, and a golf cart. Sometimes he'd usher around prospective campers and their families. He didn't have a legal pad, glasses, or a tie, the real makings of what I imagined a therapist to be. I didn't get to lie on a couch. I sat on a pilled orange sofa across from him, waiting for him to speak. I liked being there in the air-conditioning. It felt like a treat. Doc had teeth, but when his mouth was closed, it looked like he didn't. He resembled what I'd expected the Jelly Donut Man from one of Fran's stories to look like, except he wasn't wearing overalls. He was wearing a ribbed white tank top and running shorts that were so short they revealed one of his nuts. The Brain, indeed.

"Do you think you know a lot about boys?" Wait. What?

"I don't know."

"I imagine you think you do." Then he tapped his foot waiting for me to add more. Huh? What do boys have to do with weight loss? Well, wait, I guess a lot. I did want to lose weight so I'd be desirable, but I didn't think they discussed such obvious things in camp. "That magazine you had certainly didn't leave much to the imagination." I wasn't sure who had told. Maybe Harper's threats weren't empty. Maybe she'd seen the whole thing through the window. Or perhaps one of the girls in the cabin could have—but who would have?—told. And why? My "adult material" had been confiscated, he added. With a question like "Do you think you know a lot about boys?" I thought he meant did I understand boys, what makes them tick, that they prefer to destroy things and pee in their mother's flowerpots to, say, spending hours outfitting their Barbies, or even their more adult need to be solution-oriented and fix things, even when women just want to vent.

I was terrified that he was going to present me with the magazine, leafing through it in front of me. "What do you think your parents would say about this?" he'd say, his knobby finger pointed at an erect penis as it entered one woman's ass, another woman on her knees below, her tongue there to administer lubrication.

"Stephanie?" Doc asked, but I hadn't been paying attention. I couldn't think straight. I kept wondering if other kids at camp knew I was there, now, with the Brain having "the talk." Was he going to mention birds or bees next? And would it kill him to wear briefs? Suddenly, I couldn't remember what he'd asked. All I could think as I diverted my gaze from his groin was *Sweatin' to the Oldies*. Shit! Now what? I blinked and nodded, hoping my body would answer the question I hadn't heard him ask.

"I asked what your parents would think about all this."

I didn't think the word "porn" would trigger any feelings of surprise on my parents' behalf. Poppa referred to me as "Little Miss Hot Hormones," a term that still bothers me today. Hearing "hormones" coupled with "hot" from my father makes me want to run down the halls of my house with my arms flailing, chanting, "Go away go away go awaygoawaygo," until I can hear nothing but the sound of my own voice. Certainly my parents wouldn't have been surprised by a phone call alerting them that I still had raging hormones. If anything, perhaps they'd find it reassuring that I was still the very same daughter they'd last seen through a tinted bus window in a Yonkers parking lot. I wanted to say this to Doc, tell him that my parents would mostly be pissed that those bastards rummaged through my belongings and stole from me. But I wasn't certain how they'd react. If Mom answered the phone, I'm sure she'd have just apologized and replied with tsking sounds. "I just can't believe it," she might've said as if she were told I mutilated a finch. Instead of answering Doc, I just sat there, trying not to notice his oldies.

"Well, my parents are very conservative," I eventually lied, hoping to appeal to Doc's good business sense, "and if they knew stuff like this went on here, they'd demand their money back and send a car for me." I wanted a different life, one where people dressed in navy and burgundy with argyle knee socks and had parents who sent cars. My parents were hippies who rolled their own grass cigarettes in the house. "Then I'm pretty sure they'd tell all their country club friends that Yanisin is a breeding ground for sex. Me and you, well, we know it's not, but you don't know them. They'll tell everyone." I somehow made it seem as if I'd found the magazine, as if Camp Yanisin was responsible for corrupting me and not the other way around. "Please, can't we just keep this between us? I don't want to go home."

If I were a boy, I thought as Doc pondered what I'd said, none of this would be happening. When a boy brings smut to camp, it's somehow applauded, but when a girl is discovered with it, mock shrinks get involved.

Doc guided me out of his office by the shoulder—as if there was a kinship between us now that he had agreed to keep things between us. Although he never involved my parents, things didn't remain quiet. Nicknames still managed to form, and in the dining hall, during a singsong chant, that very night, kids referred to me as "Porno Queen."

This triggered a series of gentle groans on my part. The entire camp now knew I liked porn. I then wished I really had been sent home. I wanted to be back in my own bed, under the care of my parents. I piggybacked on Lea's scheduled phone-shack time, and once she had her turn, I asked for a minute alone. I cupped a hand over the phone and pressed my lips against the mouthpiece. But when I tried to explain what had happened, I didn't know where to start. I could only bring myself to beg to come home.

They said they didn't understand, that my letters seemed so cheerful. What had happened? I was tempted to confide in them, to share that I now had an additional nickname. Before I revealed "Porno Queen" to them, Poppa clipped me short with,"Well, it can't be any worse than Moose!" Then he snorted. I sat in silence, the phone still held to my ear, an uprush of anger. And as the words formed in my head, it became harder to swallow. I slammed the receiver down.

I sat with Lea in a rowboat during free play. I wondered if our parents looked up the camp phone number and tried to call back right away, if Mom touched Poppa on the arm, asking if she should drive up to get me. They'd go through their rituals that night, Poppa turning on a ball game as Mom layered on milky facial lotions. As she always did, she'd Scotch-tape the area between her eyes to prevent involuntary wrinkles in her sleep. Would Poppa and Mom fall asleep worried for me, or would everything go on the same?

"I can't believe he brought up the name they call me at school," I shrieked to Lea.

"So you told him about Porno Queen, then?"

"Don't say it!" I shouted, releasing the oars.

"I'm sorry, Steph. I love you." Lea was ten. Who cared if she loved me? What the hell did she know?

"No, I didn't tell him. I was gonna, but he brought up . . . Moose," I said in a small voice. I hated being fat.

THE FIRST TIME I WAS CALLED "MOOSE," I WAS IN A HALL-way at school. A legion of older boys chanted it between classes, when the corridors were busy. I recognized a few of them from my block. The Saviglias had recently moved in, two houses from ours, with their two children. One year my junior, Meredith looked like a ballerina and smoked cigarettes while waiting for the school bus to arrive each morning. Her older brother, Michael, wore eyeglasses in the shape of aviators and reminded me of the retarded Greek boy who lived in the house next door. Except Michael wasn't retarded. He was what Mom referred to as a "bike nerd." After school he and his friends mounted dirt bikes—whose handlebars and front tires could spin a full 360 degrees—and practiced tricks in the middle of our street until sundown. I'd never spoken to any of them, but when I was at my locker, exchanging my books, one of them approached me.

A tall senior named Otis tapped me on the shoulder. When I turned around, he megaphoned, "Mooooooooose," in a voice so deep and loud that the clump of students around us parted. People stopped walking and stood for a beat to measure my reaction. I turned back around and continued to fumble with the items in my locker, hoping that if I ignored it, others would too, but no one moved. My breathing quickened, and I noticed a pulse mounting inside my chest. His friends laughed and boomed it along with him. They continued to repeat it, even after I'd slammed my locker closed and ripped down the halls. I heard the low even tone, *Moooooose,* now accompanied by a rhythmic stomping of feet, even after I turned down a new corridor. A deep foreign sound came from my mouth, almost the sob of a man. I pressed my hands to my mouth and tried to contain it. I coughed and breathed through my nose, pushing harder against my mouth as the tears slipped out. I didn't know where to go.

I sat in the back of my classes that day and didn't speak, not a word, syllable, or letter, until I was finally home.

"Sweetheart, what's the matter?" It was Poppa. "You know you can tell me anything." I was heaving into my pillows, damp with sweat. I'd hidden away in my room that day, skipping the kitchen altogether. Apparently cruelty was one of the only things that didn't trigger mindless eating.

"I want to go to a new school," I sobbed without turning to face him.

"What's this all about?"

"Can't you send me to boarding school?"

"Whatever it is, it can't be that bad. Talk to me, and we'll figure it out." He was rubbing my back in circles with his hand. "That's it. Breathe. Another one. Here, I'll do it with you. Okay, now that's better. What is it, honey?"

"The boys at school"—I closed my eyes and swallowed—"they . . . they called me Moose." After I'd said it, once the words were out there, I looked up at him, waiting. He bent forward a little, as if to console me. I wasn't sure what he'd do next. I turned to watch his reaction, assuming that he'd tell me to ignore them, that I was wonderful and beautiful. Maybe he'd say, "Stephanie, one thing I can tell you, as an adult who has been thirteen, is kids tease. If you're tall, they make fun of you for that. If you're short, they pick on you. It's all immaturity. And when you get older, you'll realize these boys teased you because of their own insecurities. And what I learned is, what was so easy for everyone to make fun of then becomes so insignificant once you're older. Can you imagine if people still did that at my age, Stephanie? They'd be calling me Baldilocks." Then I'd laugh and maybe feel less alone. "It's a minefield out there, from the kid who poops in his pants to the girl with the mustache. Just realize, you are beautiful, and I'm not just saying that because I'm your father. You really are beautiful, just as you are. And when people are teasing you, it might be hard to remember, but one day when you're older, you'll remember this conversation and know that I was right."

But that didn't happen. Instead, his body began to shake. He held his stomach and pinched his eyes closed. I realized he wasn't doubled over in pain. He was laughing so hard that sound couldn't escape. His entire head turned red and tears streamed from the corners of his eyes.

"I'm sorry," he said, "I can't help it. That's just funny; what a great name." Then he wiped the tears from his face and repeated, "Moose," shaking his head as if he was recounting the punch line to his favorite joke. I buried my head back in my pillow. "Look, they're right, Stephanie. If you want to be happy and stop being teased, you'll lose weight. Then believe me, they'll be knocking the doors down to get a date with you."

When I recount that memory now, I have to be talked down. I'll ruin a perfectly fattening meal, tensing up with a stiff mouth, holding back any trace of emotion. *It can't still affect me. I was a kid. I'm not anymore. Get over it!* But I can't. It was heartbreaking hearing my father tell me it was my fault people were cruel to me. They'd stop, he said, if I stopped being fat.

While my upbringing didn't make me fat, it played a part in shaping my priorities. And of utmost importance to me was my appearance, not for vanity reasons, but because I wanted to be loved. Poppa thought he was doing me a favor by telling me no man would want me if I was fat. It was his clumsy way of trying to spare me years of frustration in an unjust society. "Ideally, no one would judge a book by its cover, Stephanie, but we don't live in that world." It's the baggage I carry.

Many people have suffered cruel childhoods, awash with harrowing moments and unspeakable memories. I'm not one of those people. I was fiercely loved by both my parents. And I knew, even then, that their love for me was uncompromising and unflinching. I didn't, however, believe it was unconditional.

Mom kept healthy food in the house, encouraged me to eat fruits and leafy greens, drove me to Fran's house, and insisted I join her at the local roller rink on Wednesday nights for Rollerobics. She didn't just talk the talk. She Jazzercised it. And she wasn't your typical controlling mother who wanted a thin daughter because having a fat one, she feared, was some reflection on her. She wanted to help because she saw how miserable I was. She was always supportive and led a healthy, not obsessive, lifestyle. Then on our ride home from the roller rink, she'd ask me if I thought she should get liposuction.

I might not have known it then, but what I needed, quite desperately, was a strong female role model. Mom was never a confident, independent woman who took pride in her own power, in her own body and mind. I never saw from her what it meant to be a satisfied woman who gathered strength and pride from her own efforts and accomplishments. Without this, I was forced to rely on Poppa's tough-love approach, one that hurt more than I'd like to say.

He'd step in, shaking his head and puffing out his cheeks, when I attempted to eat more than my portion. "Men are shallow dogs, Stephanie," he'd say, "and no one wants to be with a fat girl." In disciplining my eating habits, Poppa cited external reasons as motivation to lose weight, communicating that I'd be liked, I'd be loved, I'd be worthy of being sought after if I was thin. It'd be pretty absurd of me to suppose I was entitled to these things based simply on who I was as a person. "You'll feel so much better about yourself," he'd say, but I knew what he really meant: *We'll feel so much better about you.* He delivered the message without room for ambiguity: love came with strings and bundled with ifs.

I became convinced that if there were less of me, there'd somehow be more to love.

If I took care of my appearance, looking just so, if I lost weight and became the envy of others, Poppa would love me more. I thought this for a very long time. And I felt it with every boy I ever dated, certain each suitor would want me more, want me longer, want me back if I lost a few pounds.

My father said I could be prettier and happier. I wanted so much to be someone other than me, to give him an angelic, beautiful, trim daughter, instead of what I was: Moose.

And when I didn't get unconditional love from my father, I sought it elsewhere. Near Make-Out Rock, on a hidden dirt path in the woods, with an older boy from South Florida named Jared Held who wore pleated Z. Cavaricci pants and gave me my first hickey. The counselors punished me for missing curfew, for being caught in the bushes with a boy. They humiliated me on Girls' Hill; I became the entertainment for all the counselors sitting OD on their porches. They forced me through a paddy wagon, crawling on the ground, between their legs, being spanked for my behavior. It didn't stop me.

Jared eventually became a Jon, a Justin, and a Juan. Then Jonathan Plessett and Jack Greenwald, and then other boys with other names beginning with letters other than J, would fill in over other summers of my life. It became my ritual, the way I soothed my ego, and when boys didn't work, there was always a refrigerator or a cabinet that needed to be cleared. Emotional eating and then some, and I didn't need any kind of shrink to wrap my head around that.

nine

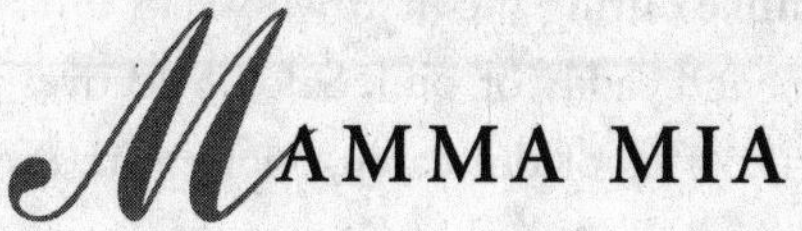

Mamma Mia

I'm sooooooo upset!!! There are these nasty rumors going around about me here at camp. 4 example = when I wuz going out w/ Jared, it was said that I gave him head in the woods, which I promise didn't happen!! Then I started spending my time w/ Jon Riser, this really, really hot guy. Jon kind of asked me out, undid my bra and kissed my breasts. I feel guilty now, though. Really guilty!!! I feel sick. I miss Leigh. Anyway, as I wuz frenching Jon goodnight, there is Hams saying that I'm a half an hour late 4 curfew, and I had better go back!! My punishment wuz to act like a monkey and go through the paddy wagon twice!! Now all the counselors are giving me shit! I hate it! I just wish that everything would vanish and the rumors would stop.

THE DESIGNATION OF QUEEN, ALBEIT PORNO QUEEN, ENtitled me to the first hot shower of the night. Okay, no. Not really. I was due first shower because I was LATRINE that morning and still had the smell of Comet on my fingers, even following an afternoon at the lake. The shower curtain in my cabin smelled of mildew, and with a whisper of a breeze, it clung to me. I found myself leaning up against the wall, just under the showerhead, trying to get my hair wet enough to shampoo. Once suds formed, I realized how sore my arms were. I soaped my stomach, sucking it in, trying to see how flat it could get. Not very, I determined with a sigh, then pondered what I'd wear to dinner.

Unlike during the first two weeks of camp, I no longer carted my clothes and caddy of pink Salon Selectives products to the shower toward the back of our cabin. Along with everyone else, I now changed from my damp towel into my warm evening clothes in the cabin, facing my cubby. It was a step for me, closer to comfort. There were still five and a half weeks left of camp, allotting me a bit more room for change. Perhaps with my weight loss, a breezier, more carefree attitude might stick. But for now, I maneuvered my underwear up, relying on the strength of my pits to keep my towel secure. I dressed strategically, fastening my bra over my towel. And when prompted about it, I said I kept warmer this way. "Can't you see that I'm drenched?" I'd say, flipping wet ropes of my hair through the air. "Well?"

"Well, what?" Hams asked, her hand on her hip.

"Well, doing it this way keeps my back dry."

"Yuh-huh. Keep selling it to yourself, Queenie." Then she turned, mooning me with her dimpled brown rear. "Just keeping things cheeky 'round here."

It surprised me how even the beefiest of the girls in our cabin snaked about, walking tan lines, just going about their business, like nudists with zinc oxided noses eating crab salad. Like, no big deal. This is who I am, and while you're at it, meet my ass. And then there were the extremists. I mean, who trims her cuticles on her bed, naked? In front of people! It's just weird, like those women at the gym who blow-dry their pubic hair with the gym hair dryer. I don't care what they say about being completely comfortable with your body; *everyone* isn't supposed to be comfortable with it. This is what came from several summers of "Yanisinning it": insouciance. Sure, this exhibitionism was justifiable at normal camps. It wouldn't be weird, I thought, if you had a balletic figure. I was mistaken. It's weird if you're anybody.

Summers later though, when I'd return to Yanisin as a counselor to eight-year-old girls, I'd stand corrected. One afternoon, on our cabin porch, I'd realize that it wasn't about fat or thin; it was about innocence. Girls fresh from the lake, full of spirit and whimsy, would wear their towels as superhero capes and run naked in the warm summer air, outside the cabin, squealing with delight. And I'd laugh to myself, amazed, really, wondering if I ever had been that free.

Puberty brought about some modicum of modesty, at least for me. But I wasn't the only one who didn't flitter about our cabin like a free bird. Beulah Tsaoussis, as it happens, didn't take to changing or showering at all. During shower hour, she played tennis against the wall outside our bunk. The single time I saw her with damp hair was after swim, and even then, it looked slicked back, as if she'd been dipped in oil. I suspect Harper coaxed her into showering during free play when the rest of us were out of the cabin riding go-karts or playing Ping-Pong. Maybe she felt too fat for fat camp.

After my shower I felt clean and manicured, as if I was wearing all white. I loved this time of day. With all the sweating from activities behind me, and the night stretching out ahead, I had time to compose a slimming outfit. My jeans were getting looser. I couldn't tuck a shirt in yet, but it wouldn't be too long. My tan bloomed after my shower; my cheeks flushed. I'd wear something off the shoulder, a long rope of faux pearls knotted in the center just as the magazines illustrated. Two coats of mascara, bronzer, and "a shimmer shadow applied just beneath the brow line," the beauty section advised. I didn't know enough about makeup or what clothes would flatter my figure. Was I an Apple or a Pear? I looked down and determined I was a Cantaloupe.

I knew it didn't matter how we looked during the day. The afternoons were for grunting our way up Bitch Hill, for hair drawn into a frizzy knot, for who the hell cared what we looked like. At least four times a week we'd feel the burn through Slimnastics—which was not, as the name implied, a version of gymnastics requiring strength and agility intended to slim us down—looking downright absurd as we tried to keep up with our instructor, Lydia, as she coerced us into following her choreographed aerobics routines. Lydia was an odd bird, with hair worn loose to the backs of her knees. She took to whistling and hooting us on at the most inappropriate times. She didn't do it when we were winded and about to give up but as we simply marched in place during a cooldown or a warm-up. "Right on!" she'd cheer, then stride into a grapevine move, adding a kick and a clap during the chorus of George Michael's "Monkey." Each time she'd say, "That's right, pump those arms like you're climbing vines for bananas." So we became accustomed to making complete monkeys of ourselves during the day. But at night there was no excuse, so the way you came across at the DJ dance was how you really were. It was you, in color.

As I approached my cubby, I noticed that Jordan and Grayson were eyeing the collage of photographs I had tacked behind my bed, along the panes of my window. I'd taken care to tape up images of pretty people. Glossy girls with high ponytails, coordinating outfits, and dimples you could slip into. Each of their faces tilted in a sweet smiling gesture, the way children learn to pose for their parents. Only it wasn't my camera for which they stood still.. And they weren't my friends. I'd cut their photos from our yearbook and fell asleep each night on that top bunk staring at the girls in my grade who didn't like me, who'd call me *loser* to my face. "So, Stephanie," Caryn Young had asked as we changed for gym class, "are you going to wear a bikini to the end-of-school beach party next week?" At camp, I pretended she and her clique were my friends from home, so people who didn't know me would believe I was worth liking.

In the collage, there was a photo of my parents standing in the entranceway of our home, posing in formal attire in front of our coat closet. It was from New Year's Eve, before a night of dancing.

I was excited that Grayson and Jordan had come to visit me.

"Is that your mom?" Jordan asked, pointing to the New Year's photo. I wished at that moment the photo had been taken somewhere more posh, that we'd had a cherrywood-paneled parlor with extensive built-ins, silver accents on polished shelves, and framed prints of hunting scenes. Evidence of a tailored life. I felt ashamed that I didn't have a bigger house, that I didn't come from "more," that when asked, I had to say my dad was in the moving business. "He owns a transportation business," I'd say, thinking it was an improvement on "trucking company."

"Mmmm, yeah. That's her." I was peering over Jordan's shoulder, as if I hadn't realized the photo were there. I wished Mom's smile wasn't so forced, that she didn't use so much concealer. Mom was prettier when she didn't know anyone was watching. In the photo her hair was much longer than it was the last time I'd seen her. I didn't understand why mothers of a certain age felt the need to crop their hair to their shoulders, as if they were cutting off an earlier, more decadent life.

"She's really pretty."

"Thanks." Despite her makeup, Mom did look lovely, in a soft, delicate way, and just then, I was thankful for it. She was a natural beauty, an auburn earth mother; the kind you imagined in white Grecian robes with Spartan men kneeling before her, a tress of her hair examined in his calloused hand. Maybe I'd grow up to look like that. I'd be thin when I was older. Perhaps Mom was the guarantee because girls grow up to be their mothers, even in Nike ads that insist we can choose what we take from our mothers. We might inherit their eyes or thighs, but we can choose to reject things, to carve out our own lives. I wanted to look exactly like Mom, but I wanted to be nothing like her.

"We're wearing these at dinner and thought you'd wanna wear one with us." "These" were collegiate outfits comprised of T-shirts, boxers, and matching sweatshirts. Jordan was sporting Michigan attire. Grayson had a Duke sweatshirt rigged around her waist.

"Yeah, sure," I said with a shrug, as if it meant nothing, as if I didn't feel like the coolest girl ever.

They left a stack of Syracuse items on my bed. "Do you have socks that match?"

The three of us shuffled off to my cubby in the back of the cabin, searching for the right color of slouchy E. G. Smith socks. "Rad jeans," Jordan said while fingering a pair I'd splattered with bleach a week before. "Can I borrow 'em?"

"Sure." Might as well have told me I'd won a date with Jordan Knight. That's how cool I was.

"You can come to our cabin and borrow anytime, too." I was in girl love, long before girl crushes were in vogue.

Girls were girls during shower hour, trading clothes, makeup, and secrets. Dressing the same, becoming part of something. It felt good to be seen as something other than fat. I was the girl with the good singing voice who excelled at swimming, the girl with the cool clothes, with the jeans they wanted to borrow. I felt more like myself. I wanted to take Grayson and Jordan home with me, to show the kids at school that I had popular, pretty friends.

"See you at the flagpole," Grayson said as she left, which reminded me that I'd promised to meet Lea at the rec hall before her Lower Camp lineup.

I eased up my collegiate boxers, wondering if I looked any different. Was my weight loss showing? How about my new popular status? Could you see it in the drape of the clothes? The threads weren't mine, and up until now, this hadn't been my life. What shoes do you wear with borrowed boxers and new, more shapely legs? Slip-on Keds. Before pulling Jordan's shirt over my head, I traced the outline of the Orangemen mascot. He was a smiling orange with skinny white stick-figure legs: a typical Jewish body. Top-heavy, no ass. I didn't have this body, the body of my paternal grandmother, Beatrice. Mine was a heavier version of Mom's, except I had boobs. The Syracuse mascot on my shirt looked like a cartoon of the sun; the round apples of his cheeks didn't belong on an Orangeman. I slipped on the shirt and took a moment to decide what I needed to add to the outfit. Dangling earrings, I concluded.

I flipped onto Kate's bed, my stomach stretched across her mattress, and worked a soufflé of mousse through my hair, then diffused and crunched my curls upside-down for volume. I'd apply my makeup on the porch for good light. I carted my Kaboodle makeup caddy with me, unsure which shadows would complement my new orange attire. Frosted blue, I determined, with electric blue mascara. As I made my way past the screen door onto the porch bench, I watched Beulah, still hitting a tennis ball against the wall. I wondered how she'd look with a crimped side ponytail and cheekbones. Maybe some pink blush to find them. It was a shame, I thought, that she didn't have an older sister. At least she had friends: a cluster of little girls carrying plastic buckets filled with mud and salamanders would usually call for her before dinner. They too would still be in their bathing suits, unshowered, hair matted, curls springing up at the ends like strips of bacon. Beulah's friends were eight.

Predinner preening: in the honeyed haze of evening, girls scuttled between cabins wearing nothing but a towel, then returned with an armful of borrowed clothes. They'd examine their new finds in front of a hand mirror. Surprisingly our cabin wasn't outfitted with a full-length mirror. Perhaps the owners didn't want us to obsess (any more than we already did) about our bodies. Maybe it was their way of ingraining in us that we should want to lose weight for health reasons, not social ones. Maybe they simply couldn't find a spot for it. Without one, we were left at the mercy of our compact mirrors and the word of our bunkmates. One girl's fat clothes became another girl's thin ones. "Let me just see how close I am to zipping this." Tucked behind our cabin doors, the changing began. It was part of the excitement, slipping into new clothes and lives.

Through the screen door, Jessica Fallis sang her Punky Power heart out, belting into her brush handle as she hovered near her clothes, deciding what to mismatch. She knew every last word to the song "Walk Like an Egyptian."

Kate joined me on the porch, vigorously reaching behind her as if she were trying to scratch her own back.

"Did ya kill it yet?" I asked with an exaggerated expression of fear.

"Huh?"

"Whatever's on your back."

"I hate wearing a bra!" she brayed, now snapping the back of it into place. Kate was always picking at things, adjusting bra straps, tugging at her shirt as though it would never fall right. She'd yank at her crotch and ass, always looking to dislodge some form of wedgie. "You play with your balls a lot," I eventually told her.

"For the love of Christ, would you please shut your hole!" she wailed toward the cabin as Jessica sang out the chorus of Taylor Dayne's "Tell It to My Heart." I left the scene and made my way down Girls' Hill to meet Lea.

"IT TOOK YOU LONG ENOUGH," SHE SAID BEFORE I reached her.

"I'm sorry. What's up, squirt?"

And before her words came out, her face contorted into a pink bulb. Her eyes became squints, and she hugged me, crying into the outstretched arms of an Orangeman.

"What's the matter?"

"I miss Mommy," I was able to distinguish through her hot sobs.

"Okay, you need to breathe," I urged, taking a deep audible breath. "You're getting yourself all worked up—"

"Nephnie, I hate it here." Sometimes Lea reverted into her little girl world, where she felt safer, and certainly closer to me, by calling upon a time when she couldn't pronounce my name. She still regresses today, using tears to harvest affection, and I'm afraid I've never been very good at comforting her. I was great at pep talks, but sympathizing, consoling, and nurturing weren't my ings.

"It can't be that bad," I said as I willed myself to pet her head. Her scalp was pink, and I realized she'd grown taller since the last time we'd embraced.

"I just wanna go home."

"But they'll be here for Family Weekend soon."

"I don't care!" she wailed. "I just wanna leave; I'm not even losing weight." Lea was *ten*. Before coming to Yanisin, the watchwords of weight hadn't been added to her lexicon. Surely she didn't know from calories or carbs. Covered in grass stains, Lea spent her free time dribbling a soccer ball around cones. She was muscular for her age, tall, and by all accounts she did not need to lose weight. She was sent to camp with me because Mom and Poppa didn't want to split us up for the summer. "Prevention," it was said. Fat camp made her obsessed with fat, even the fat she didn't have.

"You don't need to lose weight!" I responded, pushing her off me.

"Yes I do, Neph! I'm the only one in my bunk who hasn't." Lea had lost seven pounds, which wasn't exactly "hasn't," and according to Fran, it was the equal of downsizing one full clothing size. I hadn't thought Lea needed to lose weight, but maybe I was wrong. Maybe she just appeared that way to me because she hadn't had nearly as much to shed as I had. Or maybe this is what you learned at fat camp: to lose weight anyway.

"You aren't going to lose what they lose because you're not fat."

"Yes I am!"

"No, this, this is fat." I gripped a roll from my stomach with both hands. "Look, it even has a mouth," I said of the crease in my shirt where my slit of a belly button showed up, parading itself as a slight frown.

"Stop laughing. It's not funny," Lea whined as she began to laugh.

"Give us a hug, little girl," my belly button said, sounding not at all unlike a Mexican cartoon character named Nacho.

Lea giggled and ran in small circles as I chased her with a handful of my fiesta bowl. "I'm being serious," she said, still laughing.

"When you've got a stomach that can talk, then have it come talk to mine about being fat." We sat on the grass, now in compare mode, where it's not viable for the trimmer of two people to complain about being fat. Many years and pounds later, when Lea would have a valid reason to lodge grievances about her weight, she'd at least be mindful of where she directed them. It's just not good form to gripe about how fat you are to someone who has more to lose than you do. Quite simply, you'll be outfatted.

The person listening to you will roll her eyes, thinking, *If you think you're gross, I can only imagine what you think of me.* And she'll gradually stop returning your phone calls. So you'll learn to be more tactful in your complaints. "God, I'm terribly disgusting . . . for me." At least "for me" illustrates that you have some perspective. Then you'll add, "You know, I can't fit into any of my clothes." And she will know, all too well. She'll also think you spend too much of your energy worrying. *Obsessed,* she'll think. *I'd rather be fat than consumed with what I look like.* "I'd rather be fat than" is a game she knows by heart. She's played every outcome of it in her head. And it seems that vapid, dumb, and ugly always outweigh fat in the undesirable category. *At least I'm not ugly. I can always lose weight. You'll always be dumb.*

I've been both of those *she*s. The thinner one still disgruntled with her appearance, and the heavier one wishing the thinner one would shut the fuck up. And the two have more in common than they'd care to admit: they're both miserable.

Though calmer now, Lea continued to express her misery in whimpers, leaning all her weight into me. She pushed out her lower lip, trembling like a feeble toddler reacting to the overblown panic of her parents after a slight fall. Lea whined, "I love you," and wondered if I'd spend more time with her like this. "Don't you love me?" she said.

"Of course."

"Then why don't you ever say it? Why when I hold your hand, don't you hold it back? You're just like Mommy," she said.

MOM DIDN'T DO "I LOVE YOU." POPPA DID IT FOR HER.

I overheard him say to her, "Yolanda, you need to tell the girls you love them." He used a soft tone, a teaching voice. When it came to constructing a buttered rum raisin sauce for bread pudding, baiting a fishing hook, or harmonizing to a Beatles song, Mom didn't need lessons. Creativity and a vigorous passion for life were in her genes. But when it came to assertiveness, communication, and the expression of love, Mom needed help.

"Did you tell them today?" I don't know why I heard these conversations between my parents, but I knew, even as early as seven years old, that Mom was coaxed into verbalizing her love because of her own childhood. "You have to say the words," Poppa instructed. "I know your mother didn't, but you have to." It was learned behavior.

My maternal grandmother, Yiya, lived in Puerto Rico until she was nine, when her mother died and she was shipped off by her father to New York with her five siblings. He found most of them homes with different families, but Yiya and her younger brother spent the rest of their youth in an orphanage. In the bond of that experience she learned to put her siblings before anyone else, including her own daughters. She had three: Georgette, Iris, and then Mom.

My aunts were repeatedly abused in front of Mom. I've only heard it in pieces. A broomstick. A garage door, pulled down on Iris's fingers. As the youngest, Mom learned to keep silent and do as she was told. A drunken beating. She lived in fear, cowering in corners and hiding in closets. A thick leather belt with a heavy brass buckle. I imagine pressed powder and thick concealers. "Yeah, we got a lot of welts," Mom recounted over the years. "And when Pop drank, well, you know. He wasn't very nice to Mom. Yelling at her the way he did, to get him another schnapps." When Mom talks about that part of her life, most of it comes out in shavings, as if she's passed the events over a Microplane Ribbon grater. I don't think it's the way she wants to remember her childhood. She prefers to tell me how her parents always danced in the living room, about the big parties and the smaller moments spent fishing off a jetty in East Hampton. But when I press her, she speaks of her painful memories as if she's unsure they belong to her. "I was just a child; I don't remember exactly. But it wasn't good."

As an adult, I correlate Mom's reticent temperament and low self-esteem with the fact that she was a witness to and victim of both physical and mental abuse as a child.

Just like Yiya, Mom put her siblings before anyone else and found it difficult to express love to her children. Before her husband. Before my sister. And before me. Mom, I always believed, and still do, loves her sisters more than the family she made. I know "more" shouldn't really come into play when it comes to love. "Just differently," some might hedge. As long as by differently they mean more, then yeah.

But as a child, I didn't believe it until I saw it. Hearing Poppa urge Mom to express her love for us made me feel less loved than never hearing it from her at all. While part of me wondered, *Why doesn't Mommy love me?* a bigger part of me thought, *Isn't Mommy supposed to love me without anyone telling her to?* It was overhearing Poppa coach her that made me question if something was wrong with her. I knew she loved me in the way she cared for me, nursed me to health with a wet washcloth when I was sick, but something must've been wrong with her if Poppa needed to instruct her on how to love us. *Was she broken?* I wondered, not realizing then that her way wasn't necessarily the wrong way. And then I stopped wondering if she was broken and began to know. I saw for myself.

I was eleven years old, and we'd just returned from Disney World with sunburned scalps and ponytail headaches. My thighs stuck together, and my feet still ached from the lines. The waiting. Slow people. Public bathrooms. Overcrowding. Lea and I were in the backseat, restless and cranky, overtired from a four-hour drive from Orlando to my maternal grandparents' house in Delray Beach, Florida. Mom sat in the front seat beside Aunt Georgette, who was driving. "Say one more word," Georgette threatened me, "and I'm gonna throw you out of the car."

For the remaining ten minutes of our ride, I kept it shut. *Let her throw me out once we're back at Yiya and Papoo's house,* I thought.

After having spent several days and Disney nights with Georgette, I realized that I didn't much care for her. She was my aunt. I knew I was supposed to love her. But I didn't. She was responsible for turning Mom into her. In the company of Georgette, our mother regressed into a foul-mouthed adolescent. Her mannerisms changed, her gestures growing grander, wider; everything became lurid and uncensored, as if she'd been drinking. While ordinarily musical and tempered, her laugh became a haughty cackle. People would stare. Even once I was much older, when Mom was around one of her sisters, she would poke fun at me, announcing in front of others that I had a hair growing from a mole on my chin that needed to be plucked. Mom pronounced words differently, picking up Georgette's cadences, uttering words as if she hadn't known they ended with *r*s or *t*s. "Wannanotha be-ah?"

Once we were in the safety of my grandparents' house after the drive from Disney, I unleashed what I'd been keeping to myself in the car. "You belong in a kennel," I said to Georgette. And what I remember most from those next moments was Lea's face as she witnessed them.

Midway through it, Lea scampered out of the way, squatting on the linoleum floor by the yellow refrigerator. Her face had its own pulse, a red beady knot, her cheeks swallowing her eyes. Through the squinting, she saw Georgette, close to three hundred pounds, lunging toward me with leaden fists. Lea was screaming, whips of hair in her mouth. "Leave my sister alone," she cried. She saw our mother across the kitchen.

Mom did nothing.

It happened slowly for me, in blurry spinning dance steps. My aunt's hand gripping my wrist. Unsure of my footing as she thrust me to the ground, then swung me, the way you swing a child through the air at the beach, stumbling on my way down, with a thrum. As I clutched for safety, I was ripped back with a violent yank. The roots of my hair webbed between her fingers.

Mom did nothing.

I remember my aunt's shirt. It was a pastel button-down with thin vertical stripes and simple white plastic buttons. I tried to rip it open on my way up, clawing my way off the floor, thinking I might have a chance. She snatched my arm with one hand, twisting it, lifting me nearer as she knocked her free fist into my head, a sandbag. I squinted, unsure of what had just happened. Again. My head jolted to her rhythm. And again. She thrashed harder. She held the weight of me in her grip, now by my hair. She punched me in the ear.

Mom did nothing.

My disabled grandfather, Papoo, had wheeled himself inside. Lea's screams were the only sound of the event. "That's enough, Georgette," he might have said. I don't remember.

What I do remember is that Mom did nothing.

I was still in Georgette's hands, hanging on like life. Her panting breath, tidal. There was an unwelcome intimacy, smelling her, a sweetness in her sweat. I was dragged across the floor, my knees scraping, stumbling to recover, to fight back, even though I'd lose. She held me still for a moment, submerged in her hot embrace. It felt almost like comfort, there in her quiet ebb, moored to her chest. Maybe she'd tell me that God had made her do it, that I was being shown the way to love through discipline. Her pendulous breasts seemed like rabid animals with their own necks and individual abilities to smother and kill their prey. As she pressed me into them, the room steadied. I saw a clear glass bowl on the kitchen counter, a wedge of lemon. A knife. I was then unfurled, like a dancer breaking away into an open position before being snapped back into a rigid embrace. I winced in pain when she jerked me back to her, ripping my hair. She had my skin beneath her fingernails. Then she threw me off her and walked outside.

My scalp bled. I kept touching it in disbelief, repeatedly looking at my fingers, as if the next time I looked the blood wouldn't be there. Was I really bleeding? Oh my God, I was *bleeding*. Lumps formed within minutes. My fingers passed over them as they swelled larger. Lea ran to me, gripping my leg, still in a trance, repeating her same chant, "Leave my sister alone!" I looked up at Mom as I made it to my feet. She did nothing and said even less.

Lea came with me as I locked myself behind our bedroom door, and from behind it, I screamed to my aunt, "That's child abuse. I'm calling a child abuse hotline and reporting you." There was a silence. No one would answer me. "I said I'm calling a hotline."

And then much closer than I'd imagined, right beyond the door, came the voice of my aunt, calm and even. "Yeah, go ahead. I'll help you dial."

I called Poppa, in a hyperventilated cry. He was in New York. He'd taken over his family business, a moving and storage operation, and was slammed with work—the way he always managed to be when Mom took us to Florida to spend time with her family.

"Where's your mother?" he wanted to know. So did I.

"WELL, YOU NEVER OPENED YOUR MOUTH TO HER AGAIN," Mom says now in a nervous half laugh.

"I was eleven, Mom. I don't care what I did or said."

"Well, what was *I* going to do?" And she says *I* as if it wasn't her place to cut in, as if she wasn't a mother, my mother, as if she were just a powerless girl herself. "*I* couldn't have stopped her," she says. Mom says *I* as if her *I* would never, and will never, be enough. Maybe it's why she never said "I love you." Because to her, in the "I love you" equation, her *I* didn't count for much.

And now, on the grass, in front of the rec hall, my sister cried to me, wondering why I was just like her, our mother. I didn't want to be.

"Is this better?" I asked Lea, grabbing her hand as I pulled her up off the grass.

"Much," she said. We walked together, squeezing hands, toward the flagpole. "But, Neph?"

"Yeah."

"Don't you miss Mommy, too?"

"Yeah," I said. And I did.

IN THE DINING HALL, I JOINED GRAYSON AND JORDAN AT a table, taking a seat facing the boys' side. In the weeks I'd been there, Adam Fink and I had only spoken to each other in short bursts. I'd been busy in all-consuming three-day relationships with other boys. But it didn't keep me from pining for Adam. It was just as Fran had said when she lectured us about willpower.

When it came to food, I knew I shouldn't be eating certain coveted confections, but they were always in our house for one reason or another, wrapped in the body of an aluminum swan, some deliciously fancy leftovers in our refrigerator, and as much as I craved that dessert, I'd eat around it. *Everything* around it. A bowl of mashed potatoes, a fistful of stewed string beans, three fingers of peanut butter, deckled brisket padded by white bread, spiked with pickles, onions, and a honey mesquite barbecue sauce. Each was a new attempt at burying my want.

Eventually, I'd give in, realizing I'd not only pleasured my way through the cranberry-walnut pie, but I'd inhaled the whole of our kitchen. It seems I didn't just do this with food. I did it with boys. I Crosby, Stills, and Nashed my way through adolescence and loved all the ones I was with. If I couldn't be with Adam, I'd be with everyone else.

Still, not only did I linger by the dining hall steps after meals, I arrived early to lineup and dawdled when leaving the pool if I knew Adam's division was up next. I liked the way he sometimes pursed his lips and kinda chewed on the inside corner of his mouth when he was thinking. Then he'd somehow smile, just by twitching his nose. I'd look away when he noticed me noticing him. Not tonight, though. I'd force myself to actually say something, and it would *not* be some airhead comment on the food. Original. Sharp. Whimsical. Brilliant! What could I say?

"So, what's up with that grody girl Beulah in your bunk?" Grayson asked as she glared over her shoulder at Beulah, who was eating with one arm surrounding her plate, her chin nearly resting on the lip of it, as she scooped through a molehill of rice like a worm burrowing its way through dead wood.

"She smells." I shrugged, then looked back down at the chicken thigh on my plate. They hadn't removed the skin. Fine feathers were visible, pores, and follicles. I peeled it back and examined the underside, poking at the gelatinous lining. The actual meat of the chicken had a violet vein strung through it. When I looked up, Jordan and Grayson were staring at me, waiting for me to say more. "What'd ya wanna know?" I took a deep cleansing breath, as the subliminal weight-loss tape had instructed.

"Isn't her bed right next to yours?" Jordan asked, interrupting my mental count to ten.

"Yeah. She grosses me out." I tried breathing again, this time with my eyes closed.

"If I were you," Grayson said, "I'd play a game of decorator. Then I'd, like, move all the beds to the opposite side of the cabin."

"Well," I added after silently counting backward from ten to one, "there's more to the story."

"What?" Jordan asked, leaning in closer. I felt important being the bearer of such secretive news, their eyes on me, waiting and edging closer. They weren't looking at me because I was fat, or even thin. Maybe they didn't even care about the clothes I was wearing. They liked me because of something I had to say. Because of what I had to add, and it made me feel like shiny silver tap shoes.

A silence hovered, and I took my time, savoring the attention before sharing what I'd learned from Kate. I regaled my new friends with the Beulah Tsaoussis saga, explaining, with the slightest trace of superiority in my voice, how Beulah had come to camp without underwear. Her mother, it turned out, packed for her and simply forgot to include any.

"Beautiful story," Jordan giggled into her cup of sugar-free lemonade. Jordan spoke mostly in "B" adjectives. Bodacious. Bizarre. Bummer. Brutal. Ballsy.

"She did *not* come to camp without underwear!" Grayson said as she dropped her fork in disgust.

"Ugh, I think I'm gonna barf."

"And that's not all," I elaborated. "Apparently she was too embarrassed to tell anyone, so she stole underwear from us." Jordan's nostrils flared. "I mean, she stole my underwear in the middle of the night." Beulah hadn't stolen from me, but the story sounded better this way. "She didn't get caught until Candy noticed that her Thursday and Saturday days-of-the-week panties were missing. Then I noticed that some of mine were missing, too."

"I hope you, like, burned them when you got them back."

"Beulah was hiding the dirty underwear in a duffel beneath her bed."

Grayson and Jordan looked at me, then at each other, their mouths agape.

"So," I continued, "can you please pass the water?"

Jordan handed me the pitcher. They waited for me to fill my glass, then watched as I knocked it back.

"So, what happened?" Grayson asked.

I raised my index finger, indicating that they'd need to wait for it as I finished my water. I poured another, then offered each of them the pitcher.

"Tell us!"

"Gina had to call Beulah's parents." I whispered this next bit for effect. "Her mom sent a box of underwear a few days later."

"A few *days*?"

"Yeah. Days!" I said. "She wore her bathing suit beneath her clothes until they came. Have you seen her bathing suit?" Beulah's suit stretched only to mid-nipple. "It fits her so well. *Not*."

"Ew. Don't make me gag."

I realized, then, that all it really took to be popular was to have information, to be cruel, and to own a footlocker of college-sport clothing.

Kate ran past us, crying. Everyone turned to watch.

"Oh, I wouldn't worry about her," Grayson said with a broccoli spear tucked in her cheek. "She'll be fine. She probably just learned what lactose intolerance means." Grayson was a snap. I felt closer to her the meaner we got.

Once she saw Wendy Fink run after Kate, Grayson announced she had some news of her own. "Well, I heard that Adam has a crush on you," she said, twisting her mood ring.

"Oh." I hesitated, unsure of what to say next. I wasn't ready to let my affection for Adam be known.

"Duh," she said, waving her hand in the air so fast a disc of carrot wheeled across our table. We paused to watch it roll off the table. "You so totally like him."

"Nah," I lied. It was a small white lie; so small I could hold it.

AFTER I TRADED IN MY DINNER AND DECLARED I WAS NOW a vegetarian, there was no lingering in the dining hall. I couldn't very well talk to Adam in front of Grayson. Instead of grabbing him at the dining hall, I'd dart back to the cabin, add some of Harper's perfume, and change into something green to accentuate my hair. It would be my chance to speak with Adam at the evening activity. What if it was true, that he really had a crush on me? I had to hurry.

Kate was on her bed, her expression pained, as if she'd been injured.

"What's the matter?"

Kate didn't speak. She sat hugging her knees and sobbed. *Please, not tonight. Later, fine, but not now.* "Do you want to talk about it?" I asked softly. As she sniffled and wiped snot on her arm, I took the moment to pray she didn't. *Please don't tell me.* I was sure she'd say something about how hurt she was that I didn't sit with her at dinner.

"It's my mother." Kate looked up, stifling a cry behind a forced smile. "She's malignant; she's going to die." I was a selfish girl. "You know what's horrible? I don't want to go back home. I don't. I don't want to see her. I just—" Kate swallowed everything else in moans and trembles. And I just stood there, frozen, trying to decide if I should go over to her, or if I should continue toward Harper's cubby for the perfume.

I didn't say anything. No one I loved had ever become sick or died. What words could *I* offer that would soothe her? I had no idea what she was facing or feeling. I didn't know what losing your mother felt like, what it meant for your entire life to change. What would hugging her do? I'd become a diluted version of Mom.

After what seemed like a few minutes of looking at my hands, I kicked off my Keds and edged my way beside her. I was only half on the bed and felt awkward trying to balance, acting as if I was comfortable. I felt the cold metal frame that held the limp mattress in place as it dug into the back of my thigh. I halfheartedly rubbed her back, knowing this was what people did to comfort others. What next, though? This was something I didn't know, something I had never learned.

We didn't leave the cabin that night. That's the best I knew how to do for her. As much as I wanted to talk to Adam, I stayed in.

I tried to change the subject, bringing levity with talk of Oprah's recent weight loss, but Kate was unresponsive. I pet her head, but it felt strange touching her hair, so I pulled my hand back and fidgeted, picking at the hem of my sock. What did she want me to do? Certainly there was nothing I could do to fix things. I could be there. I could listen, I guessed, but she wasn't saying anything.

"Here I am worrying about losing weight when my mother's dying," she finally said.

"I'm sorry." It's what people say when they hear bad news. They apologize that you have to be going through it. They express regret for your loss. It was if her mother were already gone.

"Shit, no one cares what *she* weighs," Kate said in a laugh that morphed back into tears when she added, "She's dying. Why do they give a Mary what I weigh?"

When we die, no one remembers us for what we weighed. Our weight isn't etched into our headstones beside our identities as daughters, wives, and mothers. We live life, in part, for the legacy we'll leave behind. But at thirteen, you're immortal and just beginning to contemplate your identity. You starve yourself at the expense of your health, willing to make a Faustian pact with a Devil Dog if promised a thin life. I didn't fret about building my character and accomplishments, or how I'd make my mark in the world. I worried instead about my profile in photos, my round jawline, and my inability to wear skirts because of chub rub. And even realizing that no one would remember what I weighed didn't once diminish my obsession with my own appearance. It should have, sure. Death has a way of putting life into perspective. If only it had the same effect on thin.

Even today, when I hear people say, "Holy shit, get the fuck over it already. There are people starving in Africa, people with missing limbs, stricken with poverty and homelessness. You didn't survive Vietnam, family tragedy, rape, or a debilitating case of depression. How do you have the nerve to carp on about the cellulite on your pasty white ass?" I can stop them midsentence and agree. I've been extraordinarily fortunate, but it doesn't make my struggle any less real . . . "for me." It temporarily puts things into perspective, sure, but the emotional issues don't dissolve upon the intellectual acknowledgment that it can always be worse. And the "I've had it worse" game is one I have no desire to win.

"I love you, Scully," Kate quoted with a John Candy smile after blowing her nose. "And that's not the booze talkin' either."

The next morning, Kate had her winning personality back.

"Fuck those little intercamp pork-swords. I've got back fat bigger than them."

We applied talcum powder to our inner thighs, then stuffed our way into our camp uniforms. Of the powder I set back on the shelf, Kate advised, "We better take the whole damn thing, Klein. I sweat more than the pig who built his house out of straw."

ten

WHEN EVEN "MISFIT" MISFITS

I don't know who I like. All I know is that I want someone. Someone to call me up all the time and ask me out every week and tell me how much they like me. And I want to like them just as much. How? is the question. Who would like me?

A QUILT OF FOG HUNG IN THE THURSDAY MORNING AIR, making all of camp seem pale and gentle, as if it were still asleep. Kate and I got a head start on the rest of our division as we set off for the intercamp buses. The whole of Yanisin was heading out to compete against Camp Timber Stream. Sadly, there'd be no pie-eating contests. This was all athletics, and all quite serious from what I'd been told.

I'd done intercamp before, back when I went to normal sleepaway camp. The entire camp traveled to a nearby rival, where we competed in various sports against kids our age. Come the end of the day, we watched the older boys contend for some all-important hockey cup. Then we'd sing, "We've got spirit, yes we do. We've got spirit, how 'bout you?" in rounds across their recreation hall, each camp trying to convince the other of our spirit with the escalating volume of our words. Being forced to exude spirit about something in which I had no interest had always irritated me. But I cheered from the heart when it was all over and we'd get to have dinner in the other camp's mess hall: plates of toasted Reubens and thick slices of apple pie. We'd chant, "Food, waiter, waiter, food, waiter, waiter," slamming our fists on the tables as a server brought forth the goods.

I wondered what the Yanisin owners were thinking in setting us up to fail against Timber Stream. I'd hoped they'd call the whole thing off due to slippery fields and an imminent threat of rain. Why would they set us up against a normal camp? Yes, *normal*. Because whatever statistics indicate about the growing rate of childhood obesity in America, no chubby child ever felt normal. We didn't feel normal in gym class, in stores that didn't carry our size, and most certainly not beside the athletic kids at Timber Stream. Sure, the excursion added variety to the summer, but why set us up to fall short in the face of the tall and thin? What morale lifting would be accomplished on the two-hour bus ride home full of bruised knees and already threadbare egos? The lot of us were at Yanisin because we already knew we were misfits, the social pariahs back home, so pitting us against athletic kids would surely magnify it. Were the owners hoping this would serve as a reminder that there was a real world beyond our isolated fat one at Yanisin, and we'd return to it at summer's end, so we'd better keep motivated?

As Kate and I negotiated yet another hill toward the buses, we spotted Matty Catalano and Harris Smalls, two boys our age, taking a breather midclimb. Harris had the body of a beanbag chair and was already winded, his camp uniform marked with Ring Dings of sweat. Upon our approach, Kate exchanged a purposeful nod with Harris, while Matty and I were left to swap awkward boy-girl smiles. Along with a cleft chin so pronounced it looked tooled by hand, Matty had sable hard-rock hair that fell to his eyebrows and was considered "Yanisin good-looking." Anywhere else, he'd be Joe Lunch Bucket, but at Yanisin, he was Joe All Star, especially while standing beside Harris

Smalls. Charting in at well over 350 pounds, Harris required the scale at a nearby truck stop for his Saturday weigh-ins.

According to Kate, during these off-campus weigh-ins, while Harris's counselors stole away for a smoke, Harris found refuge at the truck stop vending machine. As quickly as he could manage, he'd punch in the codes. B8. C11. D2. The most coveted items in the sugar vault: king-size Snickers, king-size Twix, and the old standby, Reese's peanut butter cups (the four-pack). The jumbo confections were aptly plunged into the crotch of his pants. Back at Yanisin, Harris sold his crotch candy for fifteen dollars a pop. Eventually, he curried favor with some of the counselors who wanted a cut of the Yanisin black market. Together they set prices, with an oath from Harris never to rat out his suppliers. I wondered how many of the would-be profits he ate himself. His counselors sweetened the pot by expanding it. Now along with vending chocolates, Harris distributed egregiously marked up "value meals" from McDangerous and Taco Hell.

"I don't get it," I said to Kate when she'd first shared all this with me. "Why is he here then, if he's not even gonna try to lose weight?"

"He's a charity case. The owners let him stay here free all summer because he's a child of the state." I felt funny asking what she'd meant by "child of the state," as if I'd seem stupid for asking. Did he sleep in an orphanage? I pictured the staged scene from *Annie,* seeing little girls with rag curls slipping along the floors having a pillow fight after singing into the handles of their mops. I thought of their small white beds, the line of single cots, and wondered how Harris fit in just one. How would he find a family to love him if he remained that big?

"Not everyone here wants to be saved," she finally said, as if she were patiently explaining the nativity of Jesus of Nazareth. I still didn't get it. My thoughts were stuck on Harris's being poor. Forget his inability to pay for fresh produce; how could he afford all the food, even the cheap food, it had to take to sustain that weight? Didn't orphans have rationed portions, where they were each handed a single serving of gruel? They got a fat lip for even thinking, *Please, sir, I want some more.*

I couldn't comprehend anyone's being overweight and not wanting to do something about it. Actually, I couldn't imagine anyone not being all consumed with it. Not just Harris, but all the kids who paid for their illicit goods. Mostly I couldn't understand the idea of being fat and not being miserable about it. And then I remembered Kate and the Snickers she'd stowed in her tennis racket cover at the beginning of camp. Maybe she was nothing like me. Maybe she was happy.

Kate possessed a strong sense of *amor fati,* accepting her fate for a fat life. She didn't want to resculpt it to put others at ease, to make the doctors feel better, to abide by charts of normal. "I'm not here to be saved, either. Shit, I was born fat," she shrugged. "My whole family is fat, and as much as I diet, I always come back to this." She yanked at the loose flab that hung from her arm, flab a close Jewish relative of mine referred to as the Hadassah Wave. "There's no use in trying anymore; this is who I am." I don't know if she loved her fat, or fate, or life, but she was resigned to living it just as it was.

Before Harris's black market was in place, Kate said, "Beggars can't be choosers," so campers ate whatever made it over the fence. If a camper had been thrown out of camp for drugs or sex or some general fatty misconduct, it was an unspoken rule that later in the night, the ousted camper would return, launching expletives and hamburgers over the barbed wire fences near the periphery of camp. Yes, barbed wire, the same intended to restrain cattle and convicts. With the black market in place, though, there were no longer beggars; there were buyers. And large fries and Big Macs were delivered still warm. As long as a counselor was greased, you got yours—grease, that is.

"So, Harris," Kate asked, "is it really true that you dumped Andrea because she wouldn't give you head?"

"Damn straight," Harris announced as he did the We-Goin'-ta-Sizzla dance. His armpits had rolls, and the back of his neck resembled a pack of hot dogs. He couldn't keep his pants up, even with his makeshift fabric belt gnarled into a knot. And he was severing all romantic ties with a girl?! I couldn't believe it—not just that he was breaking up with someone but that someone wanted to date him in the first place.

The boys punched fists with an "Oh, yeah." Then Harris let out a turn of laughter, the infectious kind that made me simultaneously want to do the Twist and eat crescent rolls.

"Hey," Matty asked me, "you're from Lawngiland, right?" No matter the effort I made enunciating "Long Island" as two distinct words, I always got that oh-so-innovative emphasis. It's about as clever as a knock-knock joke. I nodded.

"So, you know Emma Steele?"

"No."

"Yeah, I guess she's older. She's at Timber Stream. Such an ultrafox. Maybe you'll see her today; I know how you girls stick together." Matty hailed from Greenwich, Connecticut, and assumed everyone from Long Island knew one another. "Like hottie magnets," he added. Matty had basically just called me pretty, which despite his obtuse comment made me like him.

It amazes me even now, the way people can ingratiate themselves with the smallest of compliments. I walk into a nail salon. There's a half-hour wait, which they promise will be only "few minutes. Pick-color." Then they tell me, "Too skinny. You lose weight, no?" And I stay and smile and tip too much for a second-rate pedicure. And it was the same at camp. It seemed more often than not that I liked being liked even more than the people who liked me.

And then the people who liked me showed up.

"Case in point," Matty said while fanning his hand in an exaggerated gesture toward Jordan, Grayson, and me in our matching camp uniforms. I wondered if Kate noticed he wasn't gesturing toward her. I was too afraid to read her face, so I turned away.

"Come on, Steph," Grayson prodded, looping her arm through mine. Along with Jordan and Matty, she led me up toward the buses. And as I let her steer me away, I marveled at the idea that I'd made my way across the line between *them* and *us*. There were your garden-variety chubs at Yanisin, and then there were the corpulent kids. We all attended fat camp thinking it was the one place we could be ourselves, without judgment, where the fat was factored out of the popular equation. But it didn't really work that way, not for everyone. The plump kids made fun of the obese kids. And the obese kids made fun of the morbidly obese kids. Maybe not always with words, but in our choices. There were the Harrises and Beulahs of camp, and then there was *us*.

I'd have more in common, I was sure, with the girls at Timber Stream, than I did with most of the kids from Yanisin. And I was absolutely right, only not in the way I'd imagined.

As we continued to make our way to the top of the hill, I turned back to face Kate. "Aren't you coming?" I shouted.

"They're all yours, Klein."

That they were, and I was thrilled.

THIS WASN'T THE NFL, NHL, NBA, OR MLB. BUT THREE distinct letters come to mind upon recalling our opponents in their indomitable uniforms, complete with shin guards, cleats, coordinating socks, and war-painted faces.

WTF.

To watch them, you'd think they were part of the Grapefruit League. I did not, I quickly determined, have anything in common with these girls. For us it was a field trip; intercamp saved us from drills and caterpillar sprints to the sign and back and provided a welcomed reprieve from calisthenics and circuit training. If nothing else it was a change of scenery. And we were here now, not competing in golf, tennis, or even a legitimate equestrian event, but to play *softball,* an after-work activity associated with jerseys sponsored by the corner deli, middle age, and a few cases of beer. Sure, it can be fiercely competitive among adults, but for teenage campers it's not supposed to be hard-core. But the red, white, and blue girls of Timber Stream played hardball.

The boys were across the way playing soccer, the younger kids distributed between Newcomb—a game of catch over a volleyball net—and floor hockey. We sat in our shaded dugout, folded over our soft cores, as Wendy Fink attempted to compose a batting order. Shouldn't we have done this on the bus ride here? I pulled at my shirt, bagging it out, hoping I'd be relegated to the end of our lineup. Some of the Timber Stream girls were warming up, stretching their torsos and calves, deftly gunning softballs across the field in measured angles. A brunette with red bandana wristbands practiced swinging, using two bats at once, while the batter beside her tossed a series of balls a short distance in the air, then batted them herself. The girls built upon a rhythm and knew where to sling the ball next, recognized just when to hurl a grounder and how to recover it. Each fluid step, turn, and follow-through appeared to be a reflex.

A few of their girls stood in a clutch, strategizing maybe, but most certainly sizing us up. "Size eighteen, at least," I imagined them saying.

"What are they looking at?" I said. I was taking their glares personally.

"Our shirts," Beulah responded. I was startled, not only by her voice but by the fact that she wasn't wearing her Minnie Mouse shirt.

As for our shirts, I'd nearly forgotten about them. I thought for sure that the Timber Stream campers had been lectured before our arrival, cautioned about the stretch marks that wiggled along our arms like yawning pink maggots. Certainly they'd be told to ignore the varicose veins that crept down the backs of our calves, our double chins, knee cellulite, and back fat. *No pointing.* Maybe they'd even been schooled about how to act around girls who smelled like Beulah. *No fat jokes.* They were warned, but no one readied them for our shirts. *No staring.* The Yanisin tees, the ones we were forced to wear whenever we left camp for a field trip, were *orange.* And along with fuchsia, orange is suicide for any redhead. But this was beyond the color and far beyond me. All of us suffered with the revulsion that was our camp logo. Prominently located on the upper-left-hand corner of our shirts, I'm afraid to report, was a cartoon of an overenergized vegetable couple. A celery stalk with its fists clenched victoriously in the air stood beside what can only be described as a dancing carrot stick.

In the spirit of sportsmanship, Timber Stream campers would sometimes swap shirts with Yani-"sinners"—another tee to add to their overrun collection, a souvenir from the day. Later in the summer it was rumored that a Timber Stream camper had masqueraded as the Crisco Kid, stuffing his Yanisin shirt with a pillow as he shuffled around the Timber Stream campgrounds, a cowbell fastened around his neck, doing his best impersonation of us. Perhaps he'd pretended to be ravenous, releasing a barbaric grunt, before grabbing someone's arm and asking, "Are you going to eat that?"

As our opponents took their positions on the field, I wondered if any would mock us once we'd gone. Each of them was sporting their bull's-eye-red shorts hiked high on the leg, revealing lissome upper thighs, not just tanned, but toned. Players and their counselors wore the same red lipstick, with glitter and stars painted on their faces to flaunt their allegiance. They looked like cocktail straws. I wanted to be on their team, the team of the mostly thin and seemingly brave, a part of their *us,* where *us* meant banding together in cheer, with linked arms, coordinated steps, and thighs that didn't chafe in the choreography of it all. They were going to annihilate us.

Their pitcher had sun-washed stripes of hair tousled loose from a low ponytail. Some were streaked red with Kool-Aid. I knew if extended the opportunity to do the same, we'd have sooner ripped open each packet and stabbed our way through it with our tongues than waste it as hair dye in the name of camp spirit. I wasn't even particularly fond of sweets, but since being denied them, I would have consumed the envelope whole, sucking on the mealy bits of paper stuck in my molars. The pitcher rifled a pitch across the plate as if she'd thrown it overhand.

And our very own Jessica Fallis actually got a piece of it. A big piece.

Usually softball was all about dead air. It was by far the easiest and most sought-after activity to play at camp because it consisted mostly of standing around, waiting for something to actually happen. It accommodated lazy dugout gossip, and if positioned in the field, tanning rays. So when Jessica got some lumber on the ball, we were all caught off guard. We let out a delayed cheer as the other team's lanky center fielder, who'd been using her mitt as a sun visor, missed the ball. After stumbling for it, she lobbed it past second base. Due to the "one base on an overthrow" rule, Jessica and her leg warmers booked their way to third.

That's the way,
Uh-huh, uh-huh,
We like it.
Uh-huh, uh-huh.

We cheered from the dugout, most of us now standing in anticipation. Marguerite was at bat; Hams on deck. This was a surprisingly unclassic start.

Many of the Timber Stream girls could be categorized as classically attractive, but an anomaly, their catcher, was in another league of "classic" altogether. With the body of an upturned parfait glass (a wave of hips, ass, and thighs), she was a thriving major leaguer in the classic "such a pretty face" mode. I'd never seen anyone that fat maintain such sharp features. Marguerite watched the first pitch hurtle by, flashing a self-conscious smile at the catcher, whose face was so angular Marguerite thought it might give her some pointers. *So that's why they're called Anglo-Saxon,* I remember thinking.

Another strike landed in the catcher's glove. How must their plump catcher have felt, seeing that some of us were actually smaller than she was? By no means prettier, but definitely far more trim. Her thighs bulged like small round terriers when she leaned back for a tripped-up ball. She had to hate that we were there. Our presence threw size into focus and served to highlight the parity between us. She easily could've been a Yani-sinner, which had to fuel her desire to pulverize us.

"She's on the wrong team," I was surprised to hear one of her cabin-mates sneer. It pissed me off. I was shocked not only that she'd said it, but that I'd even heard it at all. I couldn't quite get past the sound of our own sardonic cheers.

One, we are Camp Yanisin!
Two, a little bit louder!
Three, I still can't hear you!
Four more more more!

We had to pick that one, right? Obviously we always wanted more. That's why we were banished to Yanisin in the first place.

We want a pitcher, not a belly-itcher!

Bad idea, I thought as we repeated the homespun chant. Even *I* was staring at Marguerite's belly now.

You gotta want it to win it, and we want it more.

Well, uh, obviously. We just covered that with the whole *Four more more more* bit. Marguerite struck out. We needed new cheers.

Several innings later, as we took the field, the Yanisin boys our age straggled over, stacking up on the metal bleachers behind home plate. They'd finished early and come to offer their red-faced support. Their vegetable shirts seemed parboiled in two parts perspiration, one part mud. Even playing left fielder, a position I affectionately referred to as "left out," I could hear the guys as they razzed the batter and got a bit of chatter going.

When you think someone might be watching you, you watch yourself. Adam was leaning on his forearms over the back of our dugout as he stole swills of Crystal Light from his sister Wendy's water bottle. I sucked in my stomach and cheeks, tightened my ponytail, and prayed the ball didn't have eyes for me. I had a rag arm and knew enough to know that I'd need to relay the ball infield if it did. I punched my fist into my glove, bent my knees, and shifted my weight to give the impression I was ready.

Anyone familiar with the "misfits make good" genre knows how this next bit plays out. The picked-on, spat-on, underdog outcasts either win or they lose, but most important, they still feel proud and gleeful because they did their best! And doggonnit, they had F.U.N.

Unfortunately, no, that is not at all how it went down. There will be no description of a chunky adolescent in left field moving in slow motion, mitt outstretched, eyes pinched closed, when to the surprise of everyone, the ball magically lands in her glove. The ball never reached me. Their catcher hit a home run, prompting what seemed like all of Camp Timber Stream to draw nearer, waving their arms and exchanging high fives. And eventually, when I was up at bat, I did not hit the ball with my eyes closed in prayer. I'm saddened to say there most certainly will not be a pan left, directing you to witness the mouths of my teammates hanging agape because I'd just knocked one out of the park.

Here's what did happen: With Grayson at bat and two outs, I paced in the dugout. My hands were shaking. I tried to jump around a bit, shaking out my nerves.

One of the girls in our division looked up at me. I wondered if she had some advice for me. She did.

"Shelby, honey, drink your juice."

The *Steel Magnolias* potshot, insinuating that I was midseizure, did little to calm my nerves. My mouth felt pasty, as if I'd just licked a bunny. Water wasn't helping. And as much as I knew to try, I couldn't visualize the ball making contact with my bat—as Harper had coached me to do. I wasn't even attempting to stir up an imaginary arc, mapping out where the ball would go. I couldn't focus, and I was pretty sure I'd just busted a pit. I was too self-conscious to check. And then it came upon me: I was going to vomit. Would they call me bulimic if I threw up at home plate?

"We want another one, just like the other one," the Timber Streamers cheered to their pitcher.

You have no idea what it's like to want another one, I thought, and then Kate asked, "So, when's lunch?"

"Does it even matter? It's bagged," Joy replied in an unapologetic yawn as she pulled stray crimps of her hair into a banana clip.

"You're shittin' me," Kate said.

"Don't worry. I'm sure they'll make us eat it in their dining hall, just so we can watch them eat everything we can't."

Please strike out, I thought just before Grayson leaned in to golf the ball for a base hit. And now it was my turn.

I hate this. I hate this. I hate this.

At Yanisin they told us we didn't need to be great, or even good; we only needed to try. Platitudes of that kind weren't going to propel the ball into the air for me now that we were on foreign soil, now that Adam was actually watching me! The emphasis was no longer on learning a new skill or working up to our target heart rates. Now, things were competitive. Their team had not only designated a camper captain but also a cocaptain who called time-out for huddled meetings with their pitcher. They said things like "flutterball," "keystone sack," and actually used the phrase, "Whip out your Lord Charles," in reference to a curveball they'd hoped their nimble pitcher would gun over the plate. "A curve ball for a curvy girl," I also heard. And what I saw was limited to girls communicating across the field in unusual tics and suspect seizures. When the third baseman patted her tummy, I was convinced it was a fat joke at my expense.

All right, you fuckers. I tapped the bat on home plate, as if doing so proved something. I'd seen the Mets do it on television but never understood why. Was it a distancing technique initiated to help position the batter? Hell if I knew, but maybe it made me look as if I did.

As I stood at bat I didn't think of our outs but of my ins, of how many bases I'd need to round to be seen as their *us*. Strike one. Swaying over the plate waiting for the next pitch all I thought was, *Just make contact. A little something. If you bunt, act as if it was on purpose. Just get a part of it to let them know you're not that far apart.*

I didn't strike out. I struck her.

I couldn't believe it. Not only had I cracked it good, but I actually slonked the pitcher in the shoulder.

"Klein, you waiting for an invitation? *Run!*" And I did. Holy shit, I'd hit the goddamn ball! And now a force within me had me sprinting, my chest pulled forward and my elbows tucked close as my arms pumped. Who was I?

I'll tell you who I wasn't. There was an obvious dichotomy, at least in my head, between the well-seasoned athletes and the fatties in our dancing vegetable shirts. They were perfect; we were pathetic. My uniform and my friends, with their puffy mushroom-capped hair and slow ways, humiliated me. But when I hit the ball, rounding my way past first base as their pitcher clutched her shoulder in pain, with my team screaming wildly, the line between *them* and *us* blurred. I was just a kid in that moment, not perfect or pathetic, not a fat kid, not a thin kid, certainly not an athletic kid, but a kid in the summer playing an intercamp game.

Before that afternoon I didn't know softball meant throwing the ball underhand. I thought it was just an oversized—and therefore less compact, less *hard*—ball. It didn't just come down to a ball the size of an ostrich egg, one base on an overthrow, no leading, and an attitude that said, "It's still playing ball, and who you callin' soft?" Our parts might have been softer, but down at the core we were the same.

BILLY JOEL'S "GOODNIGHT SAIGON" BLARED FROM SOME kid's cassette player on our bus ride back from intercamp, where, incidentally, we got our asses handed to us. We sat, each of us, withdrawn into ourselves. We were tired. Shin guards on, stained knees propped against green pleather seats, we peered out the windows. As we passed a town with signs for farm-fresh eggs, malteds, and ale, I wondered what was for dinner and what shower I'd get since we skipped inspection that morning. Then I thought of the soggy lunch we didn't quite have. Just because it included two slices of bread and a bruised piece of fruit, they called it a meal. Anywhere else, it's what you eat while you're waiting for your lunch to arrive.

We weren't permitted to eat "away food." Instead, we devoured our lunches like greedy little animals, hunched over brown paper bags, blades of grass sticking to the backs of our thighs as we waited for all the divisions to complete their games. We smelled what we couldn't have: frying oil, never-ending platters of grilled cheese sandwiches, thin.

Kate offered me her diet soda, all backwash, only to throw her hands in the air and declare "No backsies!" We watched Lea finish up a game of Newcomb, the girls of her division being chastised by the Timber Streamers. Lea fended for herself with the patented and highly overused, "Yeah, well, we can lose weight, but you'll still be ugly." It was strange hearing Lea say, "*We* can lose weight," as if she defined herself as one of us, despite looking more like them. When our bus pulled off their campgrounds, Lea mooned them out the window.

I closed my eyes for the remainder of the ride, humming along to the chorus. *Yes, we would all go down together.* I replayed the events of the day in my head. *I really did smack it,* I thought, as I gave way to an unconscious smile. In that moment, it wasn't about getting even, being picked on, or wishing I were someone else. I became the curious kid who overturned a piece of slate from a footpath in my backyard just to see what I'd find, discovering adventure before suppertime. I was that free again. Just a kid who liked lemonade stands, trying to catch inchworms as they fell from trees, and who had to be reminded to come in and eat. Who liked carving jack-o'-lanterns, snow days, and being someone else's pillow in a game of Ha beneath a shaded maple tree. I was normal. *We* were normal. Maybe our version of normal, but I understood why the owners had the nerve to pit us against a normal camp. Because that's how they saw us. Sure they saw us as fat, maybe not the most athletic kids. But mainly we were kids. Normal kids with crushes, bruises, truck-driver mouths, and favorite songs.

I easily could have been the clumsy lanky girl who fumbled for the ball at the start of the game. We weren't all that different, *them* and *us*. And what I hadn't yet realized at that age was exactly how much we had in common. What I shared with some of the girls at the neighboring camp, aside from the ability to fit in an airline seat, was precisely what I shared with my own father: prejudice. The world was rife with small-minded people who discriminated against the big. They had contempt for overweight people, making assumptions about their cleanliness, habits, and health. Believing they weren't worthy of love. And I was one of them.

Guilty. I couldn't imagine anyone wanting to date someone Harris's size, didn't think he'd find a family who'd want him. As much as I disassociated myself from kids like Beulah, I was still one of *them*. The picked on, the humiliated, the camper who spent her time sulking in the shade, cursing her mother for not packing her underwear. I wasn't that different from her, not really. Because back at home, that was me. I was a *them* instead of an *us,* and I was certain the only way to cross the line was to become thin. I was as bad as the teammate who told the catcher she belonged on the fat team. Although I didn't say it, I still thought it.

The Timber Stream camper who'd one day stuff his Yanisin shirt with a pillow would get it all wrong. People would look at his waddling, watch as he tried to dig out a deep-seated wedgie. And they'd all double over in laughter together. Which isn't true to what it's really like. Because when you're obese, you're never the center of attention. Unless they're snickering, no one even looks at you. People divert their eyes and refuse to look into yours because you make them uncomfortable. You're literally the elephant in the room. I know. I was one of them—the kid who looked away when I saw someone morbidly obese in the supermarket. I was a hater of my own kind.

eleven

AMERICAN PIE

My favorite words:

Rotund = Plump.
I can't finish.

Love,
Stephanie

FRIDAY WAS FINALLY UPON US. IT WAS THE LAST PERIOD of the day, free swim, and I was looking forward to the divisional evening cookout on the boys' side of camp. The pool was congested, a frenzied swim, with most of us togged up in our boxers and V-necks, our suits and bodies obscured. Paige blew her whistle in three quick jolts, indicating that we should paddle to the edges of the pool and grab the hand of our designated swim buddy.

"Can someone please tell me what it says here, just below my feet?!" Paige fumed once we'd settled into a hush. Her lips, tightened and pursed, resembled a small white dumpling. No one spoke. "'No diving.' That's right. Can anyone tell me why we have these rules?" So they can be disobeyed. "That's right, to protect you from getting hurt." I rolled my eyes at Jordan, who called my roll and raised me a sneer.

"When are you people going to learn?" By "you people" she meant Tallulah Devens, who'd just generated a tsunami with her running dive.

I first learned to dive by jumping off the second *N* of the NO DIVING sign at North Hills. Mom had me leap from it into her arms when I was four and three-quarters. At that precise age I loved, probably even more than pretzels dipped in apple juice, spending time with Mom. I'd pet her hair, examine her necklace, and sometimes knead her soft face with both hands, as if positioning clay. "You're so pretty, Mommy." She smelled of blow dryer, Keri lotion, and gingersnaps.

Typically she preferred playing doubles on the tennis court, or lounging poolside with a magazine chock-full of recipes for her family and diet tips for herself, to swimming. In fact, "swimming" isn't the right word. She never swam. She *bathed*. She'd take a dip, only up to her armpits, and never stayed for long. More often than not she'd grit her teeth, then declare, "No, no, it's too cold!" when I'd beg her to go in with me. Sometimes she'd watch me blow bubbles, flipping her magazine closed, her finger a bookmark.

"Mom, are you watching? You weren't looking! Ready?" This is usually the way it went. "Mom. Okay, but Mom? Did you see me, Mom? Did you?"

So when she offered me the opportunity to leave the suspiciously warm kiddie pool and join her in the grown-up one, I was over the moon. I jumped on the cement, without a care for the condition of my feet or friendships, having just abandoned my friend Janis and our card game of Old Maid. I couldn't stand still.

"What's wrong with you?" Mom asked. "It's like you've got ants in your pants." I looked down at my bare legs. No I didn't. I wasn't even wearing pants; I was wearing water wings.

"Come on," I whined, yanking her toward the big pool with both hands.

"Okay, okay. Hold your horses. I'm coming." She had me wait as she set her tennis visor on a chaise and unfastened her sarong. I wondered what she'd meant about the horses and was about to ask when she called me to her and removed my wings.

After taking flight into her arms in a series of frenetic leaps off the NO DIVING sign at the shallow end of the big pool, I ran toward the middle, where the water was deeper. "Okay, hold on now," she said, making wide strides through the water toward where I was standing. I propelled my arms, as if ready to fly, but she stopped me, asking that I sit on the ledge of the pool. I pouted, thinking I was being scolded. "No, we're going to try something new now," she reassured me. While seated on the ledge, I formed a sliver of pie with my arms, as she'd instructed: "Yes, like pizza."

"No, apple," I insisted.

"Yes, like apple pie."

"No, blueberry!"

"Yes, all right, blueberry then. It doesn't matter."

"Wait, Mom?"

"What?"

"Cherry!"

"That's right. Now, just roll forward." My body became a wobbly sippy cup, teetering on the pool's edge. "Yup, just like that, your chest to your knees, then keep rolling forward." I was old enough to be afraid. "There's no reason to be scared. I'm right here."

"So?"

"So, come on," she urged, but I wasn't convinced this pie-diving was going to work. "Stephanie, I'm not going to let anything bad happen to you." That one worked.

When I resurfaced she was clapping and saying "Yay" in a sugary mommy voice. And I smiled so big it took up my whole face. I loved delighting her. I wanted to do it again and again and again.

As I grew older, I graduated from surface dives in the lap pool and moved to the yawning waters of the partitioned diving area. That's when Mom called it quits. She wouldn't put her face in the water or get her hair wet, so she left me in the care of the pool lifeguard and Holly

Valens, one of the older children of another club member. Holly was six years my senior, with breasts, braces, and a bob, and she promised me a pack of grape Bubble Yum if I'd dive off the high board. Mom didn't allow many sweets in our house, aside from the goodies she hid for Poppa. A baked apple with ground cinnamon and a fanciful turn of maple syrup was right there, Weeble-wobbling, on the edge of "allowed." Her idea of sugar cereal didn't extend beyond Honey Nut Cheerios, so a product offering no nutritional value whose first listed ingredient read "sugar" was forbidden.

I pined for grape gum, and if asked, would have written it a sonnet. The pieces were enormous, plump cubes of bursting grape goodness. I can still remember feeling the sugar inside my cheek, like sandy grains of a pear. It twirled in my mouth and thickened my saliva. I would have this gum even in the face of grave danger.

As I scaled the fifteen-foot ladder, my legs quivered. My body was dripping, fresh out of the water from having just pounced off the lower board. I was frightened when I reached the top, unable to inch forward on the board. Holding tight to the railings, I drew in a quick breath and warily stole a glance below. "Now, don't look down," Holly warned. I felt paralyzed and wanted her to charge up and rescue me. A small knot of club members formed.

"Come on, Stephanie, don't be a wussy," my cousin Damien shot up through cupped hands. Damien cried when we watched *Old Yeller*. I wasn't the wussy.

"Then let's see you do it!" I wanted to yell back, but I was too nervous to speak, as if the vibrations of my sounds might unsteady things. The high board wasn't as springy or wide as the low one. It felt more like a platform. I swallowed, trying to will my hands off the handrails.

"You're thinking too much," Holly said. "Just do it. Come on. One . . . two . . . three!"

By now my suit had dried and my hair was curling again. I was petrified, not of the height, but of the time I'd be in the air, the amount that could go wrong in that distance. The slightest bend in my body while airborne could result in a water slap. If I hit it right I'd disappear, like a needle into skin. It amazed me that something I could dip and swirl a finger into and lift and splash and spit from my mouth in an arc could also be hard and spank me, turning my pallid body crimson on collision. I couldn't take one more step.

"Come on, grape gum, Stephanie." Holly waved the pack in her hand. Okay, okay, I'll do it! I held my breath, took a sacrificial step, overlapped my hands, and just . . . just couldn't.

"Come on!!!" impatient voices shrieked up to me. There were more of them now.

I had a commanding view of the snack bar, the tops of sun umbrellas, and I could see all the way to the tennis court gate. The birds flew off trees. I peeked one more time at the chewing gum waving in Holly's fist, and could nearly draw in its sweet perfume. My toes curled at the edge of the board, the blue water waiting beneath me. I clasped my hands as Mom had taught me, my thumbs clicked together, my elbows locked. *Just follow your hands,* I thought as I willed my body to roll forward.

It happened fast. It didn't hurt so much as it startled me. The water was colder than February. My body somersaulted up through the water, breaking the surface to a melody of cheer. A soft gasp escaped my mouth. *Had I?* I was lost in space, unsure of my bearings. *Had I really done it?* I looked around, almost frantic, treading water, wiping it from my eyes. A new and surprising warmth coursed through me. *Yesssss!*

"Stephanie, you did it!" Holly said, with a vibrancy in her voice I'd never heard before. I'd really done it. I couldn't wait to tell my mom. I'd go right now, draped in only a towel and scream it from the sidelines of the court. Holly offered me her hands to pull me from the water. Both of us were brimming with excitement and adrenaline, our smiles beaming.

"Can you believe it?" I screeched. "I bet you thought I'd chicken out." I giggled as I tightened my grip on her hands.

Midhoist, Holly's face seemed strained. She lowered me back in, bringing her face down to mine. She smiled gently. "Stephanie," she whispered, "why don't you swim to the ladder."

My smile softened as I processed what was happening. Without warning the corners of my mouth betrayed me with a slight and continuous tremble. I slipped under the water where it was quiet, where no one would hear me cry. I wanted to disappear. No one could tell the difference between water and tears.

I *hated* my big fat life.

I slugged my way to the ladies' locker room. It was empty. I walked toward the back, turned into a row no one ever occupied, and sat on a bench, a towel wrapped around my shoulders. My feet were still wet on the tile floor. I looked down at my reward, cradled in my palm. I'd chew the entire pack from that bench, adding one piece at a time. Each a decision. I craved, needed, and coveted that gum, and with the same vigor, I despised it. I can't remember when candy was fun.

Food as motivation, I now know, is far more hazardous than throwing yourself headfirst off a fifteen-foot-high diving board. And as great a motivating force as food was in my life, I quickly learned it didn't hold a flashlight to hate.

AFTER FREE SWIM AND SHOWER HOUR, I'D TYPICALLY participate in a secretive Friday night water party in Grayson and Jordan's cabin. With most of our division already making their way across camp to the boys' side, we'd sit cross-legged on the floor doing shots of water. Wendy never dissuaded us, only demanded that we were all out of the cabin come the official start of the divisional cookout. We'd rock, paper, scissors our way through 3.5 liters each by bedtime. I wasn't sure at first what a liter even was.

"It's one of these," Grayson said, holding up a thirty-two-ounce water bottle. Wouldn't one stop drinking water the night before weigh-in? Dehydrate. That's not the way it worked, I learned. To miraculously lose water weight, you first had to find it, flood in it. But you had to time it right. In the four weeks I'd been at camp, I'd become quite adept at this trick. Throughout the night and early the next morning, I was a fountain. My system cleansed. Pounds lighter. But this particular night, I had last shower and wasn't able to make it to Grayson's cabin. I'd catch up with them over dinner, promising myself to pound at least six cups of water before my first bite.

Kate and I had only made it as far as the Lower Camp valley when her jeans unfurled. As she slumped to roll them back up, I saw a large plot of flattened grass, which Kate identified as a "Cropsy."

Almost every overnight camp has its own flavor of the Cropsy tale, revealed in an ominous tone during a campfire. Cropsy had been a local good old boy, but when a camper took his son's life, Cropsy snapped, vowing to exact revenge by returning each year on the anniversary of his son's murder to behead a camper with his rusted axe. The markings in the grass beside Kate's foot were too large to be the footprints of a ghost, even a fat camp ghoul. The trodden area resembled the outline of a body at a crime scene.

"I don't believe in ghosts," I said.

"Ghosts?"

"Yeah, not Cropsy, or that dude with the hook hand who scrapes at the car window if you're making out with some guy."

Kate stopped walking and leaned on her knees, shaking her head like an asthmatic trying to gasp in more air. "Damn, you're a pisser!" she wheezed.

"What's so funny?"

"Not *that* Cropsy, Klein. It's a fatty crop circle. A *cropsy,*" she exhaled with an emphasis on the *o*. "It's slicker than deer guts on a skinnin' knife out here."

I reexamined the damp flattened grass. It was the distinct marking of a camper who'd bit it.

"Don't look at me like that."

"You slay me, Klein."

"What, you say 'Cropsy' and I'm supposed to know you mean fatsos who took a spill on a hill?"

"It's like cow tipping, except we're awake."

"I know, I know, and we're the cows." I was getting the hang of it. There was a certain comfort in making fun of ourselves, repeating all the fat remarks of which we'd been the target all winter. It took the sting out. "Look at all of them," I said of the markings in the approaching distance. "It's dangerous out here."

"Not nearly as dangerous as your breath."

I nervously checked, cupping my hand over my mouth. We were running late as it was; there wasn't time to brush. "Really?" I puffed again.

"I don't know whether to give you a mint or some toilet paper." Kate spent many a rest hour committing an entire volume of yo' mama jokes to memory.

I breathed through my nose the rest of the way.

Skin So Soft lingered in the air with the hovering buzz of mosquitoes. Most of our division was already there, sitting in small half circles, crouched on the sidelines of the basketball court, fast eaters practicing layup shots. I liked that Friday night cookouts weren't the whole of camp, but was just our division: thirty-five girls, twenty boys, and a mix of fourteen or so counselors spread between the court and a campfire ring just behind it. Food was dispensed between the two, along three folding tables covered with plastic red-check tablecloths and an assembly line of rectangular chafing dishes and bins. The real kitchen staff had Friday nights off, so it was up to our counselors to act as the servers and chefs. Since cabins were invited to the tables one at a time, counselors could keep tabs on those who hadn't yet been served and those trying to sneak in seconds.

As Kate and I neared the group I had the suspicion I was being watched. Not Cropsy-watched—I wasn't panicked, glancing over my shoulder, alarmed to find a menacing figure hiding behind a tree trunk, axe in hand. I sensed I was being admired from afar, as if I was about to descend a sweeping staircase before taking a turn about the ballroom. I flipped my hair to one side, flexed my hand, and flounced toward the cookout a bit differently. Straighter, taller, adding a smile, as if observing my own reflection in a store window. The attention made me giddy, and I was thankful I'd taken care to cut the crewneck ribbing out of my oversized shirt, leaving me with an asymmetrical dress that I wore bagged and belted over stirrup pants. *What a feeling. Bein's believin'!*

I grabbed plasticware and a paper plate and took my place behind Kate at the tail of the dinner line. The sky was beginning to darken; an airplane flew overhead. *I'm glad I'm here,* I remember thinking as I watched it trail off. As if up until that moment I wasn't so sure, but now, standing in line for a puck of a veggie burger, it was decidedly so. *I'm happy.* Perhaps if they'd only offered me a vinegar-soaked mushroom cap, I'd have felt differently, but mostly I was beginning to like the stride of things at Yanisin, my friends and our banter, the rigid order of our days: general swim, flag lowering, dinner, and free play. Evening activity, curfew, lights out. And my body. There was now room to tuck in a shirt. It wouldn't have looked good, but at least there was room.

As I advanced toward the front of the line, I studied the boys' cabins, wondering what it was like inside. Did it smell like armpit? Was their work wheel reversed, giving the simplest chore of GROUNDS first shower as a form of punishment? Were their cabins laid out the same as ours? I tried to imagine Adam's bed and couldn't decide if he'd have photographs from home pinned up. Would that be too sentimental for a boy?

I looked back toward the basketball court, trying to determine where I'd sit. Grayson was across the way, inside the key, seated beside a mix of campers, mostly boys. Jordan was standing behind her, eating a slice of watermelon. I admired her tucked-in outfit and catalogued its colors: lime green, turquoise, carnation pink, and poppy red. She looked like a preppy picnic.

"Didn't you two eat already?" Wendy asked, turning to find the rest of our cabin in a circle, their plates nearly finished.

Kate and I both shook our heads, overlapping in our explanations. "I was last shower."

"I needed to cram a tam, and then I had to go back for a few extra party supplies." Kate had taken to calling tampons her "party supplies," which always made counselors laugh just enough to forget they should be lecturing her on punctuality.

"Okay, okay," Wendy said while plunging her gloved hand into the first bin of food. *Thank the God above.* I was starved. Since lunch, I'd played volleyball, completed a reverse loop—3.8 miles, down Heart Attack Hill, up Bitch—and practiced my butterfly stroke before free swim. They worked us hard on Fridays, knowing that the next morning was weigh-in. The pilgrimage to Boys' Camp alone surely burned off the 120-calorie bun. I steadied my plate as Wendy pressed a handful of shredded lettuce onto a soft, powder-topped hamburger roll. Next came my alternative to the flattened gray hamburger, the prefrozen kind, impossible to cook medium rare: an orange, irregularly shaped patty with visible chunks of broccoli and kernels of corn. It looked like my craps, only not as fuzzy. *You are what you eat.* They weren't kidding. Harper had even said my skin was beginning to look too orange from all the carrots I was eating.

I was issued only a single packet of ketchup—*Too much sugar,* they'd said. I then had a choice between a half ear of boiled corn and a leaky scoop of coleslaw. I didn't see how they were equals, given that corn was a starch and their coleslaw was basically cabbage dipped in milk. I opted for the slaw and two pickle spears and refused the pale, spongy tomato slices. It was a texture thing, mostly. Tomatoes, as far as I was concerned, were slime. I sidestepped the rings of red onion and hoped Jordan was carrying her spearmint Binaca.

"That was some hit yesterday." I whipped around to see Adam, who was standing behind me in a navy blue button-down and a tattered white baseball cap. I had been oblivious and wondered if he'd been there the whole time, analyzing my food choices. "I said, some hit yesterday," he repeated as slowly as a Southerner, even adding a drawl for emphasis.

"Oh, thanks." As soon as I'd said it, I realized my "oh" was a major exhale. I'd need to talk without breathing. But what would I say? Oh, God. I was so good at this in my head, but in front of him, I was a tangle of awkward. Had he purposefully waited for me to arrive before getting in line? Had he been thinking of what to say to me, or was it all just coincidence? Shit, had I just made a face? Because now he was making a face. Was he mimicking me, or was that a reaction to my breath?

"So did you nail that pitcher on purpose or what?"

"Or what," I said hesitantly. I had to keep it short. As he seized three tongs' worth of carrot sticks, stacking them on a separate plate, I took the opportunity to adjust the sling of my studded belt. My stomach looked okay.

"Leave some for us," his sister warned him with a wink. Wendy and the other counselors weren't allowed to eat until after we'd all been served.

"Klein, where we sittin'?" Kate turned to ask.

"Wherever." When I switched back to Adam, he'd already traipsed off, carrying his two plates toward an empty log near where the campfire had just begun to smolder. Kate picked a spot for us on the other end of the basketball court, near other girls from our cabin who'd nearly finished eating. I wanted to run after him, to explain, to say something clever. But I'd missed my chance.

I inhaled to the mental count of ten, then exhaled my way back to one. I'd think of something. While seated, and after a judicious amount of water, I diced my pickle spear and decorated my "burger" with a pile of slaw. What else did it need? Another burger. As much as I tried to savor the food on my plate, I was still ravenous once I'd finished. I'd already powered through the cups of water I normally would've consumed during one of our water parties. This called for drastic measures—namely mustard. While ketchup was restricted, mustard, along with carrots, was a "free food," so during cookouts I'd load up with extra packets. I'd bite open six or so, squirting their contents on my plate, then poke my way through the dip with carrot rods, leaving nothing but a faint yellow smear. More often than not, I'd take to eating the packets one by one. Some campers believed mustard had a magical weight-loss property, that the spice of it could make you sweat, hence burning calories. Others said it was high in carbohydrates and should be avoided at all costs, despite the Yanisin insistence that it was a free food. I didn't care so much either way. No one is fat because she eats mustard. A freak, yes, but fat, no.

I'd just eaten nine packets. It got to the point where the inside of my nose felt numb and all I could taste was vinegar, even after a wedge of watermelon. I sucked on the plastic of my final packet, pushing the contents through like toothpaste. Which reminded me: I needed some.

As the flames climbed high into the night, a camper who kept his thick dark hair pulled into a stout ponytail during the day regaled us with his acoustic guitar, his hair loose and feral. He knew all the words to "American Pie"—as would I in the coming weeks—and smelled of patchouli. He's now most likely married to a woman who wears paisley scarves over her head, shops using her own canvas bags, and prefers retreats in the Catskills to city life. I bet their outgoing answering machine ends with a message directing callers to pray for peace.

I picked my way past him, careful of the burning embers. The crowd surrounding Grayson had bloated to midcourt. They were competing in a round of charades, with Jordan playing center forward, her ass to me while she jumped repeatedly, waiting for people to correctly guess the movie she'd been given. *Hoosiers,* maybe? Only Jordan would get a basketball film to pantomime while on an actual court. She roused the spectators into a lively uproar when she liberated her first of several grunts.

"Like that," I thought I heard her say to her captive audience. It wasn't just a faceless crowd, but people I knew. As I drew nearer, I realized it wasn't charades they were playing. I looked at their enchanted faces. I could hear her now, midstory. "You *had* to see it," she said, laughing with delight. Then she jumped again, this time with her hands fisted in front of her waist. "Gray and I wiggled into her one pair of jeans." I smiled as her face strained into an exaggerated grimace. She looked like the boy in the advertisement. Standing sideways, her arm outstretched, as if she were wearing an imaginary pair of clown pants. "You know, those bleached pieces of shit she walks around in." My smile faded. I squinted, sure I'd misheard. Jordan was talking about Beulah, not me. *She couldn't have meant me.* But Jordan had borrowed my jeans the other night when she'd lent me that Syracuse outfit. My nose felt it first, a crescendo of pricks and tingles. My eyes came next, pooling with tears. Then the corners of my mouth turned. I might as well have been wading in the deep end.

People with whom I had strategized on the volleyball court earlier in the day were smiling. "The two of us together fit in there," Jordan mocked. People I'd dated. "Hysterical." Mouths I'd kissed. "You had to see it!" Counselors who'd handed me my mail. "Jesus, she thinks she's such hot shit. She probably thought she'd be the thinnest one here."

An ache thrummed in my chest. There wasn't room to breathe. Most of the people laughing were heavier than I was. They weren't laughing because I was fat. They were laughing because I was me. Because they thought I was a stuck-up bitch. I could read their minds, as their foreheads wrinkled, leaning in expectantly, waiting for what Jordan would do next. I ached for quiet, for the chorus of their laughter to die, for all the attention to be directed anywhere but there. I wanted to slip underwater and disappear.

I was too humiliated to see who it was standing beside me laughing in high-pitched fits. I just stood there watching, confused. *But, wait. I thought you liked me.*

When Grayson saw my face, she scooted toward the middle of the court and kicked Jordan's foot.

"What the fuck, Gray?" Jordan said, continuing her charade, this time with her eyes pinched closed, wiggling from a squat into a stand. "And we both fit in there. That's the saddest part!" When she opened her eyes and looked into the pupils of mine, her response to my presence was measured, slow and exacting, as though read from a recipe for disaster. She just smiled and turned away.

I FELT WORSE THE NEXT MORNING. BY THEN I'D HAD TIME to stew with the events of the night. I'd lost 3.5 pounds at weigh-in. I watched them move the heavy anchor from the 150 spot down to 100, achieving my first goal. I should have felt proud, should have done a celebratory touchdown dance. 147.5 pounds! Only 3.5 pounds more, and I'd be down a 20-pound bag of kibble! But I didn't. More than ever before, I hated not just what I looked like but who I was.

My public humiliation was undoubtedly punishment for how I'd talked about Beulah and thought about Harris, assuming I was part of an *us* apart from *them*. I deserved what I got. A profound sense of shame came upon me in a humbling moment as I moped back to the cabin after an untouched flapjack breakfast. *Just because you're thinner, it doesn't make you better.* I vowed to never make fun of anyone again. I never wanted to make anyone feel the way I had at that cookout.

I might have tried to bargain my way out of the humiliation, silently praying to God to please fix it. Make everyone like me. I promise I'll be nice and will never feel superior to anyone ever again! But it would have been a promise I couldn't keep. Years later I'd feel slightly superior *because* I'd once been fat.

That's the thing about being a former fat camp champ: when asked if I'd change my past if I could, I think for a moment and always answer no. The pain of being an overweight kid, the humiliation, makes you think twice before ever cutting anyone else down. There's something almost perfect in the ugly duckling syndrome. Something just. Something that *just* makes it mildly worth it. Because a sensitivity is tattooed on a part of you no one else can see but can somehow guess is there. It's always with you. A scar, maybe, some hurt that really does make you better. And you do feel a sense of superiority, not for winning some supposed battle against all your bulges, but because you'll never be insensitive or cruel. You know what it is to experience the pain of being chastised and therefore feel superior, morally composed, with an enduring, hearty even, robust sense of character. You think that because you've overcome, you'll always rise to defend the underdog. You've already lived through rejection and loneliness. At the age of thirteen you've felt it profoundly and won't ever be malicious and will always remember that you somehow made it out okay.

But none of it's true. You are mean again. Because as you live, you forget, and the sensitivity dulls. You forget the pact you made that day, promising never to hurt anyone. While I believe I'm especially sensitive, I also know I'm human.

When you're going through it, though, you wish it all away. You climb onto your mattress, the springs squealing beneath you, as you curl into a fetal position and wish your summer away. Your pain leads you to make promises you cannot keep. "I'm going to keep my nose clean," you write in your diary. You'll do anything to make the hurt stop. You'll even turn the pain into anger.

After I beat myself up all morning, my feelings transitioned into something more by late afternoon. As I did lunges in the shallow end of the pool during water aerobics, I dissected the rules of ridicule. I estimated that one could safely sling insults at the portly when the remarks were disguised behind concern. "It's such a shame," for instance, tacked on quite nicely to "She's disgusting." Your jabs somehow seemed like an acceptable form of discrimination because it was, after all, "for her own good." You'd get a stern talking to, however, if you sneezed "FatBitchSaidWhat" aloud. Because there, your words aren't softened with sympathy. Yet it seemed perfectly tolerable to jeer at overweight kids for being fat if they deserved it for any reason other than their weight. If they needed, for example, to be knocked down a few rungs on the feel-good ladder. It's cruel to mock a heavy girl when she's timid and seems kinda helpless, drawn into herself, hiding behind her bangs. But when an overweight teen shows the slightest hint of ego or the faintest color of personality or confidence, it's perfectly acceptable to level her. Tease her all you want if she shows any signs of liking herself.

Any semblance of self-esteem could be mangled into an accusation of being "conceited." That brochure they sent to prospective campers had it wrong. A positive self-image wasn't really fostered at Yanisin—maybe in an introduction paragraph touting their philosophy, but in the living, they couldn't safeguard us from one another. Counselors could patrol the grounds to break up necking campers, but they couldn't point a flashlight at the subtleties of mean. *I'm encouraged to look good,* I thought as I checked myself in a hand mirror before dinner, *but I'm never allowed to believe it.*

By the time twenty-four hours had elapsed since the cookout and nightfall was upon me, I'd come to appreciate the legacy of poltergeists and began to understand just what kept Cropsy haunting campgrounds for decades. Hate fueled his motivation. And now I felt what it meant to hurt so deeply that the only balm is revenge.

twelve

Hurts So Good

Hmm. What guys do I like? I'll try and figure it out right now on a 1–10 scale. The second number is all looks, nothing more, nothing less. A check mark indicates who I may really like.

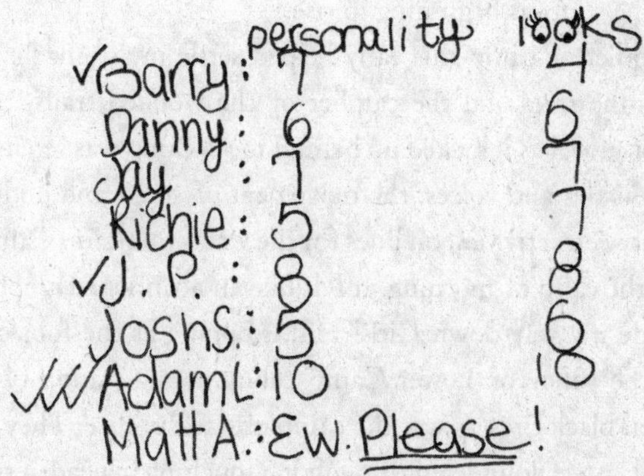

personality looks
✓Barry: 7 4
Danny: 6 6
Jay: 7 7
Richie: 5 7
✓J. P.: 8 8
JoshS.: 5 6
✓✓✓AdamL: 10 10
MattA.: Ew. Please!

I can't make ↑ my mind. Jay is really nice. He sticks ↑ for me at school, and he's cute. I don't think I like him though. Barry, well, I love him, but I don't think I like him.

I COULDN'T GET OFF THE TOILET. THIS TIME IT WASN'T because of a water party. Although a full day had passed since the cookout, I still had anxiety, a far superior diuretic and diarrhetic. What would I do? What would I say? Who would I sit with now? It was still dark in our cabin. I worried that the diarrhea that had been ripping through me might wake someone, so I tried not to push. There was nothing left anyway.

It was early Sunday morning. They worked us hard on Fridays and Saturdays, holding all leisurely activities in abeyance until Sunday. It was my day of rest. But I couldn't.

When I left the bathroom, the light flooding our cabin had bloomed from an inky silver to a russet sable. I felt my way to my cubby, picking through a pile for my nylon Umbro shorts, a bulb of cotton socks, a T-shirt, and the stiff fold of a sports bra. Once dressed, I cleaved my way into my sneakers, struggling with a tongue. I'd fix it out on the porch. The sun was beginning to rise.

The quiet of camp this early helped settle my stomach. The soft drape of the trees and the camber of the wooded trails, the gentle sounds of gravel as it kicked up behind me—camp was serene without all the whistles and voices, the movement of songs and bodies across fields, between activities, on lines for the water fountain. Camp was all mine in the calm of morning. It felt like an abandoned amphitheater.

I made my way down Girls' Hill, stopping at the foot of it. Just behind the valley of Lower Camp cabins was a station of a dozen horizontal black tires. It was the camp obstacle course. They timed us each week as we floundered through it, crouching beneath a succession of makeshift limbo bars, scaling an eight-foot wall, hurdling a bench, balancing across a wooden beam, sprinting up the hill, doing forty-five crunches, jumping rope, weaving between orange cones. Then we'd transfer our weight as we danced through a series of tractor tires. All that was missing was a rope swing over a pit of mud.

I was now leaning forward, my foot flexed on the edge of a tire, half-heartedly clutching my ankle with both hands just as they'd directed us to do each morning over a loudspeaker during the all-camp stretch. On those mornings we were instructed to take cleansing breaths, feeling them deep in our diaphragms. Our arms moved in a sun-up sweep above our heads, in one fluid motion, pressing our hands together in a namasté prayer. Begin at peace and invite in the day and its bounty of glory.

Yeah, okay.

They might have considered having this touchy-feely one-with-the-universe stretch on a grassy hillock—the give of earth beneath the soles of our feet, our bodies awakened by small flashes of light from a yawning lake—instead of assembling us on a makeshift hockey rink composed of concrete and rounded wooden walls suited for hotheaded hip checks and brutal body slams. At least I had this: the ability to do it my way while everyone else was still stretched across their mattresses like sleeping dogs. And "my way," I decided, meant not stretching at all. I didn't bother to grip my other ankle.

I happened to be an expert at lengthening my limbs, cupping my elbow as my arm extended across my body. As far as I was concerned, though, stretching was a ruse. It never appeared to prevent injury or mitigate the acute aches that followed intense activity. All it really accomplished was forestalling the inevitable pain of running. Stretching should have been called stalling.

Still, I wanted to be a runner. They had sculpted arms and lithe thighs, muscles distinct from bone. And it seemed as though they could endure anything. Hills and life were easier for those who could run through it.

I'll do this every morning, I decided as I set off into a gentle trot. Maybe if I forced myself, I'd hate it less. Maybe I'd come to know why people willingly tortured themselves with exercise. "No pain, no gain" and all that. *Go as slowly as you need, just don't stop.* I could have walked faster than I was jogging, but I wanted to say that I'd gone running. Walking was for fat people who thought they could slim down by window-shopping at a mall.

All of two yards into it I was reminded that there's a reason overweight people don't run, and it has nothing to do with a tension in the lungs or the fang of a cramp. It's not because I was out of shape. It's because my fat *hurt.* Running made my skin sting. The fat depot of my caboose and thighs jiggled violently. I grabbed at it as I ran, thinking if I flexed and squeezed hard enough, there'd be less to hurt. There wasn't.

Okay, you can stop when you get to the next tree. Not that one, the next. I white-lied my way along the periphery of camp. My calves were splatter-painted with dirt. I ran cramped, thinking it'd only worsen if I stopped. I didn't run with my Walkman as I had in the afternoons, because this was thinking time. I wasn't thinking about crossing my legs or wearing a two-piece bathing suit. Of sleeveless shirts, collarbones, or that backless cocktail dress. I thought about Jordan. My legs kicked up behind me. I thought about girls at school. It was harder to breathe, but I didn't care. I thought about the boys who called me Moose. I was in a full-blown anger sprint.

I wanted to lose weight to spite them. The more they hurt me, the more they'd strengthen my resolve. I wasn't inspired by those who'd successfully lost weight, or were at least striving to do so. Watching heavier kids squeeze out the last set of power crunches on the obstacle course didn't motivate me. In fact, "motivate" and "inspire" were the wrong verbs. I was "provoked" and "goaded" into losing weight. I was a hurricane of hate.

The "thinspiration" collage I'd constructed along the edges of my mirror at home needed to be dismantled. I could no longer tolerate my horde of weight-loss tapes, with tales of "everyday people" who'd finally shed half their body weight by Jazzercising in a Los Angeles exercise studio. The "Wow, if she could do it, then so can I!" stories just wouldn't work.

I sprinted across the soccer field until I couldn't keep up with my body, until I collapsed onto the ground, gasping for air, coughing, my head between my knees. Endorphins were a lie.

When I lifted my head I determined I was sitting in the stopper position of the soccer field, just beside where the two fullbacks would stand, right in front of the sweeper. Back home, Mom and Poppa insisted I participate in some type of after-school sport, not for the camaraderie, discipline, or skills acquired, but for the exercise. Evidently, running my mouth didn't seem to qualify. I chose soccer because it looked like grazing. And grazing I could do.

As part of the lethargic defensive team, I wasn't half bad. Simply put, I took up more space on the field. The rest of the girls flitted about like wind chimes, but I could put more force behind the ball. And no one wants to run toward the big girl. Though when they did, I'd grunt for effect. I preferred taking a defensive position to being a halfback or forward because the ball rarely came close to the goal without the ball-hog forwards of my team trying to rescue it.

At camp, most of my time on the soccer field was devoted to "pantsing" my bunkmates. That is, as they stood, carefully tracking the movement of the ball, I'd creep up behind them and yank their shorts to their ankles, then watch the terror as it worked its way across their faces. "Jesus on a muffin!" Kate had hollered, frantically recovering her shorts. "Ooh, you just wait. You're so gonna get yours, Klein!" I kept the drawstring of my shorts double knotted.

Playing defense afforded me the ability to putter around for most of the activity period, saving my energy for the occasional runaway goal attempt, when I'd burst toward the ball, punting it clear across the field, over the heads of my teammates, making me appear quite skilled. Good, even, despite the fact that my idea of trapping was falling on someone. "Ball gymnastics," "3 vs. 1 play," and "possession games" were skills I wouldn't develop until much later in life—my penalty-kicking dating life. Still, I was tired of always playing it safe. I decided next time we played, I'd be on the offense.

I was still sitting on the ground, panting, when I heard someone clapping in the distance. I looked through the orange netting of the goal, toward a wall of cypress trees just behind it. There was a narrow path between two of the trees, a shortcut from the fields to the pool and lake. No one was there. Maybe it was the ghost of Cropsy, applauding my strides toward revenge. Or maybe it was a hunger hallucination.

I wasn't wearing my watch but figured the dining hall might now be open for brunch. I clawed my way up off the grass and began to head toward it when Adam came bounding through the trees. His head was down, and he was wheezing a John Mellencamp song aloud. His body tilted forward as he jogged in small heavy steps, clapping midlyric. "You make it [*clap, clap*] hurt so good." He continued to run following the frontier of trees, his winded breathing audible from midfield. When he reached the dirt road behind the dining hall, he threw his fists in the air, then spread them on his knees as he stopped to catch his breath. When he removed his headphones and realized he wasn't alone, his body jerked back.

"My God, how long have you been standing there?" The front of his shirt was stained with sweat the shape of a tornado.

"Long [*clap, clap*] enough," I said.

"You heard that, huh?"

"Yup."

"That's pretty embarrassing."

"Yup."

"You're not supposed to agree with me!" We both laughed, looking at each other, and then the ground. Then we drifted toward the dining hall together. I couldn't believe the moment was happening. And that it had a sound track.

BRUNCH WAS SERVED FROM EIGHT TO NOON. CAMPERS were invited to show up as they pleased. It was the one day of the week we could sleep in, when cabins weren't inspected, when we weren't obligated to sit with our division in the dining hall. Our only responsibility was participating in the all-campus cleanup at one o'clock.

During rest hour on Saturday afternoons, we were handed Sunday brunch menus, a sheet of paper listing food items and their associated caloric values. We were instructed to check off eight hundred calories' worth of food. It didn't matter if our selections were nutritiously unbalanced. We could eat like old women who dressed in purple and ate nothing but a pickle and a block of government cheese, or select two cheese omelets and nothing else. We could feast on three breakfast patties, a large segment of cantaloupe, and a tablespoon of Concord grape jelly if we so chose. We'd spend most of rest hour calculating our options, strategizing how to make the calories go the distance. The key was originality.

While a peanut butter and jelly sandwich was on the menu for 350 calories, that's not how it would be ingested. I'd mark off the sandwich along with a few additional items, and when the time to eat came, I'd smear a slice of the bread (40 calories) with one tablespoon of the peanut butter (95 calories), and then affix slices from one small banana (90 calories). The banana-nutter sandwich wasn't exactly on the Yanisin menu, but it found a place on my dining tray. I'd dollop the second tablespoon of peanut butter (95 calories) into a paper cup (which toward the end I'd tear apart, enabling me to reach every last smear of peanut butter), then add the contents of a single serving of chocolate pudding (100 calories). To finish the course, I'd smash two graham cracker squares (60 calories) into the cup, creating a homespun peanut butter cup: dessert number 1. I'd decorate the other slice of bread (40 calories) with the tablespoon of strawberry jam (50 calories) and one cup of freshly sliced strawberries (50 calories). Ah, the poor man's shortcake. It was a makeshift three-course meal totaling 620 calories, leaving me an additional 180 calories for an inventive amuse-bouche or possibly a refreshing palate cleanser. Crushed ice, a tablespoon of honey, a carpaccio of cucumber.

In the camp brochure, beside "improved self-image" and "meaningful social interactions," they ought to have added, "while honing math skills and making memories that last a lifetime." Sitting beside Adam at the dining table, I regretted my mathematical decisions. I'd been so despondent Saturday afternoon by the events of the cookout that I had locked in a morning of mild: farmer cheese, bran flakes, milk, whole-wheat toast, and a Styrofoam bowl of plain yogurt.

Adam forked through two flapjacks as I poked at my cereal with a spoon.

"You're not up this early every morning, are you?" I asked, hoping he was, so we could spend more time together.

"God, no. It's just, I've gotta start training for football, for when I get back to school."

"Ah," I said, nodding as if I understood the importance of morning miles. "What position?" He could have said anything. It was like asking, "Oh, what part?" when someone mentioned they lived in Alaska.

"Nose tackle."

"Is that really a position?" It sounded like a vulgar habit.

"Yeah, it's part of the defensive line, but I'm thinking of switching positions this year. Ya know?"

I most certainly did.

LATER THAT NIGHT, I WAS ALREADY BEGINNING TO FEEL sore, and I liked it. I reached far back into my cubby for the pair of "goal" Big John–brand jeans I'd packed in my trunk at the start of summer thinking they might fit. My quadriceps hurt climbing into them, but that's as far as they'd go—to my quads. Despite having unsuccessfully tried them on only a few days before, I thought I'd be slimmer because I'd been so good, because everything was beginning to hurt. With the running, the diarrhea, and the bran, I just thought there'd be some immediate results. Oh, well. I got dressed and headed to the rec hall for Counselor Skit Night.

Before the skits began, Adam handed me a yellow piece of paper tucked into itself, a small fat triangle. "Don't read it until later," he said before dashing back to the bench where his division was seated. It happened so fast; I didn't have time to read his face or pick up subtle cues from his body language. I couldn't tell if I was now holding good or bad news.

I pinched the edges of the letter, flipping it in my hands. As the counselors impersonated campers on stage, I pretended to pay attention. I laughed when everyone else did, even strained for an improved view of the skit. But really, all I wanted to see was what Adam had written in his note. I sorted through the possibilities of what it might say. My immediate hope was it conveyed that he was falling in love with me already! He wanted me to be his girlfriend, to wear his football jersey! He couldn't wait to see me again!

As the counselors performed a choreographed sketch to the song "Food, Glorious Food," new thoughts plagued me. What if the note was a declaration that he could sense I liked him, but he wasn't interested in being anything but friends? He hadn't wanted to embarrass me with a conversation, so he'd handed me a note and darted away. My shoulders tightened when I considered the possibility that his letter might ask if I'd put in a good word with Grayson for him. What if he didn't like me at all?

By the time the counselors were on their knees, with their bowls outstretched singing for piled peaches and cream, my mind had spun a tale of rejection. I was convinced he thought I was too shy for him. I hadn't really said much when we were together, and now there'd be no *us*. He'd never know how intensely I yearned for him to be my boyfriend. At least, I thought, my pain wouldn't be broadcast to the whole of camp. I'd held my fondness for him close to me, just as I'd swallow and stow the rejection bound within this yellow triangle, silently, in furtive glances across a dining hall where only hours before we'd been sharing brunch.

I'd guessed enough and couldn't draw out the suspense any longer. At the close of the evening activity, when everyone emptied onto the rec hall steps and threaded their way to the canteen for diet soda slushies, I stole away to my cabin so I could read the letter privately. I locked myself in a bathroom stall, sat cross-legged on the bowl, and loosened the triangular note. It was a single piece of paper, but there was writing on both sides. I turned the letter over and examined the back, hoping for a clue about the contents in the closing. Would he sign with "Love" or "From"? Apparently neither; he'd simply signed his name. I began to read it backward, from his closing remarks, but I became flustered and started at the beginning.

Adam Jackson Fink thought I was beautiful.

And just like that, my whole summer changed. The day had begun in that exact bathroom stall, unable to sleep, dreading the days to come, and by nightfall my restlessness originated from elsewhere.

The following night, Adam asked if I'd take a walk with him. He tentatively reached for my hand, just my pinky at first, and I smiled, gripping his hand back. Conversation turned toward our hometowns, favorite music, schools, and our parents. He apologized for his sweaty hands.

The evening turned cool beneath a black sky, and we sat on the arts and crafts porch, looking out at the stars before curfew. Arts and crafts was housed in a converted Dutch barn, with a breezeway that led to a shingled porch. We took shelter there during sun storms. Summer love, first kisses, crushes, and overblown breakups slipped through the wooden planks of its threshing floors. From its steps, later in the summer, when we were an official couple, Adam would stay behind, watching as I made my way up Girls' Hill. "I'm crazy about you, Steph," he'd shout from the porch, his voice rising with his tiptoed stance. And I'd bark back, "It's Stephanie. I hate Steph," with a smile of amusement as I backpedaled my way into a jog. And from that point on, he called me "Klein," just as Kate did. And I loved that, along with another hundred or so things I found completely endearing about him.

On the evening he first held my hand and led me to the arts and crafts porch, he loaned me his sweatshirt to keep warm, and I slept with it that night, gripping handfuls in a thrilled disbelief. I tried returning it at the flagpole the next morning, but he insisted I keep it. Love smelled like Fahrenheit cologne. We were a couple. Adam Jackson Fink! I couldn't believe it.

We passed long-winded letters between activity periods and meals. Carrying his unopened notes had its own pleasure, a joy so intense it almost pained me. I wanted so much to rip through his letters, to devour every word, but I'd enjoy it longer if I took my time to open it. I'd peek at the beginning, then fold it closed before my eyes had a chance to take in more.

> I just said goodnight to you, but I feel like I want to talk to you some more. I've gotten to the point where I dread saying goodnight and walking away, like it was our last night together. I feel so lonely on my way back to my cabin, wishing you were with me.

I wanted to read his notes right when I got them, but I tried to hold off to savor the experience. And then I'd reread a letter throughout the day, keeping it close to me, tucked into a sock.

> I've never felt this strong about anyone ever before. I have a real feeling that we can make it work over the year, although I'll probably have withdrawal symptoms from not being able to see you every morning.

Only a few days after that first Sunday brunch, Adam and I were sitting in the movie shack with the rest of our division watching *Ghostbusters* when I swore he used his finger to write I LOVE YOU on my palm. And at the end of the week, just before Family Weekend began, he handed me a mix tape he'd made for me. He'd listed all the song tracks on the back of the cassette case, modifying the Police's song title to "Every Little Thing Steph Does Is Magic." There was an asterisk beside "Storybook Love" from the *Princess Bride* sound track. And the mix culminated with "Hurts So Good," which seemed to be true about everything except love.

thirteen

ARE YOU THERE, GOD? IT'S ME, POUND CAKE

Dear Diary,

Hey, you know I'm wondering . . . are you a boy or a girl diary? No, I'm serious. If you're a girl, you're my best friend. A diary is yourself & your best friend is always yourself. And if you're a guy, well, then, you're my boyfriend. I like to think of you as a girl, though. If you're a guy, you've got to be kind of gay. Look how you're dressed! And if you're a guy, then a book is my boyfriend—how sad!

IT WAS MIDSUMMER, FAMILY WEEKEND, AND WHEN MY parents inquired if there was anything specific I'd like for them to bring, I asked for only three things: chocolate chip cookie dough ice cream, Mom's roasted red peppers with toasted pignoli nuts over crusty Italian bread, and Charmin toilet paper. I'd have asked for clothes, but I didn't know what size I'd be. I was down twenty-two pounds.

In preparation for the weekend, the contents of our cubbies were meticulously stacked, as if each item had been folded over a board for uniformity. The floors had been swept five times, the porches cleared; the bathrooms smelled of bleach. Everyone and everything was positioned to show their Sunday best, even on a Saturday. We wore our slimmest outfits, and the finest banquet of foods were prepped for lunch—foods they hadn't served us all summer, deli cold cuts arranged in meat rainbows on platters, mayonnaise salads, cubes of cheese, and fruits and vegetables carved into animals. There was a watermelon cut to resemble a dolphin, green bell pepper halves tooled into toads, a pen of papaya swine, and a field of radish mice. Counselors' smiles were wider, their voices hospitable in a way only the prospect of a gratuity could inspire.

Most campers hoped to wait for their families by the main office, watching for their vehicles to roll in, but the camp restricted us to our cabin porches to help contain the chaos of the day. I'd been granted permission to wait with Lea at her cabin since it was stationed at the foot of the hill, but I wasn't in a rush. I sat on my bed with an Etch A Sketch for most of the morning, savoring the ability to relax. I felt sorry for the kids whose parents lived too far away to visit. Not only were they unable to see their families, but they were actually forced to exercise, to follow a typical schedule. They had already been coerced from their cabins and assembled into a group of different ages, performing drills on the soccer field. Their only respite in the weekend was a field trip to the Berkshire movie theater and mall, where they were permitted a child-size popcorn, no butter, and diet soda.

Parents residing closest to camp were the first to wind their way to our cabins. I ambled over to Lea's cabin noticing all the pallid office legs in shorts with sneakers, worn, it seemed, for the first time. Ace bandages rigged around knees. Shirts already marked with sweat. One heavyset young father negotiated his way to the Lower Camp valley with the aid of a ski pole.

"Neph, who told him we had skiing here?"

"No one, Lea; that's his cane."

"Oh," she said, sounding slightly disappointed, as if she'd momentarily hoped there were hidden indoor ski slopes beside the bowling lanes in town.

I saw firsthand why there were so many fat camp champs at Yanisin each summer. The majority of parents visiting were just as obese, if not more so, than their children. Campers hadn't only inherited their parents' lips and legs but also their eating and exercise habits. It's why Yanisin provided parents with a detailed schedule of the day's activities, including two informational sessions where parents would be what Kate and I liked to call "debeefed" about the Yanisin mission. Families were invited to participate in activities, to sign out a boat on the lake or join in a game of touch football. They were also free to liberate their children from the campgrounds for the day and night. My overnight bag was already packed.

Lea and I watched as a young camper careened from her porch upon recognizing her family, all of them bumping together, rocking in a group hug. They asked her to spin for them. "We're just so proud of you!" Hands over mouths. Outcries of joy. Tender Tanglewood moments laced with tears.

You saps.

We saw it happen again and again.

"What's taking them so long?" Lea whined, her knee bouncing.

"New York weekend traffic," I said flatly, remembering visiting days of my past, where fathers broke the ice by discussing alternate routes, optimal freeways, and secretive side roads.

After sharing a private family reunion, campers clutched their parents' hands, eager to introduce them to their friends, counselors, cubbies, and beds. "And this is where we hang our bathing suits to dry, and this is where I fell that time I wrote you about. Ooh, and this is where I brush my teeth." Everyone was proud.

"This is where you . . . uh, shower?" Proud, and a little disgusted.

"Eh, you get used to it," campers would say with a shrug, oblivious to the fact that they'd aligned themselves more closely with the standards of camp than with the people who raised them.

A young mother of a girl in Lea's cabin arrived toting cases of sugar-free gum, Crystal Light, and a bag of sweatpants in the pastel shades of sorbet. She was tan and fit and wore clothes too youthful for her age and too warm for the weather: a denim jacket pimpled with silver studs and rhinestones, airbrushing on the back. Her daughter's eyes widened when she discovered a bag filled with glow sticks, water guns, spray bottles, and tubes of flavored lip gloss. "Now be sure to share," the mother urged, "these are for your friends, too." Ruda didn't have friends. The girls called her Roto-Rooter to her face. And when the weekend ended, she'd try to horde all the items for herself.

"Yeah, but I heard your mom tell you to share," someone would say.

"Well," Ruda would argue, holding tight to the bag of goods, "I still get to decide."

Other parents straggled in, fathers quick to ask if it was safe to enter, fearful one of us might be exposed. It was the one time all summer—aside from during the delivery of our duffels and trunks on opening day—where boys were permitted inside our cabins. Brothers were welcomed to sit on our beds, to use our bathrooms to change into their swim trunks.

One father in Lea's cabin wore a straw cowboy hat and in the back, just where the crown met the brim, he'd set a pair of mirrored sunglasses. He joked to us that he had eyes in the back of his head. Then he quickly whipped around to prove it, following up with a "Yuk, yuk, yuk." He was with his daughters, one Lea's age and one a bit older than I was. The older one gestured with her hands, cocking back her thumbs, shooting blanks at her father with her forefingers. And when he turned away, she stuck the barrel of her handgun into her mouth and pretended to explode, a gesture I assumed she'd made just as frequently as he'd joked about his second set of eyes. It all seemed rehearsed.

When Lea thought she'd made out the bodies of our parents, she gripped my arm and jolted upright. "Is that them?" She strained to see.

"Take a chill pill." I rolled my eyes and glanced over my shoulder, raising my head slightly, as if I'd just sniffed. Then I squinted to make out two figures in the distance. They weren't overweight. The woman was thinner than the man.

"It's them!" Lea screamed, careering off the porch.

I decided to get up, smoothing the creases in my shorts, as I watched the figures run toward Lea. All that was missing was a wild field of poppies and the swelling of orchestra music. It'd be funny, I thought, if it weren't them. They'd all realize too late, and because of the velocity of their bodies, it'd be harder to stop than to go ahead and hug. "Oh, excuse me," they'd each say, backing away, "but hi anyway." Then the parents would anticlimactically reunite with their rightful offspring, making a mental note that Lea was much thinner.

But as the figures drew closer, I realized it was indeed our parents. I had no idea how much I'd missed them until I saw Poppa's bald head and strawberry blond mustache, Mom's long golf shorts and crooked smile.

I couldn't play it cool any longer. I leapt off the porch and sprinted toward them, flying toward Mom with my arms outstretched, nearly tackling her to the ground. "Whoa," she said with a startled laugh. When she felt that I wasn't letting go, she held me tighter, then patted my back. My body shook. "What?" she said softly in surprise, "Are you . . . are you crying?"

I pulled myself away and wiped my face. My voiced cracked. "I missed you." Then I lunged for Poppa, who, once he heard my shortness of breath, began to cry, too.

"Mommy, you're so skinny," Lea said.

"Right?" I'd forgotten what it felt like to hug a thin person. "There's nothing to hold on to," I added.

"I know," Lea said. "It feels so strange to get both my arms all the way around."

"Well, look at you two," Mom said. "I just can't get over how skinny you both look!"

"Really?" I asked, stepping away so they could get a better look. "Or are you just saying that?"

"Well, let's see," Poppa said, "I can always tell from the back. That's the true test." So like all the campers who'd gone before us, Lea and I spun around.

"You really do look fantastic," he said. "I'm really proud of you both. Keep up the good work."

"Thanks." Lea and I smiled at each other.

"This is so emotional," he said, removing his aviators to blink away his tears. And this was only our hello; I wasn't sure I wanted to see how we'd handle our good-byes.

NESTLED IN THE BERKSHIRE HILLS OF MASSACHUSETTS, the storybook town of Lenox was congested with campers and their families. While Yanisin allowed for field trips to Tanglewood (summer home of the Boston Symphony Orchestra), we'd never explored farther than its telephone booths and meticulously groomed lawns. My limited view of the historic towns of Lenox, Lee, and Stockbridge had been from a bus, through a murky window that had been jammed shut. Now shopping with my family in Lenox, I'd finally get a taste for the town. It tasted, I decided, like zucchini bread. Streets were lined with quaint shops one might find featured on a Christmas card tented with snow. The stores offered natural soaps, heirloom furnishings, and American crafts. *Adult stuff.* Antiques, pottery, and patchwork. *Sucky adult stuff.*

"This place is *bor*-ing," I said with a roll of my eyes. "There's nothing to even try on." Mom looked as if she were about to correct me. "Besides hats," I slipped in. "It's all crocheted planters and farty crap."

"Well, here, what about this store?" Mom said of a shop named Tanglewool.

"Mom, please."

"Yeah, Mom, please," Lea repeated.

"So, now what?" Poppa said mostly to Mom, hoping she had a list of alternatives in her congested shoulder bag.

We stood on the sidewalk shrugging, and in the silence of the decision, I wondered who'd be the first to suggest, "Well, should we just eat, then?"

"You sure you don't want to try on more hats?" Mom urged. "Stephanie, you looked so good in that last one with the purple flower."

"I'd rather die."

"Yolanda, let's focus," Poppa said, jingling the car keys.

"How about this one?" Lea shouted, now a few storefronts ahead of us.

I walked to check it out, skeptical, and upon seeing the display of crystals and tie-dyes, I said, "Well, if you want, I suppose we can go in." I held the door open for my family, adding, "At least it's air-conditioned."

I headed straight for the Levi's cutoffs, racing through the sizes, grabbing a half dozen pairs, then some T-shirts, an embroidered belt, and, upon Poppa's suggestion, a colorful hooded Baja poncho. I closed the changing room door behind me and placed my selections on a bench. There was something incredibly liberating about tie-dye. I couldn't believe I'd gone so long without wearing any of mine.

When I turned to undress, I saw my reflection and froze. I'd forgotten all that time we'd been shopping—in card stores, browsing through artsy posters and novelty items—to even look for it. And for some reason I wasn't, just then, expecting to see it. For the first time in over a month, I was standing in front of a full-length mirror.

Despite constantly scrutinizing my skin and applying makeup in a handheld mirror all summer, the first thing I noticed about my body was my face. With such a small mirror, I was never able to step away and examine myself from afar. But in the dressing room, I had a sense of proportion and could see everything but my feet. In that moment, my hands seemed to be the only things that were really mine. They reached up to a face, and studied its landscape, softly patting, feeling for distinct features: the plane of a cheek, foothill of a nose, slope of a lip, just as I'd seen the blind do on television. I pushed on my skin as if it were putty. "This is so weird."

"Well, you chose those clothes," Mom said through the door, waiting for me to come out and show her what I'd been trying on.

I felt for the rise I saw in the mirror: cheekbones! This, I thought, is what thin feels like. My chin was the best part. Woo hoo, I had one! *Just one.* And it was pointy without having to strain. "Oh my God," I must have said aloud once I pulled off my shirt and recognized—could it be? Collarbones!

"What? What is it?" Mom said through the door, sounding panicked.

"What?"

"You just said, 'Oh my God.' Is everything okay?"

"I have bones, Mom!"

"Of course you have bones. What kind of drugs do they have back there?"

I turned sideways and sucked in my stomach. I kicked off my shorts and checked for a rear view, but there wasn't much of one. I was sure there was still plenty of ass to go around; I just couldn't see it in the mirror. Now in my underwear and bra, with my feet shoulder-width apart, toes turned out, I did a grand plié, bending my knees until my thighs were horizontal with the floor. It was a position they had us repeat, pulse, and then hold, "feeling the burn!" during calisthenics. And there they were. Inner-thigh muscles, right behind the chub rub.

Mom knocked on the door. "Come on, let me in. I have stuff I want to try on, too, and there are no more rooms." I cracked the door open, sticking out just my head. "Did you find anything you liked?" she asked.

"Everything," I said with an enormous smile.

She wiggled her way into the dressing room with me.

It's not as though my body had become completely unrecognizable; in fact, it was mostly similar to what it had been before I'd left home for camp. While my measurements had changed, my proportions remained exactly the same; everything just narrowed and came to the surface. Thin wasn't what I'd expected it to be.

When dieting, I always imagined I was striving to become something *other*. I never compared myself with the glossy girls in my *YM* magazine. I wanted to look like Suzanne Somers. To be the sexy one who made boys drool and trip over things. The way I looked at any given moment was not at all how I pictured myself to look once I'd become thin. I imagined my hips wouldn't flare the way they did, that the lines of my body would be straighter. All those evenings spent listening to my hypnosis tapes, I'd envisioned a slightly concave stomach and hipbones. Monotone Man asked me to picture myself lying on a beach. I was to feel the sun as it passed over my body, my right shoulder at first, then down to my elbow, hands, across my stomach. The sun's warmth, he'd assured me, was melting away the fat. "As much as you want," he'd said. "Take your time, let it wash over you." Then he asked me to keep my eyes closed, to leave my beach and examine this slimmer me in a three-way mirror. "What do your ankles look like? Your wrists? Take care to notice every detail."

The thin me I imagined didn't look like me at all. For starters, thin me tanned easily and didn't have a forehead so wide it was called a fivehead. Thin was well mannered, used monogrammed soap, and had vibrant eyes in the spectrum between yellow and blue. Ignoring tie-dye, the thin me I'd imagined wore a sheer white sundress and was most always barefoot, though when shoes were required, she looked best in flats.

In my waking hours, my general thoughts of what thin looked like had nothing to do with me. Whatever the shade, hair was most certainly straight, silky, and pulled into a loose braid before sleep. Skinny women with curly manes were crazy, inflexibly religious, or social workers, whereas thin looked like a Sun-In commercial. Thin could pull off pigtails, mismatched clothes, and an atrocious name like Gertrude, Bernice, or Mildred. If you're fat *and* have the name Tallulah, you might as well snap your bra, give yourself a wedgie, and tape a KICK ME sign to your back fat.

Balletic movement and proper posture were, of course, slender essentials. Thin rested naturally in third position, the heel of one foot against the instep of the other. She was a strong swimmer, brilliant at tennis, and rounded the edges of cliffs in an Alfa Romeo convertible, a white silk scarf curling in the wind. For the thin, expressing regret seemed excessive, yet little restraint need be exercised when indulging in drinking, gambling, or recklessness of the heart. Thin looked good in red and could be a bitch, and people would still like her.

I hadn't only trusted thin to give me straighter teeth and a sunnier disposition; I'd expected it to amend my body type—to square my shoulders, lengthen my calves, and straighten my hips. But as I studied my reflection, I realized it was still me in there, only smaller. I wasn't so much disappointed as I was surprised. The Levi's I'd chosen fit. Size 31. I wasn't thin, but I was at least getting there. I roped the belt through.

"Stephanie," Mom said as she eyed my body in the fitting room mirror, "you need to buy more than just Levi's and a few tie-dyes. We need to get you fitted for a new brassiere."

"Do you have to say 'brassiere'?" I asked as I examined the way my bra rode up over the bottom of my breasts, giving me a reverse quadriboob. When I was heavier, and my bras were too restrictive, my cups runneth over, creating a visible line that appeared to dissect each breast crosswise, thereby giving me quadriboob. But now the fabric of my bra had worn thin and bagged in the cups, reminding me of the vertical lines of an aging mouth. Thin white strands of broken elastic frayed along the straps rendering the garment useless. "Can't you say 'bra,' or 'over-the-shoulder-boulder-holder,' or something?"

"Fine, you need new *bras,*" she said as she raced to button a hemp shirt over hers. "Here, you want to try one of mine?" She made like she was about to unhook it, but I knew better. Mom avoided being naked in front of others at all costs, even Lea and me.

"I'm not *that* small!"

"I know it. They're bad, right?" she asked, now looking down at her chest as she ran a flat hand across the front of the shirt. I pulled on one of the tie-dyes and tucked it into the cutoffs.

"Can I wear this out of the store?" I asked.

"More like an over-the-shoulder-pebble-holder," Mom said, still focused on her breasts. "They're like little Raisinets. Eh, better than prunes, I guess."

"Mom, can I?"

"I don't see why not. Hey, those look good." She reached toward the bench where I'd discarded the cutoffs that were too small. "Here, let me try a pair."

"They'll be way too big on you."

She wiggled out of her golf shorts and stood in a pair of thick white underwear that made me think of tennis. I sat on the bench and watched her watch herself. "Bad, right?" Mom asked me through the mirror as she used her hands to shake the backs of her thighs. "Oh, so bad. Stephanie, what am I going to do?" She bit down on her lower lip and continued to slap the sides of her thighs, as if she were calling a dog.

When we were at home, after dinner, Lea and I would regularly wiggle into the middle of our parents' bed as Mom did needlepoint or flipped through a magazine while Poppa watched a ball game or consulted *The Merck Manual* in hopes of diagnosing his latest ailment. Lea would rub Poppa's head with a paper towel, and I'd massage Mom's feet with Keri lotion. Her corns were big; I'd try to pick them off, and whenever I felt like I was about to make serious progress, she'd yell *Ouch! That hurt!* as she pulled away her foot. I'd inch up between everyone, making a family sandwich, leaning on Mom's shoulder. I could sometimes feel the breeze from her pages as they slipped too fast out from under her thumb. It felt like a whisper. And when I closed my eyes, I imagined linked train cars clicking past.

When I opened them, I'd see that Poppa was using one of his free hands to massage Mom, kneading the back of the thigh he could reach. "Why are you doing that?" I remember asking him.

"Because she likes it," he'd said. Then I looked to Mom, who nodded and said, "It breaks up the fat." I'm not sure I have a single memory of Mom in bed where she wasn't either doing leg lifts or having her thighs rubbed.

"I'm disgusted. Just disgusted," she whispered to herself in the fitting room mirror. Despite being only a size six, she pulled on a pair of the cutoffs I'd rejected and buttoned the fly. When she took a step back and tilted her head to decide what she thought, the shorts fell to her ankles. "Well, they were too youthful for me anyway," she declared. I felt stupid for thinking I looked good. She was slender and shapely and couldn't stand the sight of her own reflection.

"I hate to say it, Stephanie, but you've got my genes, and as you keep losing weight, it won't come from your saddlebags. Wanna take a guess where it'll come from?" She motioned to her breasts again, as she continued to dress into her own clothes. "Duds, honey. We've got duds." Then she looked us both in the mirror and gave two thumbs down while making a fart noise with her mouth.

WHILE I WAS NEVER BUXOM, MY BREASTS WERE LARGER than Mom's even at eleven years of age, and back then, I'd have sooner eaten a fish eyeball than have anything to do with puberty. I remember learning the word. "Puberty." I sounded it out, noticing that it mostly sounded like "pew," not at all unlike "Pew, you stink!" I didn't want to acknowledge that I was indeed going through puberty, so I refused to wear deodorant. Deodorant meant your body was changing, so I'm pretty confident I stunk. On nights when I slept over at my friend Hillary's house, her parents had us take showers, insisting we reeked up the house. While I was wrapped securely in a towel, Hillary's father would give my pits a whiff test. "Nah, you better get back in. That one still smells a little." Puberty wasn't just awkward; it seemed to make everyone weird. And upon further inspection of the word, I realized it was a cross between "pubic" and "liberty." But there was nothing liberating about getting breasts before anyone else.

At the time, I'd highlighted passages in Judy Blume books. I was thankful my parents hadn't read what I was reading, that they didn't really understand what I was thinking as I turned a page, waiting for dinner to be ready. Those books became my private teachers. And as fascinated as I was by Margaret, and her pleas to God to get Philip Leroy to dance with her, I didn't relate to her wanting bigger breasts or her period. I was eleven, in sixth grade, and I had it all: breasts, body odor, and blood. I didn't need to do exercises hoping things would sprout.

The bigger the better
The tighter the sweater
The more the boys will scream!

It didn't work that way for fat girls. I was embarrassed I'd developed and refused to wear a bra until seventh grade, when I noticed, in gym class, that some of the other girls were finally wearing training bras. *What the hell's a training bra training you for exactly?* I remember thinking. In name alone, it implied I'd be learning a new skill or job. Maybe it was like training wheels, only it kept my boobs from falling to the ground. I wasn't really sure about the implication, but I knew, without doubt, I was due for one. So one day after school, I told Mom I was going to go shopping with Hillary for "underwear" and asked for some money. She raised an eyebrow.

As an adult, I understand how a mother would want to be a part of this moment in her daughter's life, to tell her about the first time she went bra shopping, or to impart some motherly wisdom using words like "blossom" and "womanhood." I was thankful she hadn't done any of these things. Just before handing me the money she added, "And I expect some change."

Hillary and I trooped off to Great Shapes together. "If we see anyone we know, we'll pretend we're shopping for bathing suits." It was a plan.

The salesperson behind the counter was a woman who, when asked to catalog three things she could never live without, would most likely list vodka, a curling iron, and her girdle. She had a broad stance and assertive hands and insisted she help us. I imagined her hands pulling the elastic on my back, snapping it against me in a quick movement, a sting, then shaking her head, repeating in a Russian accent, "Good. Now, gells, vat else?"

Maybe she feared we would ruin her orderly piles as we nervously giggled and touched everything. "First, we need to get some measurements," she said as she held the length of a slippery tape measure between her outstretched hands.

"You go," I insisted as I pushed Hillary forward. She didn't seem to mind, as her chest was as flat as a skillet.

I was fingering a pale pink bra decorated with a lacy ribbon when Hillary dropped to the floor. The saleswoman and I stared at her. She hadn't fainted; she'd ducked down and buried her head beneath the skirt of a table showcasing folded pajama sets.

"It's Mrs. Lieberman!" Hillary whispered in an enunciated panic. The saleswoman refolded the pink bra I'd been handling, then gripped the tape measure and pinned it to me. Mrs. Lieberman was a regular substitute teacher who wore large Laura Biagiotti sunglasses and sounded like Harvey Fierstein. She liked to "kibbitz" before class and make us think she was our friend. She was the sort of woman you pictured bra shopping, somehow, fiddling through hanging bras, waving an assistant over to fetch her things in other colors. I actually liked her, but I didn't want her to know we were bra shopping. What if she'd announce it in our next class? "Oh, so great just bumping into you and Hillary like that, Stephanie. How cute. Your first bras," I imagined she would say with her back to the class as she drew two small triangles on the blackboard, then curved lines for straps, and a bow.

I wanted to crouch down too, but it was too late. I was trapped, with my arms outstretched like an opened umbrella, and I wondered if I'd always have such bad luck. The saleswoman was measuring the distance between my nipples. I remember this part, specifically. She took the thin metal tip of the tape measure and held it against one nipple, touching me only slightly, and then pulled the tape taught until it reached the other one. It felt as if I were being fitted for eyeglasses. She told me I was a 36B just as Mrs. Lieberman approached.

"What," Mrs. Lieberman rasped, "are you doing on the floor, Hillary?"

She was trying to hide from it too, this pubic liberty that had been thrust upon us by a god to which some girls prayed. I wasn't one of those girls, but I evoked his name in that moment.

"Oh, dear God," I managed to say. Then Hillary and I smiled at Mrs. Lieberman and giggled, each of us praying that the moment would remain private. And it has. Until now.

Training bras assume you're going to grow. It's practice at being a woman, knowing one day you'll leave it folded behind in a childhood drawer along with the feelings of being painfully self-conscious and uncomfortable. You'll "bloom" into a confident woman, self-assured, who takes purposeful strides with her shoulders pulled back, head held high. And when people compliment you, you'll take a moment to hear it, then accept it graciously. You won't bat it away. The awkwardness and mortification that accompany shopping for a first bra, the discontent with your reflection, are appropriate feelings for an adolescent, a woman in training, to have. Mom's lack of cleavage wasn't the only thing I inherited. She was still in training, and I was training to grow up to be just like her.

•

"POPPA?" LEA ASKED ONCE WE'D LEFT THE HIPPIE STORE, "Is it time yet?"

"Time for what?"

"Ugh," Lea huffed, throwing her hands down in a fluster, "you said before, when you were signing us out, in the camp office—"

"What did I say?" He crouched to be at her eye level.

"When I asked if we could leave camp and eat ice cream, you said, 'Now is not the time, Lea.' So? Is it time yet?"

It took him a beat to understand what she was saying, but once he had, Poppa laughed with his whole body. And we watched as his entire head flushed, which made us laugh, too. With our new psychedelic purchases, we all piled into the car for a scenic drive through the Berkshires, destination unknown but certain to include ice cream.

THE CAMP HAD SERVED US PANCAKES FOR BREAKFAST, which most campers had the good sense to refuse, not so much to save calories but to save room. Who wanted to fill up on permissible when there was a whole county brimming with prohibited to be had? Breakfast being the most important meal and all, I chose to eat mine. I didn't want to be ravenous come lunchtime. And when lunchtime approached, in fact, I wasn't ravenous, but I ate as if I were. Caesar salad and every last garlic crouton. A crock of vegetable potpie fitted with a pastry hat. Bites of this and that. And now we'd come to four spoons at the end.

The ice cream shop had a line of patrons that filed out the door. Many were from Yanisin. Parents stood in line while their kids pressed their noses against the glass cases up front, trying to decide on a flavor. Or four. The intention had been that we'd all share something, but now that we were here, in the face of so many choices, we decided that wouldn't be happening.

After choosing mine, I watched as the adults joked with one another. "What can we do?" their bodies communicated in shrugs. Poppa relayed Lea's "now is not the time" story to a father who looked like the side of a truck. He was wearing a black button-down shirt, breezy, with red and orange flames rising up from the hem. I wondered whose father he was. His hair was long, dark, and curly, with a mustache that closely resembled a strip of pubic hair that I'd seen in my confiscated magazine. Then I wondered if I'd meet any of the parents of the girls in my cabin. Was Kate's mom going to come?

Throughout the weekend Mom and Poppa met a few of my friends and their families when we'd bump into them at a grocery store, everyone loading up on all we'd been denied over the past month. It was condoned binge shopping. All the parents, including my own, seemed to regard our obsession with scouting out food in a tolerant, sympathetic way. *Poor things.* It felt a lot like Halloween, when I was allowed to eat as much as I wanted for that one day, after which I was supposed to toss out the rest, returning to my "normal" cottage cheese life. Family Weekend, we all rationalized, was just that, a weekend. "It's not like you're going to eat this way once you're home. But this is a special occasion."

Perhaps there were parents focusing on how fast it took them as a family to paddle their way across the camp lake, but I hadn't seen it. What I witnessed was the way my friends' parents hooked them up with their favorite goodies, standing in ice cream shop lines and sitting in parking lot traffic just to provide what had been prohibited all summer. These were the same Let's-Make-A-Deal parents I'd heard about in our shaded nutrition sessions. They spent thousands of dollars to send their kids to camp, bribing them to lose weight with offers of new wardrobes, cash, and prizes valued at over 10 percent of their child's self-esteem, even slapped their kids' hands when they leaned in for seconds, padlocking cabinets and refrigerator doors. Even Poppa, the way he'd puffed out his cheeks at me when he thought I was eating too much of something. They were all suddenly okay with it. It was like receiving a cake with a file inside from the person who'd incarcerated us. And they chaperoned and enabled all of it, despite the money spent, because people bonded over food. It's what all us of knew. It's what we'd all practiced at home, and now our parents were able to bring it to us, that slice of home for which we'd all been yearning.

After bulldozing through my sundae I felt sick. With the first spoonful, I closed my eyes and felt the warmth and thickness of the fudge as it slipped around the cool silkiness of the ice cream. It was chewy. I waited for a release. I felt tense and anxious and spooned the rest in quickly. I didn't even want it anymore. It was too sweet and tasted the same for too long. And then it tasted like nothing.

"So, how is it?" Poppa asked me. With the spoon still in my mouth, I hummed a *mmm hhhhmmmm* for him, and he nodded his head, as if he were proud. He'd done what he came to do. "Well, enjoy it while it lasts," he said.

It was my only chance at sweets for the next three weeks, so I finished it. Relief washed over me once I was out of breath from cramming it all in. And after the immediate relief passed, a wave of panic crashed in. My saliva was heavy, a web caught in my throat. I thought about all that exercise I'd done, the mornings I was up early sweating and running up that damn Bitch Hill. And now I'd just undone it all. Eating was thrilling and wearisome at the same time.

Maybe, I thought as I raised the waist of my shorts to better accommodate a stomach roll that had been bulging up, I was being too uptight about the whole thing and needed to loosen up, live it up while I could. Mom and Poppa wouldn't urge me to enjoy it all if it was wrong to do. This was everything I'd craved for the past four weeks. One night, I think our cabin actually studied a flyer of all the flavors the shop had to offer. *What's wrong with you?* I thought.

I felt like the Jelly Donut Man from Fran's lecture. When she handed him that donut once he'd reached his goal weight, nodding her head that it was okay, he had permission, I bet he did eat the whole thing, despite his admission that it wasn't as good as he'd remembered. Because he didn't know when the opportunity would ever present itself again, someone giving him the thumbs-up to do exactly what he knew he shouldn't be doing.

fourteen Caught

Dear Dirty Di,

I spoke to Leigh a few days ago. I really, really miss her. She is the best! I love her. Life is pretty good—my hickey is gr-8. I love the world. Peace.

Love always,
Stephanie Tara

ORGANIZED RAIDS WERE RETARDED. LITERALLY. OUR counselors dragged them out for days, using the anticipation of the event to motivate exemplary behavior. Our DL Gina tried to entice us, announcing she had something special to share with the group.

"A real treat," she said. "And I might decide to tell you about it in the next day or so . . . *IF* none of you are late getting to activities." When it came to disclosing the details of this "special thing," she took her time, prolonging the suspense. "Well, I don't know," she exaggerated to another counselor, "do you think they deserve it?" It was like threatening us with coal the week before Christmas.

"I'm sure you've all been discussing it among yourselves all day, guessing what this special treat is." Ah, no. "And no, it's not a chance to enter the kitchen and eat as much as you can carry out." Some of the girls in my division actually giggled at this. We were sitting near the equipment shack eating our afternoon snack beneath the oak tree, and Gina paced our circumference, stopping to lean in closer: "But tonight, we're . . ."

Then she straightened up again, backing away, waiting for us to beg for her to continue. And some of the girls just played into it, like kindergarteners responsive to reverse psychology. *"Now, don't you smile!"* Ugh. I hated being treated like a child.

" . . . going on a raid!" The girls bounced, squealing and clutching one another's free hands. "Shhh. We don't want anyone else to know," Gina cautioned, as if our noise had consequences. Then she extended an empty garbage bag, insisting we all stand to pitch our nectarine pits.

Come nighttime, some of the girls actually dressed in black. Beulah was flustered. She began to hold herself, stoked at the idea of sneaking out in the middle of the night. What I mean by "hold yourself" is that she was so elated that she began to clutch at her vagina, like a young lady at a party, afraid to miss out on any of the excitement by excusing herself to use the potty.

"Ooh," she brayed, "I'm bringing this full tube of toothpaste, and I'm gonna squirt it in one of the boys' noses! Or in his hair!" Then she scampered off to her bed in little frantic steps, waving her toothpaste. "Stephanie," she stopped and turned to ask, "why aren't you wearing dark clothes? Aren't you afraid of getting caught?" She stood there in her Nancy and Ronald slippers, her eyes wide and blinking, waiting for my response.

"I'm all out," I moaned with an artificial frown.

"You can borrow some of mine," she panted.

"I'll take my chances."

I know. I was a bitch. Poor Beulah, so eager to help, so easily excitable. So, she never washed her crotch. There were worse things. Like . . . Well, there were worse things. The point is, why couldn't I just play along and enjoy it?

Because I was thirteen.

Harper used her finger to trace an X across her heart, swearing no one else knew they were leading us across camp in the middle of the night. "Shhh. Let's go through the woods, so no one catches us," she whispered loudly. And I watched as other campers hunkered down low, nervous they might get caught.

I didn't see what they were getting all excited about. Even the camp owners knew we were out. We might as well have spun our flashlights and yodeled.

Once we successfully made it to the boys' cabins without being "caught," Beulah and a few other girls who'd talked about dousing the boys in baby powder and coating them in shaving cream refused even to enter their bunks. Instead they spent the entire time toilet-papering a porch, a job for which it seemed one would have to beg for volunteers. I didn't join the decorating committee, and once I realized we wouldn't even be raiding Adam's cabin, I just stood by the basketball courts and watched. I had no interest in seeing how dirty I could make a boy. I wanted to slip into bed with one and see how dirty I could be.

To my delight, I wasn't the only one. In the dining hall a few nights later, Joy suggested we plan our own raid. She was dating a CIT named James and seemed to have been orchestrating the details since the start of summer.

"One thirty," she said with a mouthful of chicken.

"One thirty, what?"

Joy continued to chew, then looked sideways at my plate. "How'd you get a pepper?"

I glanced at my meal. A rice-stuffed wrinkled green pepper dotted with small cubes of tomato towered over a bar of soy-soaked tofu. "Oh," I declared, straightening my posture, "I'm a vegetarian."

"Since when?"

"Since I decided that even the chicken here doesn't taste like chicken." In the weeks since my parents' visit, my eating rituals had changed radically. I no longer ate as if I were blocking an opponent. I fanatically continued to fill up on water at the start of each meal, only now, as I silently counted to ten, I felt its voyage: the subtle swelling of my palate, the cold sting behind my breastbone, the relief that came when it sank into my stomach. The colder the better. I'd begun to suck on ice cubes and made chopsticks my utensil of choice.

"They're a diuretic," I had announced to our table at their unveiling as I made a display of clicking them together. Any gimmick that aided in weight loss, I mistakenly believed, was a diuretic. Using chopsticks made me work for my food, making each bite a decision. I methodically poked my way across a plate, foraging for a tweezerful of sustenance. It didn't matter what it was. I'd pick through slimy button mushrooms, leaky cauliflower florets, curds of tofu scramblers, even cottage cheese and Jell-O. I'd balance a morsel between the sticks, raise them to my mouth, then draw them inside, sucking each flavor. I'd sometimes close my mouth around the sticks, chewing ever so slightly on the wooden tips. "Wood enhances food's natural flavor," Mom had said over Family Weekend, as we overindulged at Truc Orient Express. On days I was particularly hungry, I'd chew them until they'd splinter and stick to my molars, then toss them away.

Sometimes I'd get all the way to the flagpole for lineup only to realize I'd forgotten them in the cabin, forcing me to beg Harper for permission to retrieve them. "Only if you're back before announcements begin," she'd warn as she tapped a finger on the face of her watch. If I thought I had enough time, I'd sprint back for them, all the way up Girls' Hill. If not, I'd just sulk my way through the meal. I needed my crutches.

"So one thirty's good for you, right?" Joy asked. "It's the perfect time to go. Counselors are back on campus and asleep by then."

I liked being lighter and empty. It felt a little like lust, a painful joy. When my hunger prevented me from falling asleep at night, I knew all I'd been doing to lose weight was working. Which is why I was all too happy to volunteer to be the one to stay up and wake Joy at 1:30 A.M. for our raid.

According to Joy, we couldn't just throw on some black clothing and hop into bed before lights out. Harper would've foiled our plan in seconds. Black was too obvious, Joy insisted. Instead, we'd disarm any suspicion by dressing in our brightest nightgowns. Barefoot, as if we'd actually planned to sleep through the night. All our necessities were set out in advance like metal instruments set upon a surgeon's tray. The dark loose outfits we'd throw over our nightgowns were stowed beneath our pillows. We loosened the laces of our work boots, setting them somewhere we'd easily locate them in the dark. Flashlights and sugar-free breath mints were at the ready.

I lay awake in the dark wondering if Adam would welcome my visit. What if he thought I was being too forward? Why hadn't he visited me at my cabin? Shit, what would I say if Kate woke up when it was time for me to dismount our bunk bed? What if she wanted to come?

I jerked awake, realizing I'd dozed off. I felt for my light-up watch: 2:02 A.M. After slipping on my dark sweats and socks, I eased my way off the bed as slowly as my arms would allow. As I made my way to Joy's bed, a floorboard creaked beneath me. I held still, certain the sound was loud enough to have woken someone. But nothing happened. I picked my way across the floor, deliberate with each step, and when I reached Joy's mattress and felt for her foot, I realized she wasn't there. I looked up, squinting. Had she gone to the bathroom?

She was already on the porch. We signaled like baseball coaches. Soon we were outside behind our cabin. I started to ask why she hadn't woken me, but she pressed a finger to her lips, then used it to point toward the pool. Our indirect route to Boys' Camp would lead us around the pool, then down toward the fields as we snaked our way through the trees. This would bring us to the foot of Girls' Hill, where we'd need to pay special attention to our shadows.

"Once we're past arts and crafts, we're home free," Joy had said earlier in the evening. The most challenging part of the raid, both coming and going, was moving through Girls' Hill unnoticed. "Because guy counselors are so much cooler than ours." This was a universal truth among all camps.

Our minds were ahead of our feet. And it was so easy! It was as if

I were already there, waking Adam with a sugar-free cinnamon kiss. We brushed pine needles from our clothes and marched up Boys' Hill, weaving our way through iridescent lights. We took care to ensure that our shadows were always aligned with the dark night, blotted out by camp's most prevalent silhouettes: treetops, steep gabled roofs, and the surrounding hills.

"Did you see that?" I whispered to Joy.

"What?"

"There," I pointed ahead of us. "I just saw it again."

"Was it a raccoon?"

"I thought I saw a light."

We kept still and waited, looking for something I wasn't sure I'd even seen. After a few unremarkable moments in the dark, Joy signaled for us to press forward. We quickened our pace and safely reached the summit of the hill, making it official. We'd made it to Boys' Camp. Each cabin porch was well lit, abuzz with insects and moths. We'd need to rope our way between the porch lights lest any of the counselors were still awake. As we paused to consider our next move, Joy yanked me behind a bush. I winced when a bright light touched my face.

"Come on out," said a male voice. Neither of us moved. "I can see both of you." It was Tanner Becker, a CIT. Once Joy stood, I followed, stepping out from behind the bush into a circle of tawny light. "Now I know who you're going to visit, Joy. I just figured you'd take a night off. Jesus," Tanner said, switching the direction of his flashlight onto me. "But where you off to?" I was still squinting and hesitated to answer.

"Adam Fink," Joy said.

"All right, Adam!" Tanner said, clapping with his flashlight. "Way to go, little man." Tanner was dating Adam's sister Wendy. I was surprised he didn't know we were a couple. "Look, it's fine. I'm not gonna turn you in, but if you get caught, don't tell anyone I saw you." Why would we get caught? We were already across. Maybe he meant on our way back. "There's no one patrolling over there right now," he said as he flicked off his flashlight, "so hurry it up. And keep it quiet." I imagined the Get Out of Jail Free card being plucked from the top of the pile.

Joy cut straight across the gently sloping lawn and flung open the screen door to the boys' cabin. She didn't seem very concerned about how much noise she was making.

I trailed in behind her expecting to squint my way from bed to bed until I established which was Adam's. I feared I'd mistakenly kiss someone else awake. But once inside the cabin, I saw it was alive with quiet activity. Girls from older divisions were half dressed, in bed with what I assumed were their boyfriends. A few boys had pillows thrust over their heads; others had closed themselves off by tightly drawing their sleeping bags closed. Unlike our cabin, theirs wasn't divided into two sides. It was enormous and intimidating. Suddenly toilet-papering a porch didn't seem so bad.

"Adam's that way," Shiva Baum—a boy with an already receding hairline—whispered to me, tipping his head as his girlfriend sucked his neck.

Adam slept as if he'd been placed in a coffin: his sleeping bag pulled to his armpits, arms crossed, head straight. I was afraid the slightest touch might instigate a startled scream. I stooped beside him and whispered, "I'm here."

His eyes flicked open, a sly smile spread across his face, and he turned to me and yawned. "What took you so long?"

"Are all these girls in your cabin every night?" I whispered, still crouched beside his bed, feeling uneasy. I didn't like the idea that he could see other girls without their clothes on.

"I just can't believe you're here, Steph." He was grinning, that posed-second-grade-picture-day smile of his, and it made me exhale a slight laugh. "Klein, oh God, I meant Klein. Please don't go!" His eyebrows pinched together, and he reached for my hand. I'd scolded him often enough about my name. Not that I minded "Steph" so much; it was more that I enjoyed seeing him vulnerable, just slightly hurt, mostly moping, when I feigned being deeply offended. It's how I knew he still wanted me.

"Here," he said, scooting over, holding open his sleeping bag for me to climb in with him. I sandwiched into his single cot, both of us on our sides facing each other. He pulled me close, and I drew in a breath. It took me a while to place the smell. He smelled like a sweat-stained pillow, as if he'd been fighting a fever, being tended to with wet washcloths. The mildew-sweat smell comforted me somehow; it made me feel as if I really knew him. He also smelled like clay.

"It's been like this since Family Weekend," he whispered, "because if people get caught now, it's harder to send them home." I must've looked confused because he clarified, "If they were caught earlier in the summer, they'd be sent home with their parents during Family Weekend."

"Are you glad I'm here?" I asked.

"Of course! Don't I seem glad? Am I not showing you enough?" He squeezed me. It was the first time we'd been this close without Nookie Patrol breaking us apart or shining a flashlight on us in a field. I wondered if Adam wished they were around now, to save him from me.

"It's just, why haven't you ever visited me in my cabin?"

"Because your counselors are complete rags." Only I don't think Adam said the word "rags." Instead, he probably called them bitches, spelling out "bitch" then adding "es." "It's so great to hold you without those stupid PDA laws. Here, I want you to listen to this." He placed headphones over my ears and played me Air Supply.

He tightened his embrace, rocking me a little, after hearing the first part of "All Out of Love." The lyrics were about hurting, about missing, *thinking of you 'til it hurts.*

"Klein," he said, removing the headphones, "I've been thinking a lot about what's going to happen between us after the summer's over. Obviously it won't be the same, but I hope we can keep a loving relationship, maybe not as intense, but still loving. I don't think I could stop loving you, even if I ever want to." I was the luckiest girl in the world.

He'd refer to that night through the years, writing me a letter from his chemistry class, saying how we took for granted how we were able to be together every morning, and all those long good-byes at night, before curfew. We were so lucky to have all those moments between us, and why didn't we realize it then?

But we did realize it. He played me songs about being *tormented and torn apart* while we were still together. It was a luxury knowing what you'd miss, just as it was happening, even before having a chance to. It made us hold on tighter.

I pushed away Adam's hand when it roamed lower than my belly button. "Relax," he said. "I wasn't even thinking of that, Klein." I somehow knew he was relieved I'd redirected his hand. "I just love every part of you. You're so beautiful." And I believed him.

I didn't feel fat next to Adam, and it wasn't just because he was so much broader and taller. He adored every part of me, which made me not mind so much about my softer parts that dimpled, flapped, and folded.

"Was that your stomach?" Adam said, trying to pat it down, as if he could capture the growl in his hands.

"Oh, I guess," I said as if I weren't acutely aware.

"What do you have under here?" He tugged at my nightgown, a thin cotton tank top that flared into a long A-line. I wiggled free of my sweatshirt. He pulled me on top of him, and I rocked my hips against his, grinding on him. I could feel him hard beneath both our clothes.

We tried to be very quiet, aware of each sound we might be making, wondering how loud we were. It should have been exciting, trying to be silent, trying to kiss without letting our lips betray a sound, trying to go unnoticed. But it wasn't exciting. It was trying.

"She licked my ass!" a boy screamed full throttle across the cabin. Everyone perked up, leaning in the direction of the scream. It was

James, whom I remember more as a man than a boy. "She licked my *ass*!" He screamed again, this time with his fists in the air.

Ew, what, like, the hole?!

James had a car and an appetite for everything. Joy emerged from under his covers, pulling out a rope of hair that had been lodged under her neck. She looked withdrawn and distant, as if she were in the wrong place, waiting on a platform for a connecting train in the dead of winter.

Why would she do that? Maybe she feared he'd break up with her if she hadn't. Fat girls, I remember thinking, were expected to be freaky. We had to work harder at sex than thin girls. It's the only way we'd convince a guy to choose us over someone thin. Even at fat camp, where it shouldn't have mattered so much, guys still chose to date the thinner side of fat. And from the looks of it, fat girls lived up to their expectations, courageous enough to lick hairy balls and stick their fingers and tongues in private places.

Sexually, I eventually surmised, men must privately prefer fat women, with their curves and jiggles. *Privately* because they believed their choice in women was a direct reflection of who they were as men. If she was gorgeous, it meant he was desirable, too. If she was a big titty pig, she might've been a good lay, but she wouldn't be the girl he flaunted to his friends. He wouldn't want people to know he'd been with her; it'd reflect poorly on him. Would make it seem as if he couldn't do any better, and when it came to "better" in this world, I knew it wasn't about smarter or witty. It was about thin.

While stripped of sweets and candy, we campers felt as if we'd been let loose to run amok in a sexual candy land. As long as we broke a sweat while running, no one cared that it was into the brush for a game of gynecologist. Along with the shedding of weight came the shedding of inhibitions . . . and clothes. It didn't matter if a girl weighed 230 pounds, because earlier in the summer she'd been 258 pounds, and now she felt skinny, skinny enough in her own skin to want to show it off. In the coming nights, there would be group chunky dunking: a cluster of CITs and older campers would meet at the pool, where they'd race into the dark, showcasing their midnight moons and bare (cannon)balls.

IT WOULDN'T BE UNTIL MUCH LATER AFTER CAMP THAT I'd come to know a little something about the shedding of inhibitions. My father would sit me down at the kitchen table, just the two of us, and using solemn tones and intense eye contact, he'd talk with me about my self-control, or lack thereof. And as I'd listen to his words, I would remember the night in Adam's cabin—Joy's face in particular. While I would not tongue a tail as Joy had, I would, like her, have an audience during an intimate moment. To my most unfortunate surprise, Mom and Poppa would traipse through the front door of our home one night to find me in the living room with my button-fly Levi's at my ankles—caught with a boy and my pants down.

"Do you know what you two were doing today?" Poppa asked, beginning our discussion about said dropped pants.

"Ugh, it's not a big deal!" I whined, rolling my eyes.

"Stephanie, when people say something isn't a big deal, especially the way you're saying it now, chances are it's exactly that. Again, do you know what you two were doing today?"

What did he mean, did I know what we were doing? We were blowing up balloons and making dachshunds. I didn't say anything.

"You were doing something called petting. Do you know what petting is?" It was a nightmare.

"Poppa, I wasn't having sex."

"No one said you were having sex, Stephanie. It's just that . . . try to understand. Do you remember the first time you two kissed?" I nodded. "Remember how wonderful that was, what a big deal it was?"

"Yeah." There was a broken capillary on his hand that I hadn't noticed before.

"Then, after a while, kissing wasn't such a biggie anymore, right? The big deal became letting a boy fondle your boobies." He had just said "fondle" *and* "boobies." Can I go now?

"Poppa—"

"Men will have sex with anything. They'd have sex with a hole in the ground, Stephanie. It's more emotional for girls. And the last thing you want to do is let sex become just like kissing. It should be something special. I'm not going to tell you not to have sex until you're married. Just respect yourself enough to only have sex when you . . . It's just something you do with someone you love."

I LOVED THAT ADAM WAS NOTHING LIKE JAMES. ADAM WAS gentle and genuine. And as we lay in his bed, talk was swept aside in favor of touch. I flexed from the tickle of his fingers near my ribs, shouldered his tongue away from my ear in a squirm, and couldn't keep from smiling when he slobbered on me. I nuzzled against the hem of his hair, my head in his neck. Our eyes heavy. We passed in and out of sleep. My cheek sticking to his arm. The morning light filtered in through the cabin windows. And despite my dead arm, I didn't want to shift or change a thing. I didn't know when we'd have a chance to be alone like that again. With just two and a half weeks left, I wasn't ready for the summer to end.

AS MUCH AS I LONGED FOR PRIVACY WITH ADAM, AN alarming sense of doom prevailed when a few nights later I learned of his elaborate plans for us to go AWOL—our precise destination unknown, our accomplices unclear, and perhaps most terrorizing, there would be food. Less than a week had elapsed since Joy and I had successfully infiltrated the Boys' Camp, and already I was advancing in the ranks of rebellion.

After poking holes in his initial getaway scheme (which might have included a Domino's Pizza delivery guy), I agreed to consider a revised course of action involving a Mustang and a CIT. James was not a division leader, a counselor, or an activity specialist. He was a lowly counselor in training, which in terms of authority was akin to being a security guard at a toy store. CITs had food leniency, off-campus access, and later curfews. The plan was to make our evening escape once everyone had entered the rec hall for the Untalent Show, but when the time came to flee, so did my nerve.

"If we don't go now, we can just forget it," Joy snapped at me. I wasn't about to be intimidated by a girl with crimped hair.

"Come on, Klein. It's going to be fine," Adam encouraged, taking my hand. But I didn't feel fine. It wouldn't matter how few weeks were left; if we got caught, we would, without question, be sent home. And how would I explain that to Mom and Poppa? Being caught in a boy's cabin would have been one thing, but being busted for sneaking off the camp's grounds with a man-boy who referred to his penis as "Joy's stick" was quite another.

My anxiety only mounted when the popping and spitting sounds emitted from James's car preceded its arrival from the parking lawn. Black Beauty was a tatty convertible littered with old newspapers, empty soda cans (not diet, by the way), and cassette tapes. Snaked around the rearview mirror was a gothic crucifix so large it belonged mounted on a wall. He cut the engine and announced that we'd all need to push until we were farther from camp if we hoped to break away undetected.

"Look, we ain't got all night. You two gonna help push, or what?" James asked Adam.

Who then turned to me and said, "It's your call, Slim."

I didn't want to be the one to call the whole thing off, and I did want to go on a real date with Adam that wouldn't involve a bush, a blanket, or a boat. I put my hands on a taillight, fixed my eyes upon James's car ornament, and began to push as I prayed.

fifteen

INSIDE OUT

I hate my counselor Gina—she is such a bitch. I can't wait till I get the hell out of here. I'm just going to ignore the ho-bag. Kate was complaining with me about that fat assed bitch Gina—I wish she would hit me so I could get her fired! I was docked 2nite because Gina complained about me being late for an activity!! Bitch.

I DON'T REMEMBER MUCH ABOUT PIZZA HOUSE—IF IT had a swinging set of doors, or if the counter was orange or brown or tan, or if we sat in wooden chairs or slid into a booth beside a window. What we ate the night we went AWOL, if it smelled of garlic or recycled oil used to fry up battered onion rings, is anyone's guess. If there were individual jukeboxes, if the artist playing as we each readied ourselves to gorge was Paul Simon or Elvis Costello, or if there was any music at all, is beyond the reach of my memory. Were there locals watching a Red Sox game on a too-small color TV mounted to a pine wall in the back? Maybe.

I vaguely recall the pile of pencil-thin fries festooned with ketchup streamers and a confetti of salt, yet I don't know if I waited for them to cool before that first taste, if I savored each bite, or if I wished they'd been in the fryer just a bit longer. Had I devoured it all before tasting a thing? I don't remember. Any of it. The smells, the vibe, the place, or the people.

But I do remember this:

It was a single bathroom, one door, one bowl, no stalls. Unremarkable in almost every way, aside from what unfolded within.

"Well, are you coming in or not?" Joy asked, her hand on the brass doorknob.

"No, you go first," I replied, waving her through. "I can wait until you're done."

"I'm not going to the bathroom," she said as she held the door open for me. "Just freshening up."

Once we were inside, Joy pinched and twisted the lock, turned the faucet until the stream was strong, then handed me her purse without asking if I'd hold it.

"I can't believe how much I just ate," I dramatized, checking my teeth for food in the mirror.

"Oh, I know," Joy said, flipping up both toilet lids. "I'm sick about it." I watched through the mirror as she spun some toilet paper, tearing off several sheets, then folded them into a neat stack.

"Is there some reason you're running this water?" I asked, but Joy didn't look up or answer. She layered the strips of toilet paper, one at a time, not on the rim of the bowl, but into it, using a gentle motion, as if setting a candle and wish adrift on a lake.

She faced the toilet, her knees slightly bent, hair collected into a tight grip behind her neck. And that's when I understood what was about to happen. I didn't know if it was something I was supposed to pretend wasn't happening, if I should've been searching for lip gloss in her bag to give her some privacy—the way I might've if she were sitting on the toilet—or if it was okay to turn around and watch. I didn't particularly like Joy, but at that moment, I wondered if I'd been too hasty.

Still facing the mirror, my eyes darted around the room to a can of

Lysol with a pale blue top, the back of Joy's knees, the pink cleaning fluid inside a clear squirt bottle, the way the shape of Joy's hair looked like an exclamation point. But when I heard her first gag, I whipped around to watch.

The only thing coming from her mouth was sound. At first it was a series of abbreviated grunts—the kind thrown in after song lyrics about sex, accompanied by gyrating hips. But then they rounded into open pushing sounds, each punctuated with a throaty rasp. I wondered if anyone outside the bathroom door could hear.

Although it was the first time I'd ever seen anyone make herself vomit, I wasn't particularly disturbed or surprised. I knew I was supposed to be horrified, but for some reason I wasn't. Though I remember acting as if I were.

"Wait. What. Are. You. Doing?" I recall saying. I waited to ask until she was nearly finished, long after sound transitioned into saliva, and then eventually the contents of her stomach. I was fascinated.

While I had dreamed up the idea of sticking the hose of a vacuum cleaner into my belly button in hopes of sucking out fat, I had never considered reversing my digestive process with a finger. The thought just never crossed my mind. I didn't think to associate the act with a word like "purging" or "bulimia." I remembered Fran once saying to one of the girls who'd reached her goal, "Now don't go too far in the other direction," but I didn't really think it was something one could choose. How could you choose to have a disease? I just never associated decision with sickness. I also didn't think fat girls could have eating disorders. Disorders were for thin girls who when told they looked anorexic would reply, "I wish."

I knew all about clothes, raids, and boys, and plenty about sex for someone who'd never had any, but I was completely naïve about this hypnotic world of Joy's. And that's exactly what it seemed like at the time: a world of Joy. Of ease. Of "You go sweat your ass off in Slimnastics. I'm sitting this one out." Here I'd been struggling, doing it my way, with chopsticks and subliminal hypnosis tapes, early morning runs around camp, and the whole time, there was this other reality I simply had no idea existed.

I knew what she was doing was wrong, that other people would think it was a bad thing. But she didn't seem to believe it was a very big deal. Neither did I, though I knew it was something I'd need to keep private. People wouldn't understand. Or they'd be jealous, I thought, without knowing exactly why, as I watched her thrust her fingers into her mouth again.

When Joy finally stood up, she looked at me and smiled. It was neither a cunning nor a mischievous expression, nor was it coy or nervous. It was welcoming, as if she'd been asleep and just noticed I was there upon waking. "Oh, hi!" her face appeared to say. Then she tossed her head back, laughing away any disorientation, as her eyes blinked tears. A vein just shy of her widow's peak throbbed, and she seemed to exhale, "So much better."

She flushed. Twice. Then she wiped under her eyes with more toilet paper, dabbed the spots from the edges of the bowl, and discarded the wad into a half-full waste pail.

"Okay, your turn." She sighed after rinsing her mouth, her hands signaling for her purse. I'd forgotten I was still holding it.

"I don't know how. I've never done that."

"Just take your finger," pointing hers in the air, "and you'll feel something dangling in the back of your throat."

I took a stance similar to the one she'd made, hovering over the bowl. I saw bits of beige food swaying in the water, some floating, coagulating toward the outer edges, rust stains near the bottom. I didn't know how close to bring my face. It smelled like sour and garlic and disinfectant.

"Wait," she interrupted, setting her handbag on the vanity beside the running faucet. She leaned past me for more toilet paper, then spread a layer on top of the toilet water, explaining, "So you won't get splashed too bad." She stepped away. "Okay, now."

I bent forward again, though this time, Joy held my hair. I wiggled my finger in my mouth. Nothing happened. With my finger that far back, all I felt were several small raised dots on my tongue, hard taste buds I suddenly had the urge to pick off. I wiggled my finger again. Nothing.

"You feel that thing dangling in the back of your throat? Pull on it."

I took my finger out of my mouth. "All I feel are hard bumps, like pimples." Then I swallowed and wiggled my tongue in circles against my palate to scratch an itch.

"You're not reaching far enough back. You have to go *all* the way back," she said. I looked at the small white tiles on the floor, browning at the edges, as she spoke. "And when you feel that thing dangling, keep touching it, and after you pull the trigger, keep doing it." I gagged. It was working. My stomach muscles contracted. "No," she yelled, "do not swallow. I know you want to, but you can't!" It hurt in my chest.

I coughed, and when it subsided, my mouth widened, and a clump of pink and beige plopped out. Fries. It wasn't a violent explosion as I'd expected. When I'd been sick at home and thrown up it always came forcefully, a torrent of fluid, from a place that felt like the very bottom of me. This came from somewhere higher, as if it started from the top and worked its way down the longer I worked at it.

"It will probably take six or seven more rounds," she said. I felt her torso against my lower back as she leaned forward, examining the contents of the bowl. "'Cause you weren't drinking your water."

My vomit continued to clop out in thick patties, and I was able to see each layer of food as it had been ingested. After the fries came the chicken tenders I'd decked with honey, then the salad from the camp dinner. It was my stomach in reverse. When I thought I'd finished, Joy coached, "If I were you, I'd give it one more. I can just tell." So I did.

When I finished, I stood, swallowed, and caught my breath. Joy released my hair and pulled some toilet paper for me. I wiped the saliva from my fingers, then examined myself in the mirror as Joy flushed.

My forehead was so red it looked blue. I smoothed away my leaky mascara and pressed my hand against my stomach. It had flattened out, and I felt like a woman.

While I knew it was somehow "wrong" and "bad," I didn't know how unhealthy it was to induce vomiting. At thirteen I never really understood what it was to be bulimic. How often did one need to throw up to be considered one? Though I did know to hide it, that it wasn't something you publicized, not even in a whisper. I had no idea of the havoc it could wreak on the body. I figured it was something women just did and kept private, like masturbation. And I wondered what else was part of this new adult world. I was eager to learn.

Joy and I reunited with the boys, passed through the parking lot, piled back into the car, and with pure stealth returned to camp. I made it to my cabin before curfew without anyone ever catching on. Without ever being caught.

JOY AND I NEVER SPOKE OF THAT NIGHT AGAIN, BUT FROM that point on, the world was a little different. I speculated about who else—not just at camp, but everywhere—knew about "pulling the trigger," as Joy had called it. Had Fran ever tried it? Any of the girls from my water ballet class at North Hills? What about Leigh? Everyone was a suspect.

On the morning of a camp field trip to a water park, I arrived at the dining hall for an unusually early breakfast and wondered if I'd spot any trigger-happy campers.

Because of the field trip, we were directed to eat and run; the buses were waiting. With my tray of French toast sticks and coffee-flavored yogurt, I scanned the dining room for Adam, wondering if he'd already eaten.

He was sitting at a table with a handful of boys from his division. As I drew nearer I saw that Jordan and Grayson sat among them. Why was he with them? He'd seen how Jordan had humiliated me at the cookout, and in the weeks since then it had only gotten worse. I wasn't just sleep deprived due to hunger or raids; I'd heard that Jordan and Grayson were collecting cigarette butts from all-camp cleanups and were planning to dump them into my bed. I'd cried to Adam about Jordan, confiding how scared I was to fall asleep at night. "They're planning to cut off all my hair!" I'd told him when I first found out. And now he was sitting with them, and—wait, was that a laugh? He was actually enjoying their company? I hated him.

It was too late for me to turn back. When I joined their table, they all stopped talking. "How goes it, Klein?" Adam said, all bushytailed.

"I just lost my appetite," Grayson groaned, excusing herself from the table with Jordan in tow. They made a point of encircling the table for everyone to see, only to relocate at the table just behind us.

I looked to Adam, thinking he might offer something in the way of a defense on my behalf. A mere "That was rude" or "Was that really necessary?" could have worked, even if it was too early in the morning for him to scream *"Cunts!"* But he didn't say anything.

I'd dedicated an entire page in my diary to declare, "I love Peter Cetera!" I'd committed all the song lyrics of "Glory of Love," the feature track from *The Karate Kid II*, to memory. I was looking for a man who would fight for my honor! Because that's what you did when you loved someone. You didn't stand by and watch; you stepped up. But Adam just flashed me a toothy grin and bobbed his oblivious head to some imaginary song playing just for him.

"Oh, Klein, how is it that you're just so divine? And fine!" I left my tray at the table and stormed off to the buses alone.

When Adam caught up with me, he hemmed and hawed, panting words like "middle" and "slack," encouraging me to be reasonable. "It puts me in a tough spot," he said when I asked why he hadn't taken my side in our girl war.

"You suck," I said, refusing to look at him.

"What do you want me to do?" he whined. "I'll do anything."

"No, that's just it," I snapped, now aware we were about to make a scene. "You didn't do or say anything."

"You want me to go back? I will!" he said with a half turn in the other direction.

"No, it's too late now. Because if you gave a shit, you wouldn't have been able to *stop* yourself from saying something!" I wanted him to suffer. "Here, take this back. I don't want it anymore." I removed a small gold football charm from my necklace and handed it to him. He'd given it to me one night, saying he wanted something of his to always be near me. It was etched with a thin *71,* his football number. "We're so over."

Really, it was all a show. Not just a scene. Because as far as I knew, that's what girls did to boys: they made them miserable. According to Percy Sledge, when a man loved a woman, he'd "sleep out in the rain if she said that's the way it ought to be." So if there was some guy camped out in a thunderstorm to prove his love, I wasn't about to let Adam off with a simple "sorry." He'd need to prove it. Beg for forgiveness in the middle of the night holding a stereo above his head. I wanted to love the way people did in the movies.

"Say it ain't so," he said, sniffling, his chin to his chest.

"You're the one who said you wanted to be 'left out of it.' So, there you go. Consider yourself left." Then I tossed my hair and ran away without looking back.

WHEN WE FINALLY ARRIVED AT ACTION PARK IT WAS TIME for lunch. The parking lot was an elephant's graveyard of camp buses, as filthy and rundown as ours. Once again we'd be paraded in front of kids from other camps, among others, in our dancing veggie shirts. The humiliation hadn't subsided even with the myriad occasions we'd been forced to wear our orange tents: to the movies, bowling, roller-falling, and the mall. It didn't matter. Each time still felt like the first time: embarrassing.

I'd turned Mr. Celery and Ms. Carrot inside out, arguing that I was still wearing orange, so counselors would be able to spot me. It was futile. Gina made me switch it back when she was pacing the bus aisle, first for a head check, then with an envelope of canteen money, calling out names and distributing cash. Over Family Weekend, Poppa had replenished the till so I'd be able to purchase new clothes when they took us to the mall. Given the fact that I wouldn't need to buy any more stamps, batteries, or bug repellent with only two weeks of camp left, I'd put in a request for the full balance. "That's a whole lot of souvenirs," Gina had said as her eyes narrowed into the expression of a hallway monitor.

"Sure is," I countered with an artificial smile. I wanted to yank her down by her pelican wattle and clamp her greasy bulbous nose to her clipboard.

"That shirt of yours needs to be worn the correct way there, Miss. Or you'll need to stay here, and this money won't do you much good." Oh, sit on it and rotate. I rolled my eyes until it hurt, then went ahead and fixed my shirt. "Wise decision," she said. "Besides, you can always take it off inside the park." And then she smiled, as if to dare me.

Just when we thought it couldn't get any worse. Being paraded through the park entrance in our happy-salad uniform was only the beginning. Next we'd need to reveal something far more humiliating: ourselves. In bathing suits. In public. At a water park. I wondered how many whale jokes I'd overhear near the tidal-wave pool.

The bus doors opened and everyone filed out. I squinted as the sun broke into my eyes. It was crotch hot. And what was worse, we weren't ushered into the park. The staff led us away from the buses but kept us contained in the parking lot. I found a strip of grass on a curb. Brown bags were handed out. Lunch. Soggy hot tuna fish, clumps of it. Cans of warm diet soda. A packet of miniature carrots. A turd of an apple.

"Now remember," Gina said to our division as we made our way through the park turnstiles, "you've all had your lunches now. So don't try to ruin the fun with cotton candy." Oh shut up, you bag. I hated when someone fatter than I was had the nerve to lecture me about food. Uh, clearly I'm doing better than you are. Gina most definitely was not suspected of pulling the trigger.

Fat camp champs who'd been to Action Park over previous summers took to calling the place "Traction Park" because someone always managed to royally fuck themselves up on one of the many lawsuit-waiting-to-happen rides. At least that's what Kate seemed to think.

"Oh, it's true," Hams confirmed as we crammed our towels and valuables into a locker. "Last year when I came off some super-speed water slide, from my ass to my ankles was all red. And I'm black."

"You *are*?" Kate joked as she wiggled into a pair of jelly shoes.

"Are you guys keeping your shirts on?" I asked. They looked at me as if I were talkin' jive. "What?"

"Newsflash, Klein. People are gonna know we're fat with or without the fat camp fiesta shirts." Did that mean she was keeping hers on?

"Why?" Hams asked me. "You're really gonna take yours off?"

I decided I'd feel better in a bathing suit, even in public, than I did about that shirt. I pulled it over my head, stuffed it into our locker, then slapped my hands together, as if I were ridding myself of dust and the past. As they looked to each other, deciding what to do with their uniforms, I tucked cash beneath the leg of my suit, near my chunk change.

"Fuck it," Hams said, whipping off her shirt to reveal a magenta one-piece with a ruffled sash spanning her torso. She smiled without covering her mouth.

We looked to Kate, our hands on our hips.

She responded with her body first, folding her arms and spreading her legs shoulder-width apart, as if each foot were made of iron and rooted to the ground. Then in a stock-still voice, without a thread of irony, she added, "Fat chance."

"Fine. Then where to first?" I asked, unfolding a large map of the park. The Tarzan Swing? The Alpine Slides? Surf Hill?

The vending machines. It was unanimous.

OUR COUNSELORS WERE ASSIGNED POSTS THROUGHOUT the park. Food posts. They stood like totem poles, guarding snack shacks, vending machines, and the food court. Once we were turned away, we agreed to go down a long wavy slide. Only upon reaching the top, Kate had second thoughts.

"You two go on without me," she squeaked, leaning forward expectantly. No way was Kate scared! I mean, the only body language she spoke was an indifferent shoulder shrug, and well, yeah, flipping someone the bird, but she definitely wasn't one for biting her lip and wringing her hands. And when she did it, I couldn't help but picture a cartoon elephant standing on a bar stool, trembling at the sight of a field mouse. It wasn't even a particularly steep slide, where you were warned to lie flat, keeping your arms crossed. For this ride, you set down a body mat and could sled downhill headfirst if you liked. But Kate's hands were quivering at the idea of going down at all. We refused to let her turn back and eventually goaded her—with the ever effective "Don't be such a wuss!" strategy—into at least sitting on the slide.

"I just can't do it," she said peering down at the journey she'd be taking.

"Come on." Hams tried to reason with a modicum of sincerity. "What do they always tell us? 'Don't say you can't until you at least try.' You'll psych yourself out."

"Yeah, say it," I teased. "I think I can, I think I can."

"Oh, you hush now, Klein," Kate snapped, momentarily breaking from her panic to laugh.

She ultimately agreed when we pledged to all go at the same time, holding hands. A knot of Red Rover grips, and to the count of three, we pushed off. We were all moving at such different speeds, though, that our hands broke free from one another.

When I emerged from the shallow pool at the bottom, I looked for Hams and Kate to see what they thought of the ride. Hams was already out, wringing water from her hair. Kate wasn't in the pool or just outside it. I relinquished my mat to a stranger, and using my hand as a visor, squinted up behind me.

WAIT. BEFORE I GO ANY FURTHER, I JUST NEED TO SET THIS straight. The Kate I knew was a blasé, screw the establishment, wait on that while I pick my ass, screw you very much, and thanks for the ride, pal, kinda gal. If you caught her picking her nose, instead of turning bashfully red and quickly making like she'd simply had an itch right below her nostril, she'd withdraw the booger, examine it on her finger, then look up at you, then back at her finger. And then she'd flick it at you. That was Kate.

HER SLIDE MUST'VE HAD A DRY PATCH, AND HER MAT must've slid out from under her. The first thing I saw when I squinted up were her legs. They were aggressively kicking in an effort to wiggle the rest of her down. When Kate let forth a keening yelp, I couldn't keep from breaking into a peal of laughter.

"Song of Solomon!" she blared from the middle of her slide. "It ain't funny!"

We watched from the bottom as Kate struggled to look up behind her, gesticulating for the attention of the staffer who'd been setting the pace, instructing park guests when it was their turn. "Can you throw down some extra water?!" she squawked. "Or something?! Anything!" She panicked, squirming, bending her knees, trying to scoot her way down.

"Hello?! Don't you go lettin' people down!" she kept booming.

"Now, I mean it! *Hello?!*" She was like a bowling ball stuck in the middle of a gutter.

Scooting most of her way down, she eventually made it to the bottom, and then asked us to examine hers. "It's bad, ain't it? And no goddamn fat jokes!!!" Hams and I couldn't answer. "Now quit it! It's not funny!" she snapped like an enraged mother who'd just discovered her child waiting patiently in her closet, wearing a white goalie Jason mask.

We alternated between calling her the Little Engine That Couldn't and the Little Red Caboose the rest of the day. Well, no, we weren't that clever. But it makes for a better story.

That was it for Kate. She refused all other rides. With a fisherman's cap and a thick stripe of zinc oxide straddling her nose, she spent the remainder of the afternoon afloat in an immense yellow tube.

"You sure you're okay?" I asked before leaving her alone.

She stretched out her arms and with John Candy delivery said, "I'm Joe Public, welcome to my beach."

Most campers were undeterred by their bruises and scrapes, refusing to admit defeat. This was especially true when it came to food. Civilians were handsomely paid for obtaining candy bars from the vending machines our counselors guarded. Never mind the winding lines for the rides; when our counselors' backs were turned, we wiggled toward the front of food lines for frankfurters and fries, the forbidden pluck of food tasting all the sweeter shared among friends.

Sure I wanted to lose more weight, but I wasn't one to take orders from a fat camp director charged with breaking me down. Tell me I can't do something, and time how fast I do it. So, when the counselors were trading posts, a few of us raced up the refreshment-building stairs into the pavilion of fattening. Once there, I immediately swallowed the top of a friend's soft-serve ice cream cone. "Don't worry," I assured her, handing it back, "I'll get us another."

With each swallow, it wasn't as if I knew it wouldn't count. It wasn't a premeditated binge, where I allowed myself to gorge with the knowledge that none of it would be digested. When I raced up those steps with a handful of girls from my division and poured through the pavilion doors, I wasn't hungry. I wasn't thinking. I was reacting. It was a chance to hoard, to refuel on all we'd been denied. It was all giggles, not guilt. Not yet.

I snatched sugar packets from the table, ripped them open and poured the sugar into my palm for everyone to see. I made a display of licking my finger and pressing it into the sugar. Sweets didn't even do it for me. I just wanted to prove how innovative I could be. "What a great idea," I wanted someone to say. "Ooh, look at Stephanie." But no one did.

Though when Tara suggested we all stock up on sugar for our morning oatmeal, everyone leaned in, grabbing at the paper packets and stuffing them into their suits.

I ate two chicken nuggets and was dipping a third into a tub of honey mustard. If we'd had on jeans, we'd have unbuttoned. Midbite someone asked, "Aren't you a vegetarian?" I'd forgotten. I still ate the rest.

Once we'd run out of money and steam—several hot dogs, hamburgers, and corn dogs later—we sat like men stretched around a card table, taking up the width of our seats, stuffed and groaning.

"Ugh, I'm so full I'm gonna yak," one girl said, grabbing her distended potbelly through her orange farm-fashion apparel.

No one said anything. I might've lifted an eyebrow. Not such a bad idea, but how was I going to get away with it alone?

"Seriously, I'm so ill," I agreed, making a sour face. Then I sipped diet soda, very clear of what would happen next. "I think I'm gonna try to go to the bathroom," I said, standing.

"Good idea. I'm coming." And then about six of us filed into the park bathroom, and I felt like a leader. I didn't need Jordan or Grayson to feel popular. All I needed was this. The bathroom was fitted with as many stalls as a multiplex theater, yet it appeared to be empty. I took a stall far from the entrance and repeated how sick I felt. "So sick, I might even have to throw up," I said. No one would think it was weird to vomit if you were actually sick.

"Are you . . . throwing up?" one girl asked after I gagged a few times.

"I'm trying to," I said casually through the stall as if it was something all women did, like wearing pantyhose or drinking coffee.

"I'm going to try, too," she said. I saw her feet turn around. "But how?"

I didn't answer her. I was too focused on the task at hand. I'd forgotten about the layer of toilet paper, so my face was splashed with cold toilet water. This was gross, though I wasn't about to stop now that it was coming up. I continued, opening my eyes after each bout to examine the contents. I wanted to make sure I got it all, all the way back to the tuna lunch. I was glad I'd had the ice cream. Everything slid out with it, still cool, and it tasted the same as it had going down.

I wasn't as courteous as Joy had been and refused to wipe the food spray from the rim of the bowl once I saw all the dried urine and a pubic hair. I used the toilet paper to clean the thick saliva from my hands. I felt powerful as I wiped away my tears. *Good idea,* I repeated to myself. Then I flushed it all away.

Jessica Fallis continued to hack away unproductively. "Nothing's happening," she said, opening her stall for us to see.

"You can't swallow," I repeated, as she tried again. Then I walked to the mirror to rinse my mouth and fix my ponytail.

"Stephanie," another girl asked, sticking her head out from her stall, "can you please help me?"

I looked toward the door to the bathroom to see if anyone was coming in. When the coast seemed clear, I elbowed into the stall with her, keeping the door open. I didn't speak, just pulled toilet paper and lined the water in her bowl with it. "Now, just relax," I reassured her. "It's not that difficult." Then I wiggled my finger in the air. "Just keep doing it until something comes up."

"Thanks," she said. I shouldered out and closed her stall door.

Most of the girls were still in their stalls, and I wondered if it was their first time. With some it was obvious. They said it hurt too much, and they were going to quit. But as they washed their hands and heard the productive vomiting of the others, they hurried to a different toilet and tried again.

"Listen," I told one of them, "try it with more than one finger, and you don't need to thrust, just wiggle, then pull your hand out when you feel it's coming close."

Did they know it would take time to get it all out, that it would have been easier if they'd had more to drink? I was reluctant to share all that I'd learned from Joy with such a big group, and from the sounds of it, most of them were managing fine without me. I looked to the door of the bathroom again, thinking if someone walked in and made a face, I'd explain how we'd all gotten food poisoning from the fish sticks.

I didn't see it, but I heard one of the girls say that Jessica threw up blood. She was a diabetic, and I remember wondering if that had anything to do with it. Had she simply cut herself with a jagged fingernail, or was she heaving up blood? I didn't want to know. That was enough for me. I wasn't about to check up on her; I just wanted out of there.

"Come on guys, stop it," I urged, gently steering one of the girls out of her stall by her shoulder. "Let's go on the rides now."

"No! It's not fair," she cried, gripping her hair in a low ponytail. "I want to throw up, too. I don't wanna gain!"

"Guys, is this normal?" Jessica asked about the blood in her bowl.

I didn't stick around to look or answer. Those who hadn't vomited continued to work on it, and those of us who'd been successful left together. We'd all at least tried, so I knew no one would tell. They'd keep the secret between us, just as I'd kept Joy's. Then we stood in line for the Roaring Rapids, discussing when we thought color war might break, as if nothing ever happened. But my hands were still shaking when I thought of Jessica.

sixteen

TALL TALES AND HEROES

There are some girls here (Jordan and Grayson) that I'm beginning to want to hate. Hate is so strong. I would hate them if I could. I hate having to put up with them. When I complain and complain to Adam he doesn't do anything! He says that he's in a tough spot, but he's really not. I'm supposed to be the girl that he loves, but he cannot stand up for me. I wouldn't even hesitate. If someone was making him miserable, if it be Lea, Leigh, or anyone else, I would be fast as a snap to jump in to make him happier. He is such a wimp in that respect. He has never stood up for me . . . What does he do about some girl making me hurt and upset? Nothing!

ALL OF CAMP WAS ABUZZ WITH TALK OF COLOR WAR, A stretch of four or five days at the end of summer during which the entire camp was divided into competing armies of red and blue. As we counted down the remaining days before final banquet, predictions were made on likely themes. Redcoats vs. Blue Patriots? Red Samurai vs. Blue Ninjas? Sugars vs. Fats? It was anyone's guess. Amid all the speculation on how and when they'd break color war, and who the likely generals and captains would be, there were also several fake-breaks intended to prolong and heighten the excitement of it all.

On the night we returned from Action Park, a fire engine had trailed our buses into camp, the sirens blaring, insisting a fire had ignited down by arts and crafts. We were to file out of the buses but to stay out of harm's way. That's when a cluster of counselors, who'd most likely had the day off, came charging out from behind the front office, blowing whistles, clad in either all red or all blue, distributing thin newspapers with a bold headline reading COLOR WAR 1989. But upon reading the article in search of the theme and team rosters, we realized each paragraph consisted only of two repeating words: "fake out."

How totally gay, I thought, but I joined in the chanting anyway.

Fake out. Fake out. We want a break out!

There were already another two fake-breaks by the following evening. On football league night, I saved a seat on my blanket for Kate, and we discussed what we'd do if we were split apart, as if there was anything we could do. We sounded like two friends who'd agreed to finally make it. "No way will we let it change us."

"Yeah, no way."

I hoped they'd put me with Jordan, because if we were pitted against each other, she'd be encouraged to hip-check me across the hockey rink. If we were on the same team, there wouldn't be much she could do. Unless they made her a captain; then she could boss me around.

The title of camper captain was a big deal. It was recognition of your leadership skills, a reward, really, for being a good camper, a strong camper. It meant someone believed in your abilities. You got to stay up late, working on fight song lyrics and building floats, painting themed plaques. You no longer had to spend your time chained to your division and curfew. As it was, evenings provided opportunity. In the dark of night, no one was responsible. You could eat a sack of black-market goods without looking over your shoulder and kiss until your lips hurt. In the dark, we all felt free, and it was never more true than during color war.

And from my experience at the normal camps, that's just what it was: war. People sabotaged their bunkmates, dumping the contents of someone's cubby just moments before the judges arrived for inspection. Some cabins adopted the noble policy of being "color-blind" and banded together in solidarity. When a judge came upon a dusty corner and asked who'd been responsible for FIRST SWEEP, each camper would step forward to take the blame. They refused to let "the establishment" pit them against one another, which struck me as anomalous, considering they had no qualms about fighting over boys, backstabbing, and revealing secrets they'd been trusted to keep. But there was nothing like war to bring about ardent declarations of peace.

Camp romances were done in if the couple was assigned to opposing teams. By the afternoon following our trip to Action Park—which seemed like an eternity for a camp relationship—I had accepted one of Adam's many groveling apologies, and we were back to being the happily-ever-after version of Stephanie & Adam, the part you never really got to see in the movies because once the couple kissed and made up, the screen would freeze and credits would roll over their love-struck faces. You just had to assume it all worked out between them, that the next time she insisted he'd messed up again, he wouldn't throw up his hands and declare her "impossible!" Instead he'd continue to make amends with sonnets, serenades, and stalking. And the cycle of blame and apologies would always work for them. No one in movie-love ever saw through it.

My camp romance with Adam worked the same way. We loved with dramatic "it's over" endings that never stuck. We always found our way back to each other, with Adam apologizing, even for things he didn't do. I knew I had the power in the relationship, that he'd do whatever I asked. It made me feel safe knowing he'd never reject me. I subconsciously beat him up a little just to hear him tell me he couldn't live without me. It made me feel needed and loved.

Adam passed me a note on movie night saying he'd talked to his division leader and was assured we wouldn't be split up for color war. "It would ruin me if we weren't on the same team, Klein." It's all any of us could talk, or cheer, about.

One, two, three, four, we want color war!
Five, six, seven, eight, we don't wanna wait!

I WAS THANKFUL FOR FREE SWIM AT THE LAKE THE FOLlowing afternoon. Finally a time in our day when we weren't suspiciously asked to deviate from our schedule and report to, say, the tennis courts.

Few people actually used the lake shower for anything beyond rinsing their muddied feet, but I thought of what my cousin had once taught me at North Hills and decided to give it a shot at camp. I ran the numbing Berkshire water over myself as I squirmed, wiggling beneath the showerhead for as long as I could take it. I drew in my breath and quickly worked conditioner through my hair. We did things like this at the lake: conditioned. We did it because no one told us not to, because the lake was as big as an ocean to us, because some summer-edition beauty magazine said it was a beachfront activity, in the sun, for deeper penetration. I sprinted back into the algid lake, feeling warmer compared to the ache of the cold shower. My hair was a slimy coat that fanned out, translucent ribbons and swirls of Salon Selectives all around me. I decided I liked the lake where it was too deep to stand, where you didn't have to agonize about what you were stepping on, about eelgrass, minnows, or a lake floor that felt like mucus.

"Do it," I yelled to Kate, who was lounging on the dock.

"Nuh-uh. I got enough water action for a lifetime the other day, thanks."

"Come on, just do it. Go under the shower, as cold as you can take it. Now!" Kate didn't move. "The water feels so warm. It's like a trick."

"You've lost it, Klein."

"Just do it!" I squealed, but Kate remained completely still, soaking up the skin damage.

I dolphin-kicked my way past the red-and-white buoy to another arm of the dock, toward the center of the lake. It smelled green and mossy. I looked at myself underwater as I paddled to stay afloat, my skin so pallid. Everything looks whiter underwater, even in the inky nucleus of a lake.

Jessica Fallis was on the center dock with Harper, complaining that she didn't like the way Aaron kissed. Aaron and Jessica were boyfriend and girlfriend going on three days, which was your basic silver anniversary as far as camp relationships went. Jessica asked Harper what she should do about it.

"Just tell him," Harper said. I didn't know how anyone could use the word "just" when discussing kissing. And to actually talk about it, to say the words, with the boy you were doing it with?! I'd sooner talk to Poppa about feminine hygiene than talk to a boy about the way he kissed me.

"You mean she should actually say it out loud?" I asked, doing the Yanisin Roll up onto the dock. They both looked startled to see me.

"Yeah, just tell him you like smaller kisses," Harper hesitated. This seemed like bad advice to me. If a boy ever said that to me, that he preferred something else to what I was doing, I'd spend the night in my cabin crying. People would ask me what was wrong, and I'd lie, say we'd broken up because that was easier to say, easier to do even, than admit I needed to change. If I were Jessica, I'd just suck it up. Literally.

Adam kissed the way I played tennis: inaccurately. When my racquet actually made contact with the ball, I had a hard time recognizing my own strength, so I'd lob it over the fence. Adam put both his lips not on mine, but over them, making it a challenge for my nostrils to do their job. When Adam kissed me, he hit over the fence.

But I'd never actually say so. I may have wanted to threaten him with the idea of losing me, but I never wanted to hurt his feelings. Instead, when he became too eager, I'd tell him to go chew some ice. Just as I was ready to share this "go chill out" advice with Jessica, a low-flying airplane circled the lake. No way was it a real breakout, I thought as I followed everyone else's lead out of the lake. Nine days of camp still remained; it was too early. And Boys' Camp hadn't even made it down to the lake yet. They'd only break color war if we were all together. Still, I didn't want to be the last to learn the chosen theme, so I raced over to the fields like everyone else.

Lower Camp was already there, having a planned water fight to alleviate the heat. But as the plane circled overhead, they put their battle aside, wondering if this would be a real outbreak of war. We all jumped and squealed with excitement when flyers floated down. We reached high above our heads, clapping at the papers, eager to see if this was really it.

I didn't need to look at one to know it was real. Campers started hugging. They must have found their names on the roster and realized they were on the same team. I saw a male counselor with a lit torch, half his face painted red, racing down the hill from behind us, ready to encircle the crowd. He wasn't alone. Other war-decorated counselors paraded in from other directions, torches held high. And where there's fire, there's color war.

The loudspeakers blasted, confirming it. We were instructed to return to our cabins and dress in the color of our team. Keeping with the tradition that family was never split between teams, Lea and I—redheads with a mother who refused to buy us red clothing—were shit out of luck when we learned we were on the red team. We borrowed red, lent out our blues, and eventually made our way to the field beside the infirmary for the traditional first event: tug-o'-war.

We've got spirit. We've got guts.
We've got the blue team by their nuts, so pull team, pull!

As far as competitions went, I found it just a bit ironic that color war at fat camp began with the one activity where the heavier and more immobile you were, the better equipped you were for the job. Nearly everyone on the team looked like an anchor, so our generals made the game-time decision as to who'd wrap the rope around her torso. The girls on the team kicked at the ground, marking the grass with divots, just as the guys had demonstrated. Eight-year-olds spit on their hands like grown men, and I half expected them to smear shoe polish on their cheeks. As I watched their sweet faces contort into little vexed burls, I found myself sitting up on my knees, eager to see what would happen.

That was the thing about color war; it converted people. There was an elevated energy in the air. Everyone knew to take it seriously, even if they had no interest in such organized events. I got sucked into it and found I was suddenly on my feet rooting aloud, high-five'n with Beulah. It normally irritated me, being forced to cheer along, but when I saw so many people trying so hard, I couldn't help but join in.

AS I WASHED MY FACE FOR BED LATER THAT NIGHT, I thought of the days' activities. How we'd won tug-o'-war but lost the boys' basketball game. I wondered when they'd post the team point totals. Harper flickered the lights with a five-minute warning before lights-out.

After patting my face dry with a towel, I examined it for pimples in the small bathroom mirror. I used my hands to push my eyebrows apart, relaxing the muscles beneath them. I was nervous. I didn't know why.

I hated competition and knew from my earlier experiences with color war that in the coming days I'd find myself running faster and working harder—not because I wanted to lose more weight, but because someone would come to me and say, "I'm really counting on you." It's what our generals always did. Yet one of the best parts of color war was that as much as people relied on you, you didn't seem to ever be the focus. That is, there was something bigger than you going on. Bigger than weight loss, or pounds, or even food, color war rooted you out of the ordinary.

Every action, each routine, would be part of the competition—points awarded and deducted for everything. When it came to sportsmanship, I had no doubt that I'd soon find myself reluctantly bellowing, "We want another one, just like the other one" to the opposing team for a few extra points. We'd all be transformed. Unprompted, we'd clean up after other people, folding their towels lakeside, offering them the driest life vest for the kayaking event, even picking up someone else's trash before the rope burn. We'd become the kids our parents always wanted: selfless, heroic, and downright tidy.

I looked up at the bare lightbulbs on our bathroom ceiling, at the carved names, and Sharpie marker graffiti. A beige moth in the corner. It seemed as if I'd been at camp forever, and soon I'd be leaving. Maybe I was anxious about going home to Leigh and school.

That's not it, I thought as I eyed my teeth in the mirror. Now that I was down twenty-eight pounds, I knew everything would be different. I'd make friends with a new crowd, get asked out on dates, and play center forward in soccer. I smiled, then wiped away the mascara remnants from beneath my eyes. I'd had the same raccoon eyes at Action Park.

I felt like a cheater. Maybe that's why everyone thought it was wrong to make yourself vomit. It was for lazy, pathetic people. I was tired of being that. I nodded to myself in the mirror, as if we'd just made a pact never to do it again. There. It was behind me. I collected my toiletries, flicked off the bathroom lights, and felt relieved.

The morning came too quickly. I made my bed, then dressed in the same red clothes, deciding that Mom was right. Red really wasn't my color; it was too loud. I snapped up my chopsticks, then slugged my way to the large field for a team meeting before flagpole lineup. Tracy, our team general, explained that once we entered the dining hall, breakfast would be a silent meal, emphasizing how crucial it was for us all to keep quiet. "No whispering!"

One of the most important indicators of color war success appeared to come down to volume. I already anticipated sitting beneath the Snack Tree during rest hour to practice our new cheers. It'd be hot, and we'd fold sheets of paper into accordion-like fans and pant lifeless lyrics into the thick afternoon air. Then a co-captain would yell, asking what was wrong with all of us, as if the answer weren't mapped across our sweat-stained bodies. "Now this time, with some oomph!" We'd sing songs to the tune of "Eye of the Tiger." And prior to being dismissed, a selection of campers would be assigned as servers to the judges, offering to give them massages, cut their turkey meatloaf, serenade them with "You've Lost That Loving Feeling."

When we weren't encouraged to cheer and scream until we were hoarse, we were ordered into silence.

"Now, when I raise my hand," Tracy trumpeted to the team once we'd all gathered at the large field, "what happens? That's right! When the arm goes up, the mouth goes shut. Now, let's try it." Then our team screamed—not words, just actual shrieking—all eyes on Tracy, waiting for her signal. "That was awesome, you guys!" She said with a fraction of our enthusiasm once we'd complied. "That's how it should always be. You want to win, right?!" But we were too scared to agree and didn't know that she wanted us to screech again. "I said, you want to win, right?!" It seemed we spent far too much time working on our timing.

Tracy broke us into our divisions then talked each group through their day, indicating which fields and activities we'd be participating in, asking for volunteers to help paint the banners immediately after lunch. "I will," I offered, surprising myself by how chipper I sounded for so early in the morning.

"No," she said flatly. "Anyone else?" Other girls raised their hands and were chosen. *No? Wait. No?* I guess I had to learn to talk only when called on. Still, she could have at least said that. Maybe she just wanted me to save my energy. I was, after all, the very best swimmer in all of Girls' Camp. Once she finished scribbling down names and had directed us up toward the flagpole, I asked her why I couldn't participate.

"Because I didn't raise my hand?"

"No, Stephanie," she said, peeping over her shoulder. "We've got you doing something else. After breakfast, you need to go to the office."

"Why?"

"You'll see," she said, sounding distracted. Then she bolted to the next division and asked for more volunteers. What would I be doing at the office? I really hoped I wouldn't have to massage some judge's feet or sort through all the mail. I wondered who from the blue team would be going with me.

I'd become quite adept with my chopsticks and finished before most anyone else at my table. I was expecting to have to sit through at least another twenty minutes of silence, but I was excused when Tracy tapped me on the shoulder, indicating that I was now free to go to the office.

I told the office secretary my name and began to explain that Tracy had sent me when Doc came in, clearing his throat. "I've got this," he said to the secretary, then he motioned for me to follow him into his office, adding, "Come with me, why don't you," just in case it was unclear. *Grossatating.* There was no way I was crouching beneath his dangly oldies to knead his feet. Once we were in his office, though, he took a chair behind his desk and offered me the sofa.

"Do you know why you're here?" he asked, rocking back into his seat, as if he were settling in for a tall tale.

"No," I said tentatively.

"I want to talk to you about what's been going on lately." This wasn't about color war. Maybe he'd heard that Jordan was planning on putting cigarettes in my bed and wanted to be an intermediary. He looked at me as if he saw something deeply important in my face.

"Okay."

"I heard that you've been teaching the girls in your division to throw up, and that you yourself have been throwing up."

"I haven't thrown—"

"And it's very troubling to us here."

I felt my face burn, sweat prickling under my skin. "I didn't do anything!" I heard myself shout. I lifted my eyes for a moment, just beyond Doc's face, catching a glimpse of movement. Harper and Jessica were now in the entranceway of his office.

"Knock, knock," Harper said.

Doc swiveled toward them, then signaled that they join us in the empty seats. I knew what was coming next. It was an intervention. Harper sat in one of the chairs, and Jessica took a seat beside me on the sofa. I could tell she was trying to catch my eye, but I wouldn't look at her.

"Harper and Jessica are here because they're worried about you. We're all very concerned," he said. "Right, ladies?"

"We're here to help you," Harper said, nodding her head in agreement. Had Jessica said something to Harper at the lake when we'd been talking about kissing? And they just pretended like everything was fine?

"I'm sorry I told, Stephanie," Jessica announced more to the room than to me, "but I was scared when I saw blood, and now I'm really worried about you, too."

Everyone looked at me, waiting for a response. I knew there was no point in denying what had happened now that Harper and Jessica had been summoned as witnesses. I also wasn't about to bring up Joy. It would only make me look guiltier. I didn't say anything.

"Do you know what bulimia is?" Doc asked. I averted my eyes and studied the raised grain of his desk. "It's a disorder—an eating disorder."

"I really didn't want to tell," Jessica blurted out again, this time grabbing my leg.

"That's fine, Jess. Stephanie's not mad at you. She knows you're just concerned. Isn't that right, Stephanie?" No. That wasn't right at all. I wanted to feed her limbs to a meat grinder as she watched. "You did the right thing," he said. I narrowed my eyes at Doc, who was now standing by the door of his office. "Now, I've got it from here, girls," he whispered, nodding.

After they left his office, Doc leaned on his desk and flipped up a strip of paper. Without looking at me he said, "Yanisin just isn't the place for you anymore. It's better for everyone if you go home." Still consulting the paper, he began to push numbers into the phone at the edge of his desk. "Maybe you'll have something to say to your parents," he said.

"Wait. You're kicking me out?!"

Without responding, he spoke into the phone, then handed it to me. "Well, go ahead."

My knees were bouncing. I took the receiver and cupped my hand around the mouthpiece. "Hello?"

"Stephanie?"

"Poppa, they're sending me home," I cried softly, "because they think I'm . . . bulimic, but I'm not!"

"Well, are you?"

"I just said I'm not!"

"Then why are they sending you home? Who's sending you home?"

"The Brain," I said, feeling my eyes widen. "The camp shrink."

"Well, did you make yourself throw up?"

"No!" I lied. I stretched the phone cord, holding the receiver, looking for a nook of privacy in the room. That's when Doc stepped out of his office and waited in the main entrance. "I just want to come home," I cried.

"They can't be sending you home for no reason, Stephanie."

"I just want to come home," I repeated. "They're starving me here."

"Well, I'm sure they know what they're doing."

"No! I'm telling you. It's not for nutritional reasons. They're just too cheap to give us more food."

"So what does any of that have to do with them wanting to send you home?"

I thought for a minute. "Okay," I said, "so I'm starving here, right? And they take us on this trip to Action Park, so we all pigged out, but then I felt guilty and didn't want to gain, so I made myself throw up. But so did a bunch of other girls." I caught my breath and wiped snot onto my arm.

"Stephanie, it's okay. But why didn't you just tell me the truth to begin with?"

"I was afraid and thought you'd be mad at me," I sobbed, then swallowed, feeling a sting in my throat. "You believe me, right? I'm not bulimic, and I'd never do that again."

"It's very important that you understand this," he said, and I could almost picture his blue eyes, veined with red as he said it, "you can never go wrong with the truth. Do you understand me? Your mother and I might get upset, but no matter what you tell us, as long as it's the truth, you won't be in any trouble."

"I'm telling you the truth! I swear I'll never do it again," I sobbed.

"I believe you," he said, and when I heard him say it, I knew that he did.

MY FIRST OPPORTUNITY TO TALK TO ADAM ALONE WASN'T until late at night, after our last team meeting of the day. I'd sent him a note asking that he meet me at the white benches. The shoulder of the path from the dining hall up to the office was spongy and slick. I sat on the bench and wormed mud from the fretted soles of my sneakers with a stick as I rehearsed what I'd say. It was a moonless night, but I could see my breath.

His shoes made sucking sounds as he plodded up the side of the path to meet me.

I'd just say it. They're throwing me out for throwing up. Then I'd thrust myself into his arms and say I was sorry for ruining our last days together.

He aimed his flashlight up at my face, and I squinted. "What a vision!" he said, making a *thwump* with his fist as it landed on his heart. I rolled my eyes and smiled.

I was going to miss the end of color war. He was going to be in the rec hall without me when they announced the final scores. "So, what's up, buttercup?" Everyone around him, even the boys, would be crying, linked in a line of swaying as they sang the alma mater. It was always the most emotional moment of camp, and I was going to miss it.

I always felt pressure to cry at endings. At my other camps, when everyone else was sobbing their good-byes, I tried to think sad thoughts, hoping to instigate some tears. I'd think, *Dead bunnies.* What else is sad? My parents are dead. Lea has been killed. I hoped to imagine something worthy of real tears, to prove that I was capable of feeling more than anyone else. But the thought of outliving my family seemed too improbable. I never imagined the right stuff.

Waiting for Adam on the benches, I had detailed all he'd experience in the remaining days without me. I knew he'd be herded to the lake, where he'd make a wish before setting a small candle afloat on the lapping waters of the lake on Friendship Night. But if I wasn't there beside him, maybe he'd forget to wish for *us.* Maybe he'd hold someone else's hand. In the final days, he'd make a time capsule, and canter from bunk to bunk asking for addresses and phone numbers. He'd go home with signed pillowcases and other people's T-shirts and come to reflect on it all. And maybe he'd realize he just missed camp, I thought, not *me.* And that's the thought that set me up for tears.

"What's wrong?!" Adam said, trying to peek behind the curtain of my hair.

"I'm leaving early, and you're going to want someone else," I blurted out.

"What?"

"Am I not enough for you? I mean, we might as well break up now anyway. We live nowhere near each other, and who knows when we'll even get to be together again, and—"

"You're leaving early?"

"So you admit it?"

"Admit what?"

"That you don't even care if we're together anymore!"

"Of course I care! You're acting crazy!"

I was acutely unaware of just how crazy I was being when I protested, "I am not!" before storming off to my cabin. Halfway there, I turned to see if Adam was following after me. He wasn't. It seemed to confirm everything.

ON THE THURSDAY MORNING MOM ARRIVED TO PICK US up—six days before the official end of camp—I'd already said most of my good-byes and was eager to leave. I'd imagined the news of my being kicked out had spread through most of Girls' Camp and half of Boys'. I usually gauged who knew by how surprised they acted when I said I was leaving. If their eyes widened and they coupled an "Oh, my God!" with a "Why so soon?" I knew they'd already heard.

I felt ashamed and hated that people acted as if they knew something about me that I didn't or couldn't see for myself. And the best vantage point for them to get that glimpse, it seemed, was to look down at me. The worst was when they feigned concern. Girls in my division with whom I'd hardly spoken all summer approached to tell me how worried they were about me. "You really need to get help," they'd say. Some of these girls had even been with me in the Action Park bathroom, trying to vomit themselves.

I knew that feeling: pretending to care, just to make yourself feel important. You came across as such a benevolent person when you had an opportunity to express your worry, but really it was a way to sneak in and watch up close as someone else unraveled. And the more emphatically you declared your genuine distress for a person, the more they felt the sting.

This was fat camp, a supposedly compassionate, safe haven for kids with eating disorders—*overeating* disorders. And yet by the management's own admission, they were incapable of handling eating disorders. I wasn't treated with compassion. I was treated to one outgoing phone call and a few quick good-byes.

When people who clearly hadn't tuned into *The Puke Report* asked why I was leaving, I made sure to emphasize that it was both Lea and I who were going home, so they wouldn't suspect I'd been asked to leave. I alluded to something important going on back home, so important, in fact, that I couldn't really bring myself to talk about it. I'm sure I led them to believe there was some kind of sudden sickness. I even lied to Lea, telling her Mommy and Poppa were letting us leave early because I'd lost enough weight and complained to them that we were starving. She was excited.

As I packed the last of my belongings during our cabin cleanup, I came upon my goal jeans. Marguerite asked if the red team would be penalized for my mess. I assured her the judges would most likely understand, then unfurled my jeans. I didn't bother changing in a bathroom stall, or even tucking behind a cubby. I stood in my bra and underwear, right in front of our door, then stepped into them. I couldn't stand with my feet too far apart; they were tight around my ankles. I wiggled them up, amazed at how easily they glided over my hips. And they actually zipped. Sure I had to suck it in, but they zipped! Good, let them send me home!

I checked my bag for my diary and ensured that all the letters I'd received from Leigh and Adam were safely tucked away. If he ever learned about Action Park, Adam never alluded to it. He dismissed my psycho breakup babble and vowed to see me in a week. He'd come to stay with me at my house. We'd have separate rooms, but we'd finally be together outside of camp or Pizza House. Any time we missed each other, he suggested in one of his letters, we'd make a list of all the fun things we'd do once we saw each other. "But don't judge me on the size of my list, okay, Klein?" It was all going to be okay. I slipped the pen out from inside my diary and added an entry.

They think that I'm bulimic. Great, huh? I threw up at Action Park and they flipped out. It won't happen again though. I know that!! Especially since what I've been put through here. Jessica told Harper and Harper told the shrink. That's another story. Mom & Poppa know. They believe me though, thank God! They're practically the only ones. I'm going home earlier than expected. I fit into my goal jeans! How exciting!!! I can't wait to go shopping! Jeans and tight shirts and new lingerie. I'm not embarrassed anymore!!

THE HIKE UP THE HILL WAS LONG. KATE AND I PROMISED each other we wouldn't cry. That we'd keep in touch, and she'd call me when she got home from camp. She hoped everything was okay with me, and that's all that was said on the matter. I was embarrassed. I didn't want to say anything that might change the way she thought about me.

"At least you get to eat real food," she said. "Damn, I'm so jealous. I wish I were hitting the road with you."

"Me, too."

"You bitch. You're leaving me with all these flaming assholes and goddamn silent meals."

Then I kinda laughed, but decided to turn it into a fake cry.

"Oh, no you don't, Klein!" she warned, thinking my sobs were real. "We said no tears, didn't we?" She threw her hands into the air as if there were no getting through to me.

I seized the opportunity and quickly reached for her shorts. But when I tried to yank them down, they wouldn't budge.

"Yesssss!" she said, doing a small circular satisfaction dance, churning her hands in the air. "Who's got the drawstring knot now?"

I laughed, so happy to see my friend implementing my little defensive technique. "Well, preacher on a pogo stick," I mocked, "look who finally wised up!"

"Hey! I like it. I'm gonna use that one," she said. "Klein, just look at you, hotter than a pot of boilin' neck bones, you are."

Then my laughter turned into tears, this time for real.

"We're not doin' this," she snapped. "No way. Do you hear me?" But I kept crying. "Oh, fuck a duck," she said, slapping her arms around me. We stood in the middle of the hill, hugging without making a sound. Both our bodies just shaking.

"I'm gonna miss you so much."

"I know, me too. You're a real pain-in-the-ass friend, Klein. And maybe that's why I love you so much."

"I love you too, Scully. And that ain't the booze talkin' neither."

"I don't know if you've noticed," she quoted for the last time, "but I've *still* got a slight weight problem."

We laughed, wiped our faces, and said our good-byes by saying, "This isn't good-bye."

WHEN LEA AND I SPOTTED MOM, WE RACED TO HER, OUR arms extended, screaming with delight. She told us how wonderful we looked, how skinny. We asked where Poppa was. "He's at work. What d'ya think?" Then I called shotgun as someone loaded our duffels into the car. Our black trunks would be sent home on a truck in two weeks, which meant we'd get to shop once we were home! I turned all the air-conditioning vents so they blew on me, and Lea leaned forward from the backseat, eager to join in our front-seat chatter.

Our words stumbled over one another, vying for Mom's attention, and as we drove, a recognizable feeling washed over me, yet I couldn't describe or really understand it. It was déjà vu, maybe. There was an overwhelming sense of familiar in all the unfamiliar towns we passed. I somehow knew the signs, the grain of wood of the local alehouse, the way the afternoon light hit the metal decals, shaped like massive bottle caps. As our ride progressed, we settled down and had less to say. The green manicured fields gently sloped into browns, and I watched the telephone wires bob from pole to pole, growing closer as we neared home. I pressed my palms against my stiff jeans and felt a warming smile sneak across my face. Soon I'd get to go shopping for new clothes. I could reinvent myself.

It was exactly how I'd felt at the start of summer, so eager to escape my fat life of Moose in favor of a clean slate where I could be popular and no one would associate me with the have-to-haves. And now I was happy to be leaving camp, to be going home, where no one knew about Porno Queen, Jordan, or what went on at Action Park. Now that I was on the thinner side of fat, everything was going to be different.

PART

THREE

It's a good day when I feel confident. It's not just the status of your health that makes it a good day. It's also my feeling like a good mother. So if you spit up all your food and the doctor is worried that your tummy looks bloated, it's not the end of the world if I at least did something right that day. And sometimes it's hard to feel I'm doing anything the way a mother's supposed to do things, so I continue to visit you in the NICU and sing and read and pump. I nuzzle up against you and promise to be positive even when all I want to do is cry. Then you latch on, and I smile so damn big, it's gross. My hair is frizzy, and none of my clothes fit, not even Phil's clothes, but I don't care. Yes, I do care, but it's just a day, and you're a life.

—*2007, age thirty-one*

seventeen

MOOSE

Dear Dirty Di,

Austen Rand asked me out . . . again. And I said no again. He said he was begging, so ever since then, the calls have stopped. I kind of miss them though. I mean, you would too. Even if he is a geeky nerd, you'd like getting calls from a guy who always tells you how gorgeous you are. He says that he really likes me. I don't like him though. Then there is Eddie, who Leigh likes now, but who I think that I'm beginning to like too. He always says "hi" to me & hits my ass. I think that he is really cute, but I don't stand a chance with anyone as a REAL girlfriend. The ever popular with losers, Alex, thinks I like him or something, but he is such an asshole. I sometimes feel as if I like him, though. Not most of the time, though.

P.S. Adam is calling me at 11:30 P.M. It is now 11:11 P.M. I'm going to make a wish that we're always together.

IF MY LIFE WERE A FORMULAIC COMING-OF-AGE MOVIE, we'd be way past the workout montage—me on a stationary bike in baggy sweat-soaked clothes chomping a carrot, huffing my way up a hill with a slender counselor running alongside cheering my efforts; I'd shake my head, stop running, and slap my hands on my knees in defeat, but toward the end of the montage, after the close-ups of meager portions, inclined sit-ups, leg lifts, and frizzy hair framing my ruby-red face as I downed a bottle of water—or no, as I slurped from a water fountain, with a winding line of campers yelling for me to hurry up—you'd see that I was determined now, sprinting up the hill, this time victorious and smiling, and we'd be just beyond the bit where the camera zoomed in on my pensive face, behind the glass window of our family car as I neared home ready for a new life.

Next, perhaps there'd be footage of the highly anticipated dramatic intervention with Mom and Poppa, where they'd lecture me about the dangers of bulimia using stern tones and probing questions. Then we'd cut to a scene with a clinical psychologist, a real one, jotting notes on a legal pad, a crinkle between her eyes as she nodded and adjusted her spectacles. Or maybe the director would take an alternate approach, focusing on my reunion with Leigh. It would begin with the first time she sees me. "You are such a liar!" we'd hear her scream, shaking her head in disbelief. "It's like it's you, but it's not you!" she'd say, staring at my reflection in a three-way mirror as I tried on a new life and asked if they carried it in a smaller size.

But it wouldn't happen that way. Mom and Poppa never sat me down for a discussion, nor did they make mention of counseling or even what had happened that summer at camp. It had all been "dealt with" in that abbreviated moment over the phone. Unbelievably, that was it. Even now, when I inquire about it, using those same anticipated tones and probing questions, neither of them really remembers any of it as a big deal. Maybe they figured it was a phase, something all girls went through at one point, that it wouldn't happen now that I was no longer immersed in the fat camp girl dynamic.

As it turns out, they happened to have been right. Once I was home, I really did keep the promise I'd made with myself in the mirror that first night of color war, and I wouldn't make myself throw up in the coming days, months, or even years. That is, until my sophomore year of college when, along with the use of enemas and appetite suppressants, I'd once again reverse the digestive process. It wouldn't happen more than once a month, if that, but sometimes I'd eat so much that it became intolerable to sit, or even sleep, so I'd do it for relief. And it would be. My breathing would become easier, and I could fall asleep. I knew I wasn't alone in any of it.

A friend eventually confided that when she was younger, much younger than thirteen, she'd repeatedly thrown up for attention and control. As it was described to me, her mother had asked the pediatrician what she could do to prevent this behavior. So one day when my friend started throwing up, her mother acted on the doctor's advice and spooned the vomit back to her, forcing her to eat it. When she first shared this with me, I thought, *What kind of doctor advises that?* I imagined her mother gripping her daughter by the hair, ripping her jaw open, and somehow pouring the vomit into her. They'd struggle, she and her mother rolling on the floor, spitting, crying, the both of them covered in her insides. And it worked. She stopped doing it. But in high school she started up again.

I was surprised by how open she was to discussing the details of her therapy. Without the slightest trace of shame or guilt in her voice. "It's a lot like going to a fat doctor," she said. "I journal what I eat and what I bring back up. Then I jot down my feelings, like what I might have been feeling that could have led to the purge. Then we discuss it in person. I don't have to feel bad or hide it anymore."

Did she just yack with the bathroom door open, as the rest of her family continued to eat? Would she return to the dinner table and ask her mom for seconds, or maybe a sheet of paper, so she could write out her feelings between bites? I couldn't imagine what that was like. What it was to eat without guilt, not to have to hide or pretend.

Those following years illuminated other extremes both shocking and sobering to me. In my post-collegiate years, I darted up in the middle of the night, hearing a strange tapping in the common area. A rhythmic pace of *tap, tap, tap*. I squinted, pushing open my bedroom door to discover one of my roommates was exercising in the dark with the aid of a raised platform, kicking one leg as the reverse arm punched the air, to a step aerobics video she'd muted. I wasn't sure if I should apologize for interrupting her or ask her what was wrong with her. There'd be others, of course. Roommates who'd gorge after breakups, boxes of half-eaten Entenmann's cakes, donuts, and Famous Amos cookies hidden behind dust ruffles. One of them would spit her food into empty two-liter 7-Up bottles, collecting her marbleized spit-mixers beneath her bed, along with her half-chewed cakes, to toss out later when no one was around. I'd discover their secrets when I looked to borrow shoes. When I'd reach for a sweater set, I'd unearth diet pills, stashed in armoires. They each took the time to carve out hiding spots, to tuck away their secrets. And those who knew about it, girls like me, harbored the secrets, never confronting the girls, even the closest of them, because of shame. When it came to food rituals, I still couldn't imagine what it was like not to have to hide. Even when it came to the secrets of others.

I never wanted to put anyone in an uncomfortable spot, to think I was relishing their misery. I wasn't gorging, purging, chewing and spitting, or exercising like an animal (also considered a form of bulimia), but I understood. I'd learned all of it in fat camp. I wasn't about to confront any of my friends about it. Their health and bodies are their issues, I told myself. But really, addressing their issues would've forced me to acknowledge my own.

ALL I WANTED WHEN I ARRIVED HOME FROM FAT CAMP was to roll on my bedroom floor. I missed carpeting. Thick toilet paper, water pressure, and my own sink. Real mirrors. Drawers with handles and a closet! I rummaged the house for old clothes, things I hadn't worn in years, just to see if they'd fit. I loved the new me and couldn't stop staring at myself in my bedroom mirror. I compared my belly with all the images of navels surrounding it. So mine still didn't look like theirs. So what? I couldn't wait for everyone to see me.

My high school, The Wheatley School, both sounded and looked as if it was an exclusive private institution. It wasn't. Its student parking lot resembled the Rallye Motors luxury car dealership. Its classes were small, teacher-student ratios exceptional, and the percentage of graduates who moved on to Ivy League schools was downright astonishing. But it was a public school. A *small* public school. Claustrophobic. Incestuous. And the chances of meeting anyone new were just as minute. It accommodated grades eight to twelve, with maybe one hundred students per grade. *Maybe.* Aside from the occasional new kid who'd moved into the district, we'd all been picking our noses together since kindergarten, so on that first day back to school my freshman year, grade nine, it's not that I was expecting to meet anyone new. I was just eager for everyone to meet the new me. Except I couldn't quite figure out who that was going to be.

I'd narrowed it down to four outfits: two if the first day of school was a hot day, and two for a rainy or unseasonably cold day. What I wore was going to set the tone for the entire year. The drop-waist dress was still in the running. I liked that the fluorescent stripes ran diagonally across my body, but it didn't seem tight enough. Like, did it look as if I was trying to hide something under there? I'd vacillated between the acid-washed blue jeans with the white triangle on the back pocket and the black stonewashed Edwins that, according to the saleswoman at one of the trendiest boutiques on the North Shore of Long Island, were all anyone would be wearing. But at the last minute, I eschewed a bedazzled crop top and went for a pink oxford shirt and mini denim skirt paired with my burgundy Weejuns, using one of Poppa's neckties as a belt just as Grayson had. Things had to be done a little differently if I wanted them to actually *be* different. I had to start out on the right foot and decided that foot couldn't be trapped in Birkenstocks. Two new pennies were tucked into the fronts of my loafers, and I was off.

I was also late. First day of school. Freshman year. And I missed the bus. I'd even made sure to iron my hair the night before. I sprang up as soon as the alarm clock blared, having slept on edge all night anyway. It was the treadmill that tripped me up. Hoping to get it over with for the day, I exercised for thirty-five minutes and hadn't accounted for all the outfit indecision. Poppa hadn't left for work yet, so he was happy to give me a ride.

"So? You all excited?" he kinda squealed on our drive there. "Big day, Miss Stephanie! You get to see all your friends and show off how great you look. Must be very exciting."

"Poppa, please."

"What? A father can't be proud of his daughter? You and Lea fill me with such *nakhes*." Oy. Did he have to start in with the Yiddish so early in the morning? "And you know, last year was just a trial run, but now everything goes on your transcript."

"I know, I know."

"Okay, okay," he mimicked. "All we ask is that you try your best."

"Yes, dear," I said, batting my eyes. He once told me the secret to a happy relationship was those two words. I'd hear him say it to Mom when he didn't feel like discussing things, chased sometimes with "whatever you say."

When we pulled into the school driveway, my stomach tightened.

"You shouldn't be too late," Poppa said, checking the time as he put the car in park. At least it wasn't a new school; I knew where I was going.

I kissed him good-bye, straightened my skirt, then pushed through the entrance doors—thankful I'd missed the bus, so I could have this moment to myself. Drawing in a deep breath, I held it to the mental count of three, then exhaled slowly, counting backward from ten to one. I was going to be "in the moment," aware of each sensation, just as Monotone Man had prepped me for all summer. I'd feel the compliments, each smile, and every last "Ohmygod!" I'd worked hard for this and was going to savor it. Slowly. I couldn't wait to hear the shock in all their voices. *Who's that girl?* I was so ready.

As I walked to homeroom, I couldn't stop smiling. The first person I saw was Mr. Singer, the librarian, who appeared to give a slight nod of approval as I cut through the library. Then some older girls from the soccer team saw me, and I was pretty sure one even did a double take. I couldn't turn around and check because that'd be like admitting I knew I looked good. When Eddie Zarabi saw me at the back of the library, he actually held the glass door open for me and said, "Hey." But he said it like he meant it.

"Ohmygod, Stephanie!" Meryl Ferrara and Carol McKenna screamed in unison from down the corridor. The have-to-haves looked the same, except Carol's hair was lighter and Meryl was wearing too much makeup. "You look so awesome!"

"You really do," Meryl agreed, now greeting me with a hug.

"Is that a tie?"

"How much did you lose?"

"I can't get over how great you look. And you straightened your hair!"

"You're like totally different now."

It felt like that first day at camp when I was fat-flocked by the boys. Each toss of my hair inspired. I was finally beautiful.

"What period's your lunch?" Meryl shouted, now that we were each heading off in different directions to our homerooms.

"Uh, I don't know," I hemmed. "I'll talk to you later." Officially, I didn't really have a lunch period, and I definitely didn't want this year to be like the last. I hadn't exactly forgotten that Meryl had conference-called me just before the New York City trip, privately instructing Jennifer not to say anything as she listened in. Then Meryl said things like, "I don't really know about having Jen in our group. She's so . . . well, what do you think?" But seeing them again made me feel safe. And I loved how much attention I was getting. All the questions and admiration. I kinda wanted to sit with them now, but only kinda. I didn't want to pick up where we'd left off last year. I wanted different.

Even two weeks earlier, when I'd reunited with Leigh after camp, things just seemed the same. Leigh had suggested we bake cookies, eat Jiffy Pop, and rent a movie that first night we got together. I didn't scale the wall on the obstacle course, abide daily sign 'n' backs in abominable heat, and do the grapevine to some song about a monkey just to come home and watch *Willow*.

"Why don't we go to the mall?" I offered up as an alternative while we solidified our plans over the phone.

"You wa shoppin' with your mom awl day." I'd forgotten what a pronounced Long Island accent she had. Maybe I had one too, but I had shed it at fat camp. I didn't like the way it sounded and hoped when people heard me they didn't hear that. "Whaddaya need at the mawl?"

Attention. To be seen. For strangers to admire me! "Nothing, I guess."

"You think your parents'll take us to Blockbusta? My mom doesn't like to drive at night."

I loved my new body at 138 pounds. Sure, I still had fifteen or so pounds to go before I reached my goal, but in the meantime, I didn't want to spend my life hidden in dark theaters or at friends' houses playing *The Legend of Zelda*. I wanted to see the world and for it to see me back. To go to Laces Roller Rink and for a boy to ask me to skate for the couples-only song.

"Yeah, sure," I said. So we spent the night doing what we always did. Only I didn't eat as much as usual. And I could tell Leigh started to hold back too when she saw how careful I was being. As nice as it was to see her again, I couldn't help but notice some kind of strain between us. Maybe she was jealous, or maybe she was too much of a reminder of who I'd been. All I knew was that I felt cooped up and annoyed. Of course, in the coming months, she'd rightly tell me I'd become stuck up, and I'd apologize, and we'd be back to being best friends. She'd even go with me to Fran Levine's, and we'd work at weight loss together. But just then, all I thought I really needed was outgoing friends who wanted to meet boys. Maybe I'd make new ones once school started.

ROLL CALL HAD ALREADY STARTED ONCE I REACHED MY classroom. For homeroom, I'd been assigned to Mrs. Wellington. Yes, as in beef. But lucky for her, she was a slender woman, a beef roll-up.

She taught keyboarding and accounting classes in the room beside the art studio. At the end of eighth grade, when we were instructed to choose one elective course for our freshman year, I decided to select two. It wasn't that I was particularly nerdy and thought it would look good on my college transcript—okay, actually yes, that is partly why. I did it to avoid having a lunch period. It was not a "diuretic" I'd come up with in an effort to help shed my excess weight. I just hated having to sit in the cafeteria with the have-to-haves. But now that I looked good, there was no way I'd take both accounting and keyboarding. I'd drop one of them and have a lunch so I could get a life.

Some kids spent all morning counting down the minutes until lunch. They'd slap their books closed and hug them to their chests, sitting on the edge of their chairs, eyes spellbound on the clock, waiting for the bell to sound, and when it did, they'd jerk up and make for the door. I was never that kid. I wished there was no lunch. No lunch, no free time, and definitely no gym. Previously, when the bell chimed before lunch, I'd take my time and linger in the classroom, pretending to review notes until the teacher stood by the door, her hand on the light switch. Then I'd slug over to my locker, change up my books for the next period, and grab my sad brown sack of a lunch. I'd mostly try to eat it in the library, but whenever Mr. Singer caught me, he'd hover over the table I'd chosen, and without saying a word, he'd shake his shiny head and point a rigid arm toward the door.

My low point was visiting the nurse. For company. Regularly. I'd eat my lunch and ask if I could lie down on the green pleather bench. But when a sick kid came in needing a Band-Aid, a hearing test, or an ice pack and an Ace bandage, she'd make me leave. Which left me to hiding place number three: the music room.

The chairs were arranged like a rainbow. If the orchestra teacher, Mrs. Ronata, came in to set up before the next period and saw me, I'd quickly fumble, as if I'd been caught smoking.

"I just have a ton of homework," I'd blurt out, "and the door was open, and it was the only place I could find that's quiet." The irony of utilizing a music room for quiet was lost on me at the time.

She'd smile warmly and say, "No problem at all," as if it really weren't. But I imagined what she really thought was: *Problem child, don't you think I know you have no friends.* But I did have friends. I just didn't like them. They got excited about dumb things. Like field trips to the museum or school assemblies when people from Lincoln Center came to perform some interpretive dance. Kids would snicker at the male dancers. Not because they thought it was gay for a guy to dance, but because they could make out the shape of his package. It was stupid. But whenever anyone involved me in the whispers, I'd play along, making sounds I felt in my throat and nose, pretending to restrain a most unruly laugh that would undoubtedly disrupt the performance had I not tried to contain it. Showing them just how funny I thought it all was. But really, as far as I was concerned, it was all hopelessly boring. Not just the dancing, our whole choreographed routine. And now I'd get a chance to change all the moves.

When the bell rang after third period, I leaped up and made my way to the cafeteria. Kids were just beginning to file in. I chose an empty table toward the middle and fished my lunch bag from my knapsack. Diet soda, straw, a bag of red pepper slices and carrot sticks, and tomato, basil, and mozzarella on Italian bread wrapped in wax paper from the deli. I felt so settled and sophisticated, as if I were wearing red nail polish.

Then I saw a group of familiar faces. I'd been staring at their photos tacked behind my bed all summer. I wasn't completely disillusioned. I knew the popular girls of my grade weren't about to walk up to me and invite me for a sleepover. I just wanted them to see me and think, *I should give her a chance this year. Look how pretty she is.* But none of them seemed to notice me. It was as if I weren't there. Well, maybe they hadn't seen me. Or, maybe they didn't even recognize me! That's how good I looked. I'd wait a little bit, then walk past to throw something out.

"Excuse me, Stephanie," a voice said from behind me. I turned to see that it was Christina Effron, a sophomore who had unnaturally dark hair, so black you could almost see your own reflection in it. "Is this seat taken?"

Well, this wasn't anything I'd ever imagined. Why would Christina Effron want to sit with me? She drew tattoos on herself, wore an eyebrow ring, and struck me as the type who sat at home rubbing metal objects hoping a Wiccan leader might emerge in a puff of smoke.

I shook my head, letting her know she was free to sit there. Then she batted her eyes, flashed me an incredulous smile, and said, "Thanks" as she dragged the chair to another table, full of empty chairs. Then a symphony of laughter exploded from a clutch of girls who'd been watching from across the cafeteria.

I didn't want to eat anymore. "Could you be any more immature?" I muttered to myself as if I were convincing myself to rise above it. I was ready to collect my lunch and get up from the table, but before I had the chance, Meryl and Carol were back, with Lori and Wendy, pitching their backpacks on the floor. If they'd seen what had just happened, none of them said so.

"Ugh," Meryl said, unpacking her lunch, "I already have so much homework." She looked like a representative for Mary Kay products, dressed in various shades of pink.

"Who do you have for English?" Carol asked as she unwrapped a Laughing Cow cheese. I mostly listened as they all swapped school details—who they had for social studies or science, third period or seventh; the usual. I studied the contents of their lunches, silently calculating the calories. I remembered eating those same Laughing Cow cheeses, how I crafted press-on nails with the red wax shell in which they came packaged. Wendy got hot lunch, a hard corner piece of ziti with a carton of milk and a package of three large chocolate chip cookies. The ziti resembled a piece of cake with a crunchy burnt top and a tomato sauce that seemed baked into the noodles. Wendy sat with one leg drawn up, her chin propped on her knee. It's how thin people could sit.

"So what are you eating now?" Lori asked me.

"What are *you* eating?" I teased in an "I'll show you mine if you show me yours" kind of way.

"Tongue."

"No, really."

"Really," she said, lifting the top piece of bread. I peered at it, then moved closer. Were those . . . taste buds?

"That is sooo disgusting," Carol said. "Ohmygod."

"That's rude," Lori said, slapping the bread back on top.

"Who cares what Lori's eating?" Wendy interjected. "I want to hear what they did to Stephanie at that camp."

"Totally," Meryl said. "All I did all summer was babysit and watch TV."

"I know," I said. "I got your *exciting* letters."

"I mean, I knew you were losing weight, but I never imagined—"

"Stephanie, it's such a huge difference. Ohmygod," Carol said.

"You just lost sooooooo much weight," Meryl said.

I knew I was supposed to like this, and of course a part of me did. I would have been disappointed if they hadn't made such a big deal of it. But I was beginning to feel the width of all those "oooooo's." It made me feel kinda shitty hearing how different they thought I was now. It was okay that I hadn't liked the way I looked, but it wasn't okay that others noticed it too.

"You look so happy," Wendy said. "It must've been really hard, though, huh?"

"It was nothing," I said, as if it didn't mean everything.

AND THAT'S WHEN I HEARD IT. I WAS LOOKING DOWN AT my sandwich, ready to take another bite. It was the sound I hoped to never hear again; this time, it wasn't coming from behind me. The pang of a guttural *mmmm* followed with a silence, as if the entire cafeteria was inhaling, holding its breath until the blows of the *ooooooooo* and hiss of the *ssssssssss* broke the silence. Chairs squeaked, making way for even more. And again, the sound would resonate, replacing the mingled melody of catch-up conversations, though this time, there'd be a twist at the end, a ringing of an *eeeeeeeee*. "Oh, Moosey? We see you."

I'd thought they'd graduated, that they had all been seniors when I was in eighth grade. But I was wrong. Now they were seniors, and now, everyone was looking at me.

"What's wrong with you?" Meryl stood up and shouted at them. I looked at her hands, pressing against the table as she leaned forward. "Can't you see how great she looks? She worked hard and lost weight. She looks a helluva lot better than any of you do. So grow up already, you assholes."

I couldn't believe it. No one had ever stood up for me before, and pretty much the last person I ever figured would do so was Meryl Ferrara. The girl ridiculed Austen Rand for stuttering and drew elaborate plans to catch me in lies involving conference calls, and there she was, my have-to-have friend, "like a night in shining armor from a long time ago," just as Peter Cetera's "The Glory of Love" song said. So her armor was a thick shellac of foundation and pressed powder; beggars can't be choosers.

ULTIMATELY, THOUGH, MERYL'S CONFRONTATION DIDN'T change anything. The Bike Nerd and his friends, along with many others, continued to call me Moose. Screaming it across a soccer field, where I would never be anything more than a fullback. Chanting it over the lockers before gym class. Whispering it in classrooms when I was solving a problem on the blackboard. If I just had a chance at a new beginning, I thought, at a new school maybe, it would all be different.

It was how I'd felt about everything. I thought I wanted a chance to re-create who I was. Or to figure out who I was. Really, I just wanted to *escape* who I was.

But I couldn't escape me. I took that same personality—no matter what it wore on the first day of school or to the camp banquet dinner—everywhere I went. And as much as I wanted to be the cool blasé girl who actually liked listening to the Dead's relentless instrumental jams, I was the girl who liked Peter Cetera. The kid who wanted to be smart, to do well in school, who enjoyed learning. I listened to "Love Songs at Night" on the radio, where I'd call in and talk to a DJ about unrequited love.

You'd think I was some meek twerp. But I had big hair, big thighs, and an even bigger mouth. I was loud and eager for attention, not a sweet, easygoing girl who repeatedly won camper of the week. I wasn't nice like the quiet girls. I wasn't mean like Caryn Young or Julie Tesser, who screamed, "Doody!" at me, then ran away. *I'm just a loser,* I thought, who carried it with her everywhere she went, a set of characteristics people narrowed in on. An immodest arrogance, maybe. There was something in me that people either loved or hated. There still is. But back then, I wanted to change their minds and thought maybe I could do so by changing my appearance.

I wasn't much like the dorky kids who took pleasure in science experiments, and I wouldn't smoke or drink or lie to my parents like the cool kids. I wasn't funny. I believed I was a nothing, a nobody, in a body that still seemed to be its opposite: everything. Everywhere. Too big to hold all the nothing in me.

eighteen

To Fat and Back

Leigh wrote me this note saying she liked Jay, who I may like, not really, and Jay grabbed the note out of my hands and read it! Boy was Leigh embarrassed. I would be 2. It wasn't my fault though. And those dumb assholes are still calling me Moose.

IN THE COMING YEARS, I'D RETURN TO FAT CAMP. OTHER fat camps, where Leigh and Hillary would join me. And in 1993, with Doc long gone, I was back at Camp Yanisin, just before starting my first year of college. Only this time, I was an employee—which means they actually paid me to fuck up the heads of young impressionable campers. I'd heard they were hiring, so with Doc out of the picture, I phoned the camp and negotiated a salary with a new owner. By "negotiated," I mean he offered to pay me, and I said yes. During our brief phone interview, it's not as if he questioned, "Ever been tossed out of camp for tossing up you food?" The fact that I had no criminal record was a thumbs-up in his book. Still, here I'd been kicked out of camp, deemed "the problem child," and now I, of all people, was back to counsel and correct the lives of eight-year-old girls—girls who were probably genetically predisposed to being overweight, who'd most likely been sent to camp in the spirit of "early prevention." And they had me as their role model and guide.

I walked the camp's grounds and smiled when I came upon a flattened patch of grass. I wrote to Kate to say so, but I don't think she ever received it. Over the years we'd been in touch, sharing the intimate details of our lives in letters, things we couldn't say aloud, things that just seemed easier to write. We wouldn't share these details with our friends at home. Her mother had four cancerous tumors in her colon. The cancer spread into her blood. Her parents were going through a divorce. "My father has a girlfriend named Ermina. It's a weird name, makes me think of that syrup lady who talks with a do-rag on her head," she had written. Kate moved in with her aunt when her mom's cancer spread to her liver and doctors said she only had a couple of months. They sold her house. Kate never did get the Pontiac Grand Am that was tacked to the window behind our bed. "I got my mom's car. A Caravan. It's real embarrassing." She explained that her mom was in an experimental program that left her all doped up. Oddly, she closed the letter letting me know she had started a new diet and had already lost eight pounds.

Even more odd, her including her preoccupation with her body, at such a tumultuous time, wasn't odd at all. Body obsession, I'd come to learn, can even trump tragedy. Even when we're grieving, we can still feel fat.

One of the last letters I received from her said, "Keep this letter always, and always remember me, the pissing-off bitch! One day when we see each other again, you can give this letter back to me and we can laugh our asses off." But I never saw her after that first summer at camp. I still miss her. So much. Which is strange when you think about it. We only really had that one summer together, and still, I think about her, Google her, and realize the profound effect people who were once strangers can have on our lives. I missed her especially when I was a counselor and had campers telling me to piss off.

Aside from the obviously obese campers for whom I was now responsible, I wondered which among them were picked on at school because of their fifteen extra pounds. Who would be the loud-mouthed camper, perhaps with a sick mom or parents on the verge of divorce, as Kate had been that first summer? Did any of the girls have have-to-have friends at home, whom they'd hoped to outgrow by growing thinner? Which were capable of being bullies? Was there a Jordan among them? Which of them would befriend an awkward older camper, perhaps like Beulah, and ask my permission to visit with her? I would learn. And they would learn from me.

As a veteran fat camp champ, I was well versed in the rich tapestry of camp traditions. I escorted my girls to the rec hall for their before pictures, coaxed them into the pool, and helped demonstrate exactly how one did the Yanisin Roll. As the summer progressed, I encouraged sweet Amber, only six years old, to put her face in the lake for the first time; comforted little Ruthie when she was homesick, braiding her hair the way she said her mother had; taught them all how to pee in the woods on our overnight hike up Blueberry Hill, where I permitted them to eat all the blueberries they'd like; and I of course reminded them to be liberal with the talcum powder to prevent chub rub.

When they dragged their feet and moaned when climbing Heart Attack, I had them all look down at their shoes as they walked. "See, now doesn't that make it easier?" I tried to encourage camp spirit but felt like a hypocrite doing so. I taught the girls the words to our camp cheers and left it to them to decide when to use them.

For camper skit night, my co-counselor choreographed their moves, and we led them onto the stage, where we all did a bit of rump shakin' to "Baby Got Back." Unfortunately, they committed all the lyrics to memory. But far more disturbing than a six-year-old singing, "Knock-kneed bimbos walkin' like hos" was what I overhead one afternoon during rest hour.

As soon as I heard it I looked up. One of my campers was sitting on her bed folding laundry, singing. It wasn't a purposeful singing, where you sing into a broom handle or into the mirror or in the shower. The lyrics to Cyndi Lauper's "I Don't Want to Be Your Friend" were turned out unconsciously as she continued to fold. Here I hadn't only taught them the lessons I'd learned from Fran, reminding them when they went home to always eat while sitting down, on smaller plates, so their portions would seem bigger, but I'd unintentionally set them up to expect catastrophic romantic breakups. I'd blared songs about unrequited love as if they were mantras to a religion rooted in scorn. "I'll forget I ever let you into this heart of mine, baby" aren't exactly the words you'd expect to hear from a girl who wears Wonder Woman pajamas.

MORE OF MY HABITS WERE PASSED ALONG IN THE DINING hall.

"Now, if you're craving sweets at home, what will you do?" I quizzed at our lunch table.

They all knew the answer, as I held these interrogations weekly. "Try drinking a glass of skim milk," Monica said as she simpered.

"And why would Monica do this, Ruthie?"

"Because the lactose sugar usually satisfies the craving," Ruthie said.

"And what if it doesn't? What will you do, Kristie?"

"I'll take whatever it is I'm craving and cut it into quarters . . . on a plate!" Kristie quickly added. "Because—"

"Everything counts when it's on a plate," they sang in unison.

"I'll eat one quarter," Kristie continued, "then wait twenty minutes before I have the next piece."

"Twenty minutes," Jessy interjected, "because that's how long it takes for the stomach to send a signal to the brain that we've been fed."

This was our mealtime ritual. Scoops of food had been measured, then turned onto our plates. Before any of us forked through the globes of instant potatoes, we waited until all our cups were filled with water. After a short Q&A round, we'd inhale, then hold it, until I raised my hand. The girls then counted aloud with me, backward from ten to one. We then downed our first cup of water. Ruthie passed the pitcher of ice water to Monica, then to Lexie, around to Kristie, until all of us had replenished our cups. No one had eaten a morsel.

I lifted one hand to my face and pinched my nose closed; waiting until they followed, I then nodded and said, "Go!"

Using small paper cups usually reserved for salad dressing, or for dispensing pills in the infirmary, we all did a shot of apple cider vinegar, then quickly chased it with our second cup of water.

"Nasty!"

"Yeah, but Steph says it burns fat."

They might not have been eating with chopsticks, but I had girls in grammar school pounding shots of vinegar before each meal. I'd read somewhere it sped up the metabolism. As if that's what six- to eight-year-olds need. I wanted to save them from a lifetime of Moose. Despite my best intentions, I was perpetuating the cycle, helping to create more food-obsessed girls, dissatisfied with their bodies.

The division leader, my boss, finally approached me midsummer, asking that I no longer do my shots in front of the girls. "Inappropriate," she said. I took that to mean *for them*. It was perfectly normal, say, for me to flee to the Pig-Out Room after a meal, close the door, and swig vinegar from the bottle in private. I weighed 122 pounds.

The cider vinegar might have been replaced with balsamic at the salad bar, but I still drilled the girls at our table, hoping they'd remember what to do once they were home. I directed them always to eat food off a plate, even if it was just carrot sticks, so they'd think of it as a minimeal, not just a snack. I didn't want dinnertime to arrive with them thinking, *I'm starved! I haven't had anything to eat since lunch.* I wanted to equip them with skills. Except I wasn't giving them the right ones.

When I looked beyond my girls, at the campers who were my age when I'd first started to fat camp it, I could spot the ones who didn't belong. The thin ones who hadn't been dragged to camp to accompany a heavier sibling, but who were repeat offenders, back for more, hoping to weigh less. They were sad, unhappy people. I didn't know it at the time, but I was one of them, too.

I might have been obsessed with being thin, but really, I lived in constant fear of becoming one of them: a fat girl again. So I surrounded myself with them, considered myself fat, even when I wasn't. I hadn't chosen to be a counselor, or a successful fat camp champ, to hear how thin I was. I returned each year because the thin kids at fat camp didn't have to have a good personality. It was *thin* that really at the end of the day made people want to be around you. Not just boys, everyone. Because so many of us were haters of our own kind. It's why we were at camp in the first place: to stop being who we were, to change, to stop seeing what we'd despised each time we glanced at a mirror.

The thin kids at fat camp were always . . . I don't know how to finish that. Not *losers.* Just were never going to be popular outside of fat camp. While fat camp supposedly leveled the playing field, allowing people to be seen for something other than their size, had I been at a "normal" camp as a thin person, I'd be left to be liked based on my personality alone. And I'd never be as likable and as special as I was as a thin person at fat camp.

You're either likable or your not. And some people just gave you more chances if you were thin. Because after all, it was just as I'd imagined all along: thin could wear red and be a bitch and people would still like her.

SOME OF THE GIRLS WEREN'T JUST TOO THIN TO BE THERE. They were too young.

"It's never too early to learn good habits." Yeah, actually it is. I should have been teaching them how to balance spoons on their noses. And if I was going to talk about food, the least I could have done was spoken about intuitive eating, of being mindful, of realizing you shouldn't be afraid of food, that you can eat what you want as long as you learn to only eat when you're hungry, to learn to stop when you're sated, to imagine you can have as much as you'd like of that food, that there would always be more, so there's never any need to stuff yourself with it, no need to eat as if you're warding off thieves. I wish I'd made them understand that if you eat out of control one time, it's not going to be the end of the world. But these are things I couldn't teach, because I hadn't learned them myself.

I WEIGHED 118 POUNDS WHEN FIRST-YEAR ORIENTATION began. I was sitting on the steps of Low Library, where all the students of Columbia University socialized, and I couldn't have felt better. I'd spent most of the summer in the weight room, so I wasn't just lean; I was strong, toned, and fit. The sky resembled an ocean, with clouds that looked like white caps and small foamy bubbles. I'd gotten into all the classes I'd hoped to, and I'd made friends with a clutch of playful girls who'd asked me to join them downtown later that night, to go dancing at a club. "Less is always more," a frisky Brazilian who wore crop tops and a belly chain had advised when I asked her what I should wear. It was the life I'd always wanted. My new start, for real.

"Well, look who's here," one of a crush of guys yelled up to me from the bottom of the steps. I squinted to see if I could make out any of their faces. "Mooooooossssssseeeee," one of them bugled. My pulse quickened. My stomach floundered. Not again.

A voice, so deep it seemed plucked from the strings of a bass, jazzed in from behind me with a rich and even, "Whaassssuppp." I whirled around to see who was there, yelling back. I shielded my eyes from the sun, and looked up to see a football player, in dark jeans and a white T-shirt. I only knew he was a football player because on his head was a blue and white football helmet with moose antlers attached.

I'd spend the rest of my life trying to get over Moose.

nineteen

THE HATE DIET

I used to get pissed when he wanted to go to the gym. Even more pissed if he suggested we go together. He might as well have grabbed a Sharpie marker and circled my flaws because "let's go together" was interpreted as "you could stand to lose some flab there, Missy." I made it about me, began to cry at the suggestion, and then, he'd stay, setting his Walkman down on the table with his testicles. I'm embarrassed I was that manipulative. I hate how much I hated myself and took it out on others. I hate how miserable I was with myself.

—2005, age twenty-nine

THERE WAS A POINT IN COLLEGE, ABOUT A YEAR AND a half after my summer as a counselor, where I actually revisited my childhood weight, nearly eclipsing it at 162 pounds. I've recently seen the college photos, or I'd never have remembered returning to fat. It's not that I was in denial, too pained to recall the freshman forty I'd smeared on. In fact, it was quite the opposite: I didn't remember being fat because I was in love. And I'm now convinced that when Shakespeare wrote, "Love is blind," he was having a fat day.

What care I of such trite things as body weight and exteriors when in bed with a man who loves me completely, just as I am? There are more important things about which to ruminate. Namely, what's for dinner?

The way I see it, love is an amusement park, and food its souvenir.

I can trace every romance of my life back to a meal. My memories are enhanced by the tender morsels had at tables across from lovers, on blankets with friends who'd eventually become more, in banquets, barbecues, and breakfasts. And the seasons of these romances followed an intricate blueprint through fat and thin.

In the spring, afternoons were spent in New York museums and movie theaters, roving through parks where tulips peeked up through narrow beds of snow. I'd feel his fingertips for the first time. He'd hail a taxicab but convince me not to get in. Our afternoon would often extend into evening, an impromptu dinner at a local bistro. "So do I!" and "Wow, me too!" said in smiles between bites of young Bibb lettuce, wax beans, and golden beets. Linen napkins and polite talk and touch. Seared salmon with morels, blanched fiddleheads, petite peas, and a basic beurre blanc. White Burgundy. That first kiss as good as the last bite.

In the sweet summer of a relationship, brunch toasts were made "to us," the clinking of mimosas over peekytoe crab cakes Benedict, gravlax, and ceramic cups of coddled eggs. Strong coffee. A ruffle of skirt, coral accessories, freckles, and sunblock. He'd reach across the table to tuck a stray twist of my hair behind my ear. Fragrant strawberries presented with a shallow bowl of fine sanding sugar. The rest of our day planned yet lazy. Salty prosciutto with melon eaten from his hands in a rowboat. Our feet over the sides, making ripples in the water. He'd say, "I love you" without meaning to.

We'd meet at my apartment, before dinner with friends, noshing on hard wheels of salami, white grapes, aged grating cheese. He'd use the word "girlfriend" when introducing me, his hand on the small of my back.

I'd be surprised and excited and would order razor and cherrystone clams on a bed of wet linguine with a touch of cubed tomato and a scatter of parsley. I'd ask the waitress for more bread. I'd offer him a taste, secretly hoping he'd decline. And I'd watch as he twirled his fork in my food, bringing his mouth to my plate. *Not that much!* I wanted to shout. Instead I smiled when he said, "Good," his mouth full of what should have been mine.

Come Labor Day, we'd have our first big blowout fight. I wouldn't remember the details of it, only the midnight peace offerings made barefoot in my kitchen. We foraged the cabinets, finally composing tomato sandwiches with wobbly mayonnaise and crisp white toast. "Wait," I'd say, adding kosher salt. "Okay, now." We'd make up by the light of the open refrigerator. And I'd swear to myself that I'd never forget that moment.

We'd come home drunk some nights. I'd change into sweats, wash my face, turn on the television, and he'd lie in bed, still dressed, one foot on the floor. "I'm not going to be able to sleep here," he'd say, and for a moment, I'd worry it was his way of distancing himself. "The room won't stop spinning." I'd get dressed and walk with him to the diner for grease.

"This will make you feel better," I'd say, but really I'd feel better because I'd still be with him. We'd sit in the diner and order chocolate malteds, cheese fries, and hamburgers. And I'd love it—that refrigerated rotating pie life, lived behind glass doors beside plastic-wrapped cantaloupes filled with red Jell-O. Everything felt safe and preserved.

In the fall there'd be football games and foot massages. Tailgating and tagliatelle. A warmed bowl of parsnip pear puree swirled with roasted garlic. "So what's for dinner?" wouldn't be a passing comment; it would become our evening activity, *our plans,* along with a *TV Guide* lineup. Battened in layers of his clothes, we'd play dirty Scrabble, drinking shots of Irish whiskey. Parts of the Sunday paper would be read aloud while we feasted on navy bean stew and a loaf of toasted peasant bread. Nurturing our relationship with food. Pumpkin, potatoes, potpies. So my pants no longer fit; he still wanted to get into them. "Stephanie," he'd whisper, "I sometimes forget how beautiful you are." After sex, he'd need to rush to his front door to pay the delivery guy. He'd grab jeans off the floor. We'd picnic in bed. Hung over. Half dressed. *Have the last bite, baby.* His hand wiping my chin. Kissing me, food still in my mouth. Those jeans he was wearing, I'd notice midbite, were mine. I spit out the rest into a napkin, silently declaring that my diet started now.

But in his boxers come morning, I'd scoop apple pie filling from a flimsy baking tin, eating hunched over his kitchen counter. Drinking milk from the carton.

A glass of wine after a long day, his hands on my hips, fingers near my mouth. I'd drink too much, and we'd argue over plans and friends and parents. He'd fall asleep angry. I'd eat quiet foods straight from the fridge. Custard. Whipped potatoes. Lemon curd. In the morning there'd be soft-boiled eggs, strips of fried bacon, and apologies.

As real as it all felt, that's all we'd be: a few seasons. A morning. A wakening. A couple who were courteous, who asked each other if you've had enough fish and would you like more rice, but really, that's all we were. This couple that wouldn't be there tomorrow, for the bacon he liked a little chewy or the grapefruit juice I preferred to orange. The memories would taste like burnt coffee. And that's when I'd stop living my life in meals. We'd be over before the official start of winter. And by February, I'd be thin again. Thin, single, and miserable.

These patterns would cycle through seasons for years. The men and menus would change slightly, but the archetype was the same. I spent my whole single life trying to be thin just to find someone who'd love me once I got fat.

As an unattached adult with no "So, what are we having for dinner tonight?" it was far easier to be slim. My cupboards could remain barren; there were no complaints about my desolate fridge. The take-out menus I kept were limited to sushi and the health food joint down the block—because even then I was still too lazy to walk there. I was despondent, but at least I was skinny. Of course once I found myself in a secure, loving relationship again, I'd gain it all back, finally at ease.

"You let yourself go, is what you did." People who say this should get their eyes gouged out with a carrot. They're the very same people who believe most overweight individuals are fat because they're miserable. "You're trying to suffocate your emotions, eating from stress and out of depression, because you cannot stand your life." They believe when a person is trim it's because they're content. In my case, it was just the opposite.

The times in my life when I've been my thinnest, I've been a walking psycho wreck. Forget the fact that I was basically starving myself; skinny was usually due to some kind of loss. Death. Rejection. Divorce.

When I was married to a man whom I now refer to as The *Was*-band, I slipped into a cozy life. For the first year and a half of our marriage I remained quite slim at 123 pounds. But then I became more domestic, trying to please him with fresh baked goods and his food favorites. Miniature cheesecake brownie bites. We gained weight, sharing food and the guilt of overeating it, together. He baked me a carrot cake from scratch. I even checked the garbage for carrot shavings in disbelief. I was impressed and knew he loved me. I licked cream cheese frosting from his finger.

And then one day, when I was probably up twenty-five pounds since being married, he said to me, "I'm not as attracted to you as I once was."

You're a real shit, I would have thought if I were . . . I don't know, *sane*! But I'm sure I asked for it. Yeah, you read that right. I bet I wouldn't let up until he admitted it. That's the answer I was looking for, and I wasn't going to stop until he gave it to me. You know how you suspect something, but until the person actually admits it, it isn't completely true? I was secretly hoping he'd never admit it, preferring instead to believe that maybe I was just sensitive; maybe I wasn't as fat as I thought. Or even if I was, somewhere inside I wished it wouldn't make a difference, despite knowing men are visual. Because hopefully he wouldn't see me as fat or thin; he'd see me as me. Stephanie. His wife, the woman with whom he chose to spend the rest of his life.

I went three days without articulating a word to him, a habit I'd perfected since my camp days with Adam. Despite his pleading e-mails, attempts to convince me what he'd said was taken out of context, that he'd love me no matter what I weighed, I didn't believe him. I was wounded and felt it so deep in my chest that I clutched at it, reminding myself to breathe. And then my hurt turned toward anger. That's when I went on a hate diet.

Ah, the Hate Diet.

I realized its effectiveness while filling out a personal progress journal, one of those fill-in-the-blanks self-help journals, Mad Libs for the manic. I purchased it the afternoon following his admission. *Not as attracted,* I kept repeating to myself. I hid away in the bookstore, sipping water in the upstairs café. I borrowed a pen and did some of the exercises within.

In a short paragraph, the journal instructed me to "identify one person in your everyday life who is taking positive steps to be healthy and control his or her weight." Oprah was first on my list—not exactly in my everyday life, but certainly a person who'd broadcast her weight-loss successes. I paused, biting my inner lip in thought. Then I scrawled the name of a woman from work who was quite possibly anorexic. As far as I could tell, the only calories she consumed came from the milk in her coffee. And as fucked up as it is, there she was in blue ink on my role model list. I added a childhood friend I'd heard lost a lot of weight. Then Michelle, another coworker. And then the list changed.

I scribbled the name of an ex-boyfriend who once said, "You're bigger than the girls I usually date." Another who when we returned from winter break in college had said, "Well, someone's mother fed her well." I added the name of ex-friends, including the slurs I could remember. "Jordan," I wrote, "and the case of the fat pants." I added my motherfucker-in-law, and then my husband.

I'd get thin and stylish and look better than ever, and my motivation was never "so he'll love me more." It was "so the ass-hat will regret ever uttering those words." Healthy marriage, I know. That's a different book.

It was just as it had been at camp all those years ago. I was still motivated by hate. *Take that, judgmental windbag. I'm thin.* I suppose it's along the same lines as "the best revenge is being deliriously happy." My best revenge was being thin. Because you can't really see happy; people can fake that. You can't fake thin.

So I would begin, as we all do, a diet. A crash and burn bitch of a diet. But how? What would work this time? Hadn't anything I'd learned from Fran or fat camp prepared me for this? No, there had to be something easier.

I resolved to follow the advice in the journal and ask the thin people on my list how they did it. Oprah had personal trainers and private chefs and wasn't, if you can believe it, returning my phone calls. I hadn't actually seen the childhood friend on my list, so it would be quite awkward to phone her out of the blue. "Hey, it's been forever, but I heard you're no longer a tub. What's your secret to staying motivated?" I decided to ask my waif coworker how she did it.

"Don't do anything that makes you sweat," she confided, quite eager to divulge her secrets. "It'll make you too hungry. Do yoga if you have to, but not the hot kind. And don't keep any food in the house. Just turkey. That's it. And drink lots of coffee," Waif Worker said, raising a fresh cup of it.

"But I'm hungry," I'd whine over our cubicle divider.

"No, you're not. You just think you are. Let's go tanning." Instead of using our lunch hour to eat, some afternoons we'd zip to her favorite tanning salon. "Seeing yourself naked should be enough motivation to keep your mouth shut," she'd said. "Well, I don't mean *you,*" she stumbled, "just in general. Besides, tan conceals cellulite." Yuh-huh.

I liked how bossy she was. It was almost as if she personified my own self-control. My willpower was power-walking around the streets of New York in her Nike trainers. When I was around her, I didn't have to regulate myself because I knew she'd do it for me.

When I wasn't with her, I did all I could to keep my mind off food. I knew my motivation to lose weight would wax and wane, so I needed a plan I could stick to whether I liked dieting or not. I couldn't just wake up and decide I was going to eat healthfully; I'd actually need to do it. I knew myself well enough to know my patterns. Usually, I'd feel hopeful that I'd made it through the first three days of whatever diet it was. Then the diet seemed easier. "Hey, I can do this!" I'd feel proud of myself for doing what my mind was urging me to. I respected myself more and wanted less. "I will not fail at this" became my mantra, and I believed it. But after a few weeks of success, I'd slip into my old ways again, thinking I was immune to weight gain. So this time I thought all I really needed was to get out of the house, away from food, as often as I could. I scribbled ideas into the journal.

At night go to Barnes & Noble.
Hide in movie theaters.
Wake up early & get your tan cellulite to the gym.
When out for dinner, order only a small salad & an appetizer, not an entrée.

After work, instead of rushing home to prepare dinner, I'd go to Bloomingdale's and try on clothes two sizes too small. On purpose. If I chose clothes that actually fit, I might start to feel okay about myself. And that wouldn't do. *See,* I'd say to my stomach as it toppled over, *you've still got a long way to go.* The very words, by the by, Poppa had uttered when I was twelve and just starting to lose weight again with Fran.

After a few weeks, Waif Worker asked me to grocery shop for her. "It's just that Kyle Peck is coming over, and you're so good at all that domestic stuff." And? "And I don't have time to do it all myself. I have to go out and buy plates." Of course she didn't own plates. She didn't eat. Still, who doesn't have plates? I blinked at her. "I have to put food in my cabinets, or he'll think I'm a freak." You are a freak. "Can't you make me seem normal?" It would be a miracle at the 34th Street supermarket.

I food-shopped for her apartment because it never occurred to me to say, "Are you fucking kidding me? Why you gotta send the fat girl for the food?" It never crossed my mind to say no. So I went to the market and spent too much time analyzing not my own behavior, but what items would say about her.

What exactly would cornflakes seem to convey about Waif Worker? Wholesome, with an appreciation for the simpler things. I strolled amid the colorful rows of food products looking for other statements. The red and navy canister of Quaker Oats declared that she had patience. Microwave popcorn: the girl appreciates technology. I added a pound of Bavarian old-fashioned pretzels to the shopping cart because girls are always snacking on pretzels. Lorna Doone shortbread cookies. I paused. No, men like to eat Mallomars. *Impressive,* he'd think upon seeing the yellow box. *I bet she likes sports.* I'd buy nothing low fat or low sugar. She wouldn't want him to think she ever thought about her weight. Instead the goal was to wow him with her genes, a girl who can eat and still look like that! A six-pack of Dr Pepper and a tub of Jif and I was done.

I retraced my steps to the Lorna Doones despite having decided on the Mallomars. Screw it. I filled the cart with everything *I* wanted. Nacho-flavored Combos, potato skins, frozen miniature hot dogs, and a red bag of Tater Tots. A jar of Cheez Whiz. Tostitos. A half-gallon of Moose Tracks. A canister of Pringles. The cart brimmed with all the things I could never have. A tub of icing. Now we're talking. A box of cake mix—no, not just cake mix. Mix with pudding in the batter. Ooh, what else? How extraordinarily freeing. Go on and giggle, Doughboy. Oh, yes I can! How delicious to pretend I could be this free from food.

When I reached the checkout counter, I picked at my nails. People are going to think this is all for me. *Well, it's no wonder,* they'll think as they eye my arm lard. What am I doing? Just look at yourself. You have no control. *But she gets to.* Yeah, but she doesn't eat it. For her it's just decor. Go home to your husband, the one who thinks you're too fat to fuck.

I abandoned the cart in the checkout line, pretending to double back for a forgotten essential item. I left the store empty-handed.

I went home and filled my empty hands with folded slices of white pizza. I annihilated the pie and wondered how her date would go without the props that told the story of a life she didn't live. I ate until I felt ill. I stepped on the scale and became afraid of myself. That was it, my moment. That moment you have when you know you're out of control. I didn't want to undo all the summers I'd spent at fat camp, all the times I'd exercised and suffered. I didn't want to become Moose again. In that moment, everything stopped spinning and I was left with a quiet truth that wept and hung on my insides.

I couldn't continue to live like this anymore. Like Waif Worker, I too needed someone to make me seem normal.

That someone, I hoped, would be Michelle, the second coworker on my list. Maybe she'd have an answer. If she could do it, then so could I. I demanded she share with me her weight loss secrets.

"Oh, I just eat right and exercise," she said.

"Bullshit. Tell me."

"What? It's true."

"No it's not. You love food as much as I do." She'd gone from a size 12 to a size 2 in approximately eight months, and now she had sculpted arms—guns, really. A woman with chiseled triceps is never hiding fat elsewhere. It's the telltale sign that she probably even looks better naked. I wondered who'd pissed her off; that kind of thin only came from hate.

"Why are you asking me this?" *Why?* Because I'm fat *and* miserable, and that never happens.

"Because you look so great." Because I need help.

"Well," she softened. I leaned in. "Okay, so you have to promise not to tell anyone." I shook my head quickly, my left hand in the air.

twenty

FATHER FIGURATIVE

I'm noticing that my double chin isn't just happening due to the occasional bad camera angle; they're all bad camera angles lately. I have enough to worry about in my life. Weight shouldn't be an issue anymore. My first moment of disgust didn't come while shopping for bathing suits; it came while trying on ski jackets. Phil watched as I zipped my way into a black puffer coat. I smoothed the fabric over and looked to him for a thumbs up or down, thinking maybe it was too informal a coat to wear out at night. He didn't know what to say. "Well, do you think it's, I don't know, hard to zip? I mean, it looks like you could use one size bigger." I feel so small the bigger I get.

—2006, age thirty

MICHELLE MUST HAVE GIVEN ME THE WRONG ADDRESS. I was expecting an office building, a plaque announcing all the M.D.s in the complex, perhaps a single office door tucked to the side of a lobby, not a residential Upper East Side brownstone. I double-checked the slip of paper, then looked up at the brass numbers above the front door. I pressed the button and waited, staring into the black grooves of the intercom. I was buzzed in without having to declare who I was.

I walked through an unremarkable vestibule and faced two doors. The slightly ajar one with a plaque indicating "Chien Féroce," I assumed, was the front door to his home. The other was red with a round, thick window in its center, similar to a cruise ship porthole. A handwritten note said to press 4 for the office of Dr. Levine.

Dr. Levine, I thought as I ascended in the elevator, *you have the same last name as Fran. It's a sign! This time it's gonna really work.*

When the elevator stopped, I pulled the rickety metal gate aside and pushed open the door. I heard the muffled voice of a man shouting from behind a closed white door.

"What's wrong with you?!" the voice roared. This was it, and I could already tell this wasn't going to be anything close to a cruise.

I could either duck into the elevator and leave, or I could plod up the winding wooden staircase that narrowed as it reached his waiting room on the next floor. Michelle looked damn good. All women suffered for beauty in one way or another. I'd add this to my list.

His waiting room of clients and orchids was a relief. I was somewhere I could get help, even if it did mean being berated like a three-year-old by a frustrated father figure. A trim middle-aged receptionist with fluffy hair, a warm smile, and shifty eyes checked me in and instructed me to read through a pamphlet before meeting with the doctor. I took a seat beside a modern accent table strewn with current fashion magazines. A blonde with a vintage handbag folded into her hardly there lap lifted her eyes to me, flashed a practiced smile, then flipped through the February 2002 issue of *W* magazine. The doctor's patients all appeared to be thin European smokers with diamonds so big they rested on two fingers. I sat stuffed into my coat like a bird fluffing its feathers to retain warmth.

I studied the pamphlet. It had a prologue. Then a monologue—ground rules, a list of things *not allowed*, sample breakfasts, lunches, and dinners—an epilogue, and a "backlogue," and it ended with a quote: *To mold the body one must first mold the mind.* Several passages were written in bold; other times he screamed in all caps. The prologue outlined my initial visit. My medical history, then my blood, would be taken, ruling out anemia, infection, and something to do with blood dyscrasias. A SMAC would be performed "to rule out various disease entities." A series of T tests (T3, T4, free T4 index, and TSH) would measure my basal metabolism. A coronary risk profile would assess my cholesterol, triglycerides, LDL, HDL, and LDL/HDL ratio. Then I'd pee in a cup.

I knew none of the tests would come back the way I wanted them to: abnormal. Yeah, I was hoping for bad news. Sadly, the doctor wouldn't be able to sit me down and say, "We've found the culprit. All this time, it hasn't been your fault!" I assumed I had no metabolism, and part of me hoped he'd say my thyroid was acting out, pissed, quite understandably, at my hips and thighs. But deep down I knew *I* was the culprit.

In the monologue section he made his role clear. "I am neither a psychiatrist nor a policeman." He didn't much care about the *why*s. He didn't want to hear problems or excuses. Indeed, I would learn in the coming months that he was not a policeman. He was a Diet Dictator. I called him Dr. Dick for short.

What I've learned since my time with Fran is that someone real and alive needs to know what I weigh, what I *really* weigh, and write it down as proof. And that someone needs to be an authority figure, not a spouse, a relative, or a friend who could simply wave it away and suggest we share a bottle of Chianti.

Each week on the ride up the elevator, I'd peek through the small porthole at the rest of his home, floor by floor, trying to get some kind of insight into what his life must be like outside office hours. I glimpsed his taste in the framed line drawings. His wife, walking their chow (how ironic), smiled sympathetically. She wore driving shoes, and a quilted Burberry jacket, and looked like one of those Frenchwomen who'd never need her husband's services. They probably wore berets and looked at Botero paintings when they were hungry.

Most of the time Dr. Dick stared at me without saying much. Although I didn't know him to have children, he struck me as the type of parent who'd ask his child to choose his own punishment. "Well, what do you think is appropriate? Oh, I see. And that's all? Anything else?" I'd shift my eyes a lot, wondering if I'd said the right thing. He'd purse his lips as I spoke, looking me over as if I were Rubens's *Venus at the Mirror.*

But he'd crack a smile sometimes, and I got the feeling he didn't mean any of it. He wasn't really the vicious man I wanted to make him into. He was a businessman, and he was good at it. He knew what obese people needed—well, a lot of them anyway. We needed someone else to care for us. To get angry, to explode, to get us back on track. And we'd rely on him to do it for us, because it was easier than doing it ourselves. It was his shtick. "I don't know if I can treat you anymore" was by far his favorite threat.

He was as pushy and exacting with his words as Jared Held, the sixteen-year-old boy from South Florida who'd given me my first hickey at Camp Yanisin. While the good doctor would command me each week to take a seat in his chair so he could stab the fleshiest part of my arm with a B-vitamin shot, Jared didn't have me sit. On that stone-scaped path from the fields to the pool, Jared had instructed me to lie down beside him on a bed of pine needles. I complied. I'd been wearing my black bathing suit beneath a slightly damp white Hendrix T-shirt.

"You shouldn't wear a black bra under a white shirt, sweetie," Jared lectured softly as I wiped his saliva from just above my upper lip. "It's trashy." Jared had a mullet, wore a thick gold necklace, and pronounced "doing" as if it had no *g*. Apparently he was an authority.

Who the hell are you? I thought. It's not even a bra; it's a bathing suit—and *I'm* the girl. Don't you think I *know* I shouldn't wear black beneath white? *You ass-munch.* I was crazy about him.

Before Adam and I became a couple, there was Jared, a confident boy whom I'd dated for all of three days. In that time, I came to realize that I liked when he'd tell me what to do. Not that there was much I was willing to explore physically at thirteen anyway. I wouldn't let him beneath my shorts and refused to ransack his. Though according to my diary, "I felt his dick against my leg, and he had the biggest boner!"

Even more than the word "boner," I liked playing defense to his forward. I liked his aggressiveness, the way he ordered me into position. "Come here," he'd demand. "Kiss me like this," he'd say. He never seemed nervous, never fumbled or slobbered. I was fidgety and hadn't even considered expressing how I might like to be kissed. His way, I was sure, had to be better than mine. He was older and an authority on what I should like. I believed back then that age had everything to do with wisdom, despite his overbearing use of Drakkar Noir cologne. Jared called me his girl and put his arm around me at the minor league baseball field trip. He kissed me on the mouth, even when people were looking.

After our time in the woods together, I arrived at my cabin racing for my handheld mirror. I studied my reflection then spun around with it, squealing. My hand rose, my finger a soft trace along my neck, as I squinted for a closer look. What absolute bliss! I loved having proof that a boy wanted me, evidence of desire for everyone to see. Loved seeing his mark on my nape, as though he'd claimed me.

On a deeper level I liked, very much, the primitive feeling of belonging to someone. I was his, his property, so hands off. *His girl,* whom he'd tell what to wear and how to kiss. I wanted to please him, to be his "good little girl," but I also wanted to remind him that he had a good thing.

"It's trashy," he'd said.

"Well, your friend Jon doesn't seem to think so," I'd responded with a flip of my hair.

The flare of Jared's jealousy was the closest I'd come to ecstasy. The more jealous and hateful he became, the more it meant he liked me. It would be years before I'd learn that jealousy stems from insecurity, not love. And through those years I'd also learn that the need to feel submissive and controlled would actually be integral to my losing weight as an adult.

Because Dr. Levine was just a grown-up Jared. He'd even clap me on the arm, repeating, "Good girl," on weeks when I lost weight. After seeming pleased with my weekly food diary—where I was pressed to record, in a timely fashion, each bite and every last ounce of liquid ingested, not only for his scrutiny, but so I was always mindful of exactly what I'd consumed at any given moment—he'd toss the page atop a pile of his other patients' entries.

"Actually, can I have that back?" I wanted to save the record for my "thinspiration book," an adult version of the one I'd tacked along my bedroom mirror as a kid. Only this one was filled with the details of what I consumed, along with magazine makeover clippings, fat pictures of myself, and a list of all the mean things said to me. Reminders that I shouldn't get too comfortable.

"What, you writing a book?" he'd joke as he handed the diary back to me. The thought never crossed my mind.

But the following week, I'd probably stay the same or gain weight. I didn't respond to nice, didn't do well on the weeks when he'd joke. I couldn't lose weight with kindness. I couldn't pet my arms and tell them how healthy they were, what a good job they were doing at staying attached to my hands and shoulders. Love myself. It didn't work. Hating myself worked.

With all the weight I lost, I'd ask the Diet Dictator, "Am I done yet? Have I reached my goal?"

"A bit of a ways to go," he'd say, eyeing me as if I were an orphan he was considering for adoption. I was a size 4. He wouldn't give me a number, or a goal, to reach. He went by how I looked. I'd take StarCaps water pills, at more than a hundred dollars a bottle, the day of his weigh-ins, with just a half cup of orange juice, and my legs would cramp at night.

And just like at camp, Dr. Levine never emphasized health benefits. He didn't care if I exercised. But at all costs, I'd better not show up without my food diary. I'd hand in my journal after filling it out in the cab on the way there, making it seem as though I was eating more than I actually was. Grapefruit, I'd add. Grilled chicken, I'd lie. I'd concoct healthy meals on paper, written in the boxes of the diary, nutrition I never had. And he'd say, "Good girl." It was all about aesthetics, very much the way adolescence is. It wasn't until I was an adult that I realized the emphasis at camp became my physical form, not my independence. And I carried this notion into adulthood, remaining in an unhealthy relationship with two doctors, my husband and the Diet Dictator, thinking if I were thin everything would be okay.

"I'm pregnant!" I'd come to say to Dr. Dick eight months after my initial visit.

"You know I can no longer treat you," he said. "Now don't go crazy; don't use pregnancy as an excuse to eat." Just take it easy, he had said.

But it wouldn't be easy. In the coming months I'd sort through marital lies, have an abortion, move across town, and eventually be divorced. I was 113 pounds when my marriage ended. *Thin* most certainly did not fix things. I realized this at 113 pounds, not at thirteen years old. At Yanisin, I'd been motivated to lose weight from a place of hate, just as I'd continue to do as an adult. And that's when it can become chopsticks. And bathroom visits. Listerine. A locked stall, feet facing the wrong way. Toilet paper dabbing away tears. A room full of girls, retching. It can become several flushes before it all goes down the drain.

twenty-one

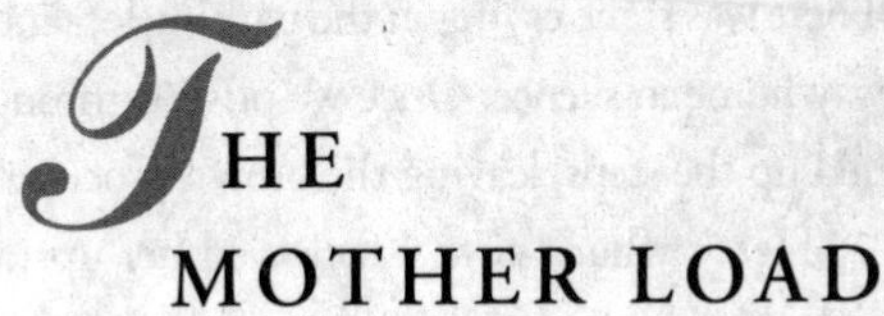

THE MOTHER LOAD

I diet because I want to be a thin mother. Because I want to hold my babies in front of the camera, as their proud mother, and not worry about the cellulite on my arms, or my chins. I don't want all their baby pictures to be with a fat mother. I shouldn't care, but I do.

—2006, age thirty-one

THE FIRST TIME I STEPPED ON A SCALE—AND REALIZED that metal bar held more in its balance than just my weight—I was about to enter fourth grade. I was standing in my pediatrician's office as he pointed to a chart and spoke of percentiles. His finger followed a curved line and stopped when it reached near the top right of a laminated graph on the wall. "Something to watch," he said to Mom.

I was in the top percentile for weight at my age. Which at first, just hearing it like that, made me think I could carry more tiles than anyone else. But when I saw the lines on people's faces as they said it, I suspected this top-tile stuff was a bad thing. I could tell by the way the doctor had looked at her. At dinner, I wasn't allowed to eat the potatoes. And later that week, after a fight we'd had over my weight, Mom locked herself into the upstairs bathroom.

She'd gone up there to sob. As I recounted earlier, we'd just come from Waldbaum's supermarket, where I'd screamed she was unfit to be my mother. There was some crying in the parking lot, and then we drove the rest of the way home in silence. Once we pushed through our front door, she continued up the steps, leaving the brown grocery bags on the hallway floor.

Here's what's new: I followed her upstairs, screaming there was no way I'd go to Fran. I shouted at the bathroom door, "Do you hear me? I'm not going! You can't make me go!" I screamed until my throat stung. She didn't say anything. She wouldn't open the bathroom door. I pounded my fists against it, ranting, "I don't need help, and I don't need you. You aren't even a mother. You should just leave us; nobody wants you or would even miss you. Nobody even loves you."

Mom eventually emerged from the bathroom after Poppa made me apologize. She sat me down and said she was going to tell me a story. She didn't want me to interrupt. I shrugged a shoulder, made an audible sigh, rolled my eyes, and waited. She asked if I remembered the time in kindergarten when Papoo got sick.

I REMEMBERED. SHE'D GOTTEN A CALL IN THE MIDDLE OF the night; her father was in intensive care. He might die. She packed in the dark, not wanting to wake Lea or me. Leaving that evening with Aunt Iris, Mom caught a flight to Florida so she could be with him.

When I awoke the next morning, I knew something was wrong. While I was sleeping, I must have heard her whispering, asking where the garment bag was, telling Poppa that I ate cream cheese on a bagel for lunch.

"Where's Mommy?" I asked him, and when he told me, I didn't believe him. I thought she was hiding. When I wanted to run away, I'd crawl under the heavy wooden dining room table and hide. Sometimes I'd stick my head in the china chest and inhale, savoring the musty cedar. Then I'd open the silverware case, fingering the velvet lining, slipping my finger along the heavy fork handles. It made me feel rich. I looked for Mom in these places, searching the house, peeking in her closet. She wasn't there.

I soon realized she was in Florida, just as Poppa had said. This is gonna be fun, I remembered thinking. I get to spend more time with Poppa now! He's going to make us lunch and be with us for breakfast! And that's exactly what happened. I loved it. It wasn't as if Mom had left us for good. I knew she was coming back in a week.

I NODDED TO LET MOM KNOW I REMEMBERED THE STORY.

"That time I was gone," she said, "when I left for Florida, your kindergarten teacher, Mrs. Dwyer, called the house asking if everything was okay at home. She hadn't known I was away and called to tell us you'd been behaving . . . uncharacteristically, I think was how she'd put it to your father." *What? No I didn't.* "She said you stopped playing with the other kids, that when someone invited you to sit with them, you refused to go over. You threw blocks when kids tried to go near you." *No. Did I really?* "She said you picked a fight with Tricia Caggiano and had to stay after school." *Ooh, that I remembered. I hated Tricia.* "You wouldn't go to sleep for your father, crying that he didn't make your lunch as I had, didn't know the same bedtime stories, couldn't braid your hair. You weren't yourself without me."

I didn't say anything.

"You see, you do need me, and you would miss me if I were gone," she'd said. "You just don't know it. But *I* do." Then she told me to get in the car. And that's when she drove me to see Fran Levine for the first time.

MANY YEARS LATER, PREGNANT WITH MY OWN CHILDREN, there'd again be crying in a parking lot. Though first, there'd be whimpering on an examination table.

"A nose," my preventative preterm labor specialist, Mimi, said when describing my cervix. "It feels just like the tip of a nose." The cold paper crinkled beneath me as she examined my girly gadgets.

"What kind of nose?" I asked, hoping to stall. "You know, do you find it to be a nose of good humor and disposition?" Mimi's head darted up and settled into a tilted pose of confusion. "And what do you know of its upbringing? Would you say it's a nose of information and good character?"

I'd been occupied with far too many Jane Austen films now that I was in my twenty-third week of pregnancy. While I wasn't on official bed rest, I was ordered by my obstetrician to lie on my left side from the hours of 11:00 A.M. to 1:00 P.M. and again from 4:00 P.M. to 8:00 P.M., which allowed for a copious amount of chick by way of flick.

"Okay, now I know she's stalling," Mimi said to my husband, Philip, who was scanning the wall of baby announcements for possible names for our unborn twins. "Up from the table," she said as she snapped off her gloves.

She walked to a chrome sink and washed her hands with foam. I sat upright in my paper gown, glancing at the chair across the room where I'd parked my shorts and running shoes. I could bolt my way out, plow into my sneakers, tighten my gown, and bushwhack my bare bottom through the forest of ultrasound technicians, genetic counselors, and maternal-fetal medicine specialists. But I was as lazy as Susan. I just sat there and grunted.

We weren't about to listen for the heartbeats, and there'd be no ultrasounds this visit. I was about to be weighed.

"Ahem," I grumbled to Philip with my finger pointing to the door. My vagina, my husband could see. But my weight was another story.

AFTER THE MEETING, I WADDLED TO MY CAR, STRAPPED myself in, and turned on the engine. I waved to Philip as he drove off, heading to the market to add more protein to our stockpile of food. I couldn't quite get past the idea that I'd need to weigh more than I ever had before. I cut the engine, picked up my cell phone, and dialed.

"Mom, they want me to gain fifty pounds."

"Who's they?"

"The preterm lady. And the OBGYN said it, too."

"Oh my God, really? Fifty?"

"Yes! And I already look like a white Fat Albert." I tilted the rearview mirror and examined my chins as I spoke. "I know I shouldn't be complaining, that there are people out there hiring women to carry their babies because their uteruses aren't fertile ground. I should be thankful for my chins and chub rub. I should, right? But I'm sorry, there are also women out there who have skinny arms and look pregnant nowhere but in their cute belly. I want to be one of those!" I was whining, regressing into the child Mom allowed me to be.

"Well, it's no time to diet. Eat." No shit, eat.

"I'm not dieting!" I ate egg whites and high-fiber crackers surely made from hamster cage shavings. I was totally dieting.

"Just focus on eating healthy, and Mother Nature will take care of the rest." I wanted to take a shit on Mother Nature.

"Do you have any idea how wrong it feels to hear someone tell me to force myself to eat, even if I'm not hungry?" They wanted to reprogram me to do everything I'd spent my whole life trying to undo.

"I know," Mom said with a sympathetic sigh—a sigh I knew well. It was as if she were sitting beside me, biting her lower lip, nervous right along with me at the prospect of my gaining fifty pounds. "It's the worst. It's like when you're sick, though. You have to force yourself to eat, so you can keep up your strength."

"I'm not sick. I'm just fucked up." My voice cracked. "You know when I left, Mimi actually suggested I go get a milk shake?"

"Ooh, sounds *good*."

"Mom! You just don't get it!" She cut me off before I had the chance to go into the details of how hard it was going to be. As if knowing how fat I'd be again after giving birth wasn't enough, I knew I'd have to reconstruct my thinking and unlearn habits I'd spent years trying to correct. I'd be accustomed to eating excess, being inactive, and using food for every reason aside from actual hunger. I was about to vent, but she'd interrupted with a calm, controlled voice.

"You'll just do it," she said, "and you can worry about losing it after they're born."

"No! Don't you see? That's just it. I don't want to have to lose it again. It's too hard."

"Well, too bad. What choice do you have?"

I didn't have a choice. I had to gain weight, whether I liked it or not, if I ever hoped to be a mother.

"Is this why people say that shit about 'once you're a mother, nothing's about you anymore'?"

"That's right," she sang.

"All right, Mom. I gotta go."

"You'll be fine."

"I know," I said. But I didn't.

Mothers endure things they never thought they could or would, things as unfathomable as pain, or even cruelty, for the sake of their children. It's what a parent does. I wasn't even a mother yet, but the idea of completely sacrificing myself for another, to quote Kate, totally "sucked the cream off a polecat's teat."

As I pulled up to the McDangerous window and took the first sip of my vanilla shake, though, I thought, *You know, she's right? It is* good. And I knew then that I'd do whatever I had to, even if it made me miserable. Because I was her daughter.

WITH MY OWN DAUGHTER, MORE THAN TWENTY YEARS after my initial weight intervention, I was due back at a pediatrician's office to discuss percentiles. This time, though, I'd be there to assess the growth of my own children. Not just a daughter, but also a son.

Before heading to the appointment, I drafted a quick response to a new friend's e-mail. She'd written asking if I was up for grabbing lunch sometime, then inquired after the babies and told me she'd love to introduce me to some other moms in the neighborhood. "And send an update!" she added at the close. "How is everything going? Weight? Appetite? Sleep? I want all the details!"

I didn't have time to include all the details, just the most important one. I replied:

> I can't even discuss my weight. It's so so hard, and I haven't lost any. Love that I'm writing a book about being the fat girl too. That soooo helps. I really want to catch up. When are you free?

She responded promptly, pointing out the obvious: that I was still psycho.

> I am laughing so hard right now . . . I'm dying. I meant the BABIES' weight, you freak! Did you really think I'd ask about yours?

Of course she meant the babies! They had been in the NICU for eight weeks. But with the months of breast-feeding, visits with multiple lactation consultants, the lack of sleep, and around-the-clock feedings, it was impossible for me to *not* think about my body.

And truth be told, even if I hadn't been an udder, I still would have thought first about my weight. It colors nearly everything in my life, and no matter the grief I endure, I will always care what I weigh.

I made it to the pediatrician's office and waited for the doctor's assessment of the babies' health. I watched as he pushed his finger along a slip of paper, up a curve, the points plotting along with their associated percentiles: measurements of success. He stopped in the middle of a curve, looked up, and smiled.

"They're thriving, happy babies, and they're gaining weight beautifully," he said. "Gaining weight beautifully" was a phrase I had come to know—and hate—quite well.

At each weekly weigh-in with Mimi, I feigned happiness when my numbers rose. "See, I'm doing just what you asked," I'd say, more for myself than for her. I had to say it aloud and have her confirm it, a reminder that I was doing the right thing.

"Yes," she'd say as she added a point to her chart. "Exactly on schedule. Just what we want to see." But I wouldn't want to see. Sometimes, I'd even step on the scale backward, insisting she just not tell me. But when I got home, I'd step on the bathroom scale anyway, lining it up just so, in the same spot as always, making sure it wasn't touching any of the grooves on the tiled floor. Obsessed. I hated every single pound, and even more than that, I hated that I hated it.

Through my pregnancy I managed to keep up with Mimi's expectations, asking in a panic, "I'm gaining enough, right?" And she'd reassure me that, yes, I was doing everything right, and she was very pleased with my "beautiful weight gain"—words I should have been eager to hear. But I despised every fraction of a pound. The numbers clicked up, and I smiled, pulling off a convincing, "Aren't you proud? See how well I'm eating?" But I felt like a failure. And despite my fattening up just as the doc prescribed, my children were still ten weeks premature.

"You should feel free to start introducing them to solids now," their pediatrician said as he snapped closed a onesie.

Starting them on solids too early can lead to obesity later in life. True or not, it's all I could think when he'd said it. I loved their meaty little legs, the rolls and folds, and was pleased that they were thriving. I also didn't want to fatten them up too much, to create too many fat cells, ones they'd never be able to lose except through liposuction. "Can't they develop allergies if they start too early?" is what I actually said aloud, because I knew how anything else would sound. Completely Psycho, capital *P*.

My children were born premature; obesity shouldn't have been foremost in my mind. But like all parents, I want to save my children from what I went through, to break the cycle, to do everything in my power to give them the best chance at leading happy, healthy lives. My parents had sent me to Fran Levine when I was eight years old hoping to do the same. To catch it early, before it became too much of a problem. They did, back then, what most doctors would probably suggest today. "Early prevention is key in the battle against childhood obesity." I'm sure someone with a Ph.D. or an M.D. is trumpeting it loud and clear somewhere. And it might be true. But it wasn't true for me.

The objective of fat camp was to boost my self-esteem and my confidence, and improve my overall health. Despite the noble intentions, I ate with chopsticks, sucked on ice cubes, and had private water parties the night before weigh-ins. I learned about enemas, laxatives, diet pills, and vomiting. So, it seems to me, my best option with my own children is to step away. Because the minute I impose any of my well-intentioned beliefs with regard to food on my children, no matter how helpful I'm trying to be, is the minute I steer them in a direction instead of letting them find their own way.

I can only hope to set a good example, to keep my mouth shut and my insecurities tucked away. To truly break the cycle, I need to focus more on my own habits and less on theirs.

I'm not sure how I'll one day manage having to watch either of my children eat the butter off their bread. Or even how I'll handle *putting* butter on their bread, *giving* them bread even. I know not to reward or punish with food, to deemphasize its role in celebrations. But I don't know how I'll raise a daughter who doesn't have body or weight issues. I don't know how it's done. I've read articles on it. Mothers should emphasize activities and exercise instead of paying attention to diet. If a child wants an excessive amount of sweets, a parent should stress fairness, reminding her that everyone received just one. Don't make it about calories or fat. I know for sure I will not frown in the mirror and will prance around the house naked (with all the blinds closed), so she knows what it is to love your body. To say thank you, and mean it, upon receiving a compliment. I've read it. But I haven't lived it yet. And as I know quite well, knowing the answers isn't the problem. It's living them.

MOM VISITED ONCE THE BABIES WERE RELEASED FROM the NICU. She didn't rush to Texas to be by my side when I went into premature labor. "There's nothing for you to do here, anyway," I'd told her when she phoned from her home in Florida. She came to see the kids and me months later. I was angry that she hadn't made it her business to be there right away, anyway. That she wasn't more take-charge, that she wasn't more of a mother, teaching me how to be a good one. It's not that I needed her to instruct me on how to swaddle or change a diaper—I learned from the nurses in the NICU—but I wanted strength and advice, words of wisdom. Mom was never one to offer comforting "this too shall pass" or strong "nothing is taken from you that you cannot learn to live without" advice. Instead she volunteered heuristics about buying Halloween candy I hated, so I wouldn't eat any. When baking, to crack the eggs in a separate bowl in case they're bloody. Advice, though, is different than teaching practical things like putting peanut butter on both slices of bread before adding the jelly, to avoid a soggy sandwich. Advice is what we cling to so our lives and outlooks can improve, so we can get through things with grace. It's not about putting a slice of bread in with your brown sugar to keep it soft, about eating parsley for good breath. This is the advice I got from Mom. Recipe tips for life. I didn't get guidance about setting limits, that they make children feel safe, because she herself never set any. Too many mothers treat their daughters as friends instead of as their daughters. They want to be liked. I don't want to be that kind of mother. I'm looking forward to the day they scream, "I hate you!" I'll know I'm being the mother I always wanted for myself: someone domineering, who'd wedge her elbows into my life and tell me how to live it, even if I had to argue back, because that's what mothers do. They pull you close to them, get in your face, and let you know there isn't space between you. That you are hers and she'll never let anything bad happen to you. But Mom loves like a passenger. I don't want to repeat her mistakes.

Despite how embarrassed of me my daughter will inevitably grow to be, part of her will be just like me, the way part of me is just like my mother. Because that's the cycle of mothers and daughters, trying to outgrow their reach on us, their habits and particular ways of speaking. We might inherit facial expressions, intonations, and cadences, but I'm going to make sure wherever my daughter goes, she knows she's mine. And I'll be hers.

"So, we going on this walk or what?" Mom asked when she was in town. I was eager to lose the fourth-trimester weight, so we hiked through the hills of my neighborhood.

"It's never going to come off," I lamented as we set off.

"Yes, yes it will. Stephanie, you know exactly what to do. You drink your water, you walk. All the stuff you know." I nodded and took a swig from a water bottle.

Midclimb, up a long stretch of hill I came to refer to as "Wheezy," Mom asked, "Do you want more kids after this?"

"You're kidding, right?"

"What, I was just asking." We walked in silence after that. I looked into the houses of my neighbors, studied their landscaping, and wondered how complete they felt. Walking with Mom, just exercising through a town, really, made me think of all those sign 'n' backs, when I'd walked off campus to that one-mile marker sign, past the homes just outside camp. I'd memorized each house, knew that when I approached a certain driveway, I was almost at the sign. I wondered what people were eating. I'd play little games with myself, imagining if I had a home, which of them I'd choose; anything to make the time pass.

"Besides," Mom added, still thinking on it, "you hit the labor jackpot with one of each. It's the best thing, immediate family. So now you're done."

I didn't know if I was done. I didn't even feel like a mother yet. I'd always wanted a big family. Not six big, but three, maybe even four. But pregnancy was too fresh in my mind to willingly sign up for more. I wasn't frightened of the additional work, the lack of sleep and opportunities to travel, or even the financial stress. I was concerned about the possible complications, about the health of each baby, but the easiest, most immediate downside that came to mind when weighing the idea of another child was: what will I weigh?

My weight is not the biggest deterrent to having additional children, but whenever I consider it, I immediately think in poly-rayon blends, in triple-hooked bras with thick beige straps, and garish wrap dresses with bell sleeves. When I imagine the worst, it's not that I envision a belly that looks like a gourd finalist at a county fair. I see the wattle, the cellulite arms, and the girl weeping in her closet because none of her old clothes fit. All the images come far too close—not to what I went through while pregnant, but to what I endured as an adolescent. And it makes me angry—angry that it enters the equation at all.

Just reaching the apex of our climb, Mom, slender as always, began to jiggle her thighs. "They're bad, aren't they? So bad." I watched from behind as she clamped them with her fingers.

I knew I'd need to respond tactfully, to dismantle her insecurities, and let her know how sympathetic I was to such doldrums.

"You sound like a jackass." She stopped walking and turned to face me. "Seriously, you're beautiful, and you sound like an idiot. You know that, right?" I was winded, but it didn't keep me from killing her fat rant. "I know you think you can be thinner, look more toned, whatever it is you're on about today, but you need to realize, right this second, how really great you look."

"Yeah, but, look at this." She widened her stance and began to lightly tap the sides of her legs.

"Mom! Stop it!" I swatted her with the water bottle. "Look, if anyone has cause to complain right now, it's me. And I gotta tell ya, you need to get some perspective, lady."

She nodded, as if she were weighing options. "It's a choice, you know," I said. "You can control your thoughts. You know, get a grip."

"Yeah, I guess," she hemmed.

"Look, sometimes I forget I was ever fat and can put on five pounds over a weekend. And I feel disgusted—"

"Disgusted. That's it. I feel so disgusted with myself."

"Did you just have kids?" But I knew it didn't matter. She wasn't trying to outfat me. She was being Mom.

"I know how you feel. Believe me, I know how you feel. Your jeans get too tight, fat pushes up, you get a lumpy silhouette. And you think, *When I weigh X, I'll be happy; when those jeans fit or are loose, then, man will I be psyched,* but really, truly, one day you'll look back at the way you look right now, and you'll think, *Why didn't I realize how great I looked then?"* It was the advice of a mother, and it was meant for me too.

I HAVEN'T CONQUERED ANY BATTLES WITH FOOD, WITH the bulge, or within myself. I still fight with my weight. Sometimes it fights back. It was messy when I was younger, and it continues to be. I can recite positive affirmations, trying to convince myself I'm no longer Moose. While I try not to allow myself to go there, it's very much who I still am inside, who I will always fear being again, whether I'm a size 6 or a 16. I still go on diets where I'll eat nothing but cabbage soup or hot dogs or no refined sugar or bleached anything. I read labels looking for 9 grams of fiber in a single slice of bread. I eat noodles made of tofu. I say it's for my health, but I don't really believe it. The chemicals in frozen dietetic foods aren't for my health; they're for my thin. Because when my clothes are looser, I smile more readily and laugh more freely. I'm happier thin, in part because I remember, and am bombarded by, messages from those I love that I'm better for it. "You look wonderful. You really lost a lot of weight." And I know they're saying it with love and good intent, but really what I hear is, "Thank God you lost weight." I'm "healthier" now, but it doesn't feel happy. It does when things zip, but mostly, it's "Was I that bad before?" And when I go shopping, I still finger the rack of oversized clothes because my mind hasn't caught up to my body. I'm still fat, passing for thin. And I realize the earliest advice I was given by Fran was exactly right. I would be fat for the rest of my life, even if I looked thin.

Still, I manage to leave the house even when I fear I'm too wide to wedge through its garage doors. One evening, I witnessed a fashion faux pas I'd always feared I'd make. There was a woman across the bar, toasting one of her friends. Her stomach bulged up over her jeans. But to my surprise, she still looked hot. And I've been her, in a mirror, worried, pulling on my shirt, looking for a different pair of jeans to mend the situation. But as an observer, all I saw when I looked at her was a beautiful woman. Mostly, I suspect, it was because she seemed so confident and comfortable. That, or she didn't realize she was a walking muffin top. It's no newsflash that confidence is sexier than hosiery and garters. But it's easier to live it when you can spot a flaw in someone, the kind you would hate to have yourself, and realize it's really not that bad.

It may not be all it takes, but it's half the battle. We get so hung up on ideals and comparisons, but at the end of the day, I'd choose the bulge girl with confidence over the waif who's checking out my shoes. I wish sometimes I could see in myself exactly what I saw in the woman at the bar with the fat fins.

Some days I do. Others, I ask my husband the question no man likes to answer: "Do I look fat?" Though, instead of rolling his eyes, he once replied, "You really want me to answer that?"

I nodded.

"Fine, but then I really need to get a look." He pulled off my jeans and lifted my top for a cheap thrill. "Hmmm," he said with his finger on his chin, "Fat, huh?" I held my breath, terrified he might say, "Yeah, you could stand to lose a good fifteen." Instead, he replied, "Stephanie, you are so hot. God, don't you realize, I don't see you as fat or skinny? You are the love of my life. I see you as absolutely beautiful. You have to remember I don't see you like you see you. Do you really want me to look at you as just fat or skinny?"

"No," I said in a small voice. 'Cause I already know I can stand to lose a good fifteen.

"Good, because you'd be doing us both a disservice. Just let me love you." Dammit, the boy didn't answer the question. "And no—I know how your sick mind works—you are not fat." I knew this before he said so.

I'll sometimes ask because I doubt myself, or because I haven't had a bowel movement in three days. Because I feel like I *ate* Jenny Craig. But naked in bed, I can sometimes remind myself, people really don't look at me the way I look at me. And thank God. No wonder those jeans made with all that elastic and "stretch" are called True Religion.

ACKNOWLEDGMENTS

SPECIAL THANKS TO DIANE BARTOLI, WHOSE INSIGHTFUL feedback and nurturing disposition quite simply enlivened me, restoring my belief in myself and the story I've wanted to tell from the beginning; to Maureen O'Neal, who encouraged me to think of *Moose* as much more than a summer at fat camp and who emboldened me to share the larger story I'd been reluctant to write; to Judith Regan, my former publisher, who early on recognized my potential and considered herself one of my first fans; and of course to Fran Levine, in whose basement I grew up.

To my crackerjack agent, Joe Veltre, for talking me down from high places, for advising me to ask myself "Is it worth it?" each time my adult self interjected within the pages of *Moose*, and who made sure I got the design credit for the jacket.

If ever there was a superhero in the publishing industry, it's Cassie Jones. Editor, evangelist, and mentor, she made William Morrow my home in more than print. Sharyn Rosenblum and Debbie Stier backed up each promise with action. Their skilled hands guided me through the inverted world of book publicity. Many thanks also are extended to the dedicated talents of Christine Casaccio, Nicole Chismar, Julie Elmuccio, Tavia Kowalchuk, and Johnathan Wilber. And to Siri Garber, my publicist and friend, whose follow-through and BlackBerry prowess are beyond compare.

I'd be remiss in not thanking Chris DiClerico for helping me turn out such a fitting title, and of course Kelly Wick Robbins and the rest of my dear friends who've not only encouraged me to eat as though I'd never been to fat camp but who've reached out to me in such meaningful ways through the years. Thank you.

To those who shaped my adolescence and find themselves within the pages of *Moose,* as evidenced by your inclusion in this memoir, you are forever in my thoughts. I am grateful to both those who offered up big ideas within small Instant Messenger windows and those who, even in their most hectic hours, took the time to read, reread, and read yet again, namely, Dan Brotman, Brenda Collier, Kimberly Gilman, Abe Greenwald, Yasmin Mehrain, Yan Perepletchikov, Charles Salzberg, and grammarian Derek Stubbs. A special thanks to the genuinely helpful Jennifer Hanser, for always reading so carefully and cheering so loudly.

Heartfelt thanks to my parents, who've had the good sense to advise me, "Enough is enough. Go to sleep already!" Along with Vernell Hutchinson, Norma Mota, and the rest of my family, who've provided equal parts perspective, guidance, and laughter with an abundance of unconditional love. Thanks to my father for the advice and the shoulder; to my mother for loving me, despite how difficult I made it; and to my beloved sister, who still owes me two hundred eighty-four favors for the candy I gave her.

My deepest gratitude is reserved for my husband, Philip, a pioneer whose fingerprints mark many of these pages, and whose unflagging enthusiasm urged me to say *can* when all I could think was *can't.* It was he who, time and again, read when the last thing he wanted to do was read. I thank him for this, for picking up the baby with the poopy diaper, and for being the man who continues to kiss my furrowed brow and calm my nervous heart. My editor, friend, and lover, he's the collaborator on all that I hold dear.

ALSO BY
STEPHANIE KLEIN

STRAIGHT UP AND DIRTY

A Memoir

ISBN 978-0-06-114799-9 (paperback)

Marriage fit Stephanie Klein like a glove . . . but unfortunately it fit her husband like a noose. She thought she had the perfect marriage, but just like that, Klein found herself "divorced when you're firm, fashionable, and let's face it—fetching."

Straight Up and Dirty demonstrates that the true measure of success isn't what's crossed off life's to-do list. It's having the grace and fortitude to move through change, curls intact and smiling.

"You could call her 'a real-life Carrie Bradshaw,' but it wouldn't do Klein justice. With a fearless voice, the blogger weaves a memoir filled with heartbreak and humor . . . a compelling writer."

—*People*